RENAISSANCE
OF ASIA
Evolving Economic Relations
between South Asia and East Asia

RENAISSANCE
OF ASIA
Evolving Economic Relations between South Asia and East Asia

EDITOR

PRADUMNA B RANA
Nanyang Technological University, Singapore

World Scientific

NEW JERSEY · LONDON · SINGAPORE · BEIJING · SHANGHAI · HONG KONG · TAIPEI · CHENNAI

Published by

World Scientific Publishing Co. Pte. Ltd.

5 Toh Tuck Link, Singapore 596224

USA office: 27 Warren Street, Suite 401-402, Hackensack, NJ 07601

UK office: 57 Shelton Street, Covent Garden, London WC2H 9HE

British Library Cataloguing-in-Publication Data
A catalogue record for this book is available from the British Library.

RENAISSANCE OF ASIA
Evolving Economic Relations Between South Asia and East Asia

ISBN-13 978-981-4366-50-2
ISBN-10 981-4366-50-1

In-house Editor: Samantha Yong

Typeset by Stallion Press
Email: enquiries@stallionpress.com

Printed in Singapore.

Contents

Tables

Figures

Abbreviations

ADB	—	Asian Development Bank
ADBI	—	Asian Development Bank Institute
AFSB	—	Asian Financial Stability Board
AMF	—	Asian Monetary Fund
ASEAN	—	Association of Southeast Asian Nations
ASEAN+3	—	ASEAN plus North Korea, Japan and China
AMF	—	Asian Monetary Fund
BIMSTEC	—	Bay of Bengal Initiative for Multi-Sectoral Technical and Economic Cooperation
BOI	—	Board of Investment
CEPA	—	Comprehensive Economic Partnership Agreement
CGE	—	Computable General Equilibrium
CMIM	—	Chiang Mai Initiative Multilateralisation
EMS	—	European Monetary System
FDI	—	Foreign Direct Investment
FTA	—	Free Trade Agreement
GATT	—	General Agreement on Tariffs and Trade
GDP	—	Gross Domestic Product
GTAP	—	Global Trade Analysis Project
ICT	—	Information and Communication Technology

IMF	—	International Monetary Fund
MFN	—	Most Favoured Nation
NAFTA	—	North Atlantic Free Trade Agreement
NTB	—	Non Tariff Barriers
OECD	—	Organisation of Economic Cooperation and Development
RCA	—	Revealed Comparative Advantage
SAARC	—	South Asian Association for Regional Cooperation
SAFTA	—	South Asia Free Trade Agreement
SOE	—	State Owned Enterprises
UNCTAD	—	United Nations Conference on Trade and Development
WTO	—	World Trade Organisation

Foreword

In the past decade, there has been much discussion on the economic rise of China and India and growing economic linkages between the two Asian giants and the rest of Asia more generally. Asia's emergence and integration and the irresistible shift of economic power to the East are no doubt of keen contemporary interest. This interesting book argues that these phenomena are not without precedence. If one looks back at the economic history of Asia, one should really be talking about Asia's "re-emergence" and Asia's "re-integration" or the "Renaissance of Asia".

We are familiar with Asia's "re-emergence". But we are less familiar with the fact that during the previous eras of globalization when Asia was prosperous, Asia was also regionally integrated and globally connected. This is an important value-added aspect of this book.

Just as in past times, Asia's integration within itself and the global economy is deepening. It is now being driven mainly by market-oriented production networks and infrastructure projects that are starting to criss-cross continental Asia. Regional cooperation policies are also being implemented, and trade and investment relations are expanding between South Asia and East Asia.

Singapore has played an important role in supporting efforts to build an Asia-wide regional architecture. We took an active part in fostering the growth of ASEAN. Then we joined other ASEAN members in creating the ASEAN+3. At Singapore's urging, India, Australia, and New Zealand were included when the East Asia Summit was established, which now also includes the United States and Russia.

In addition to historical perspectives, the book also provides a detailed set of recommendations to deepen regional economic integration in East Asia and South Asia, and to enhance economic linkages between the two regions.

In addition to the introductory chapter, the book comprises eight chapters — 3 focusing on the economic history of Asia, and the remaining on contemporary issues and Asia's future. Each chapter was prepared by a well-known expert on the subject. The editor of the book has many years of experience working at the Asian Development Bank. This volume is a welcome contribution to the growing literature on Asian economic development.

Barry Desker
Dean
S. Rajaratnam School of International Studies
Nanyang Technological University
Singapore

Acknowledgements

I have spent most of my professional life researching and teaching on various aspects of economic development in Asia. During the past decade or so, my research has focused on "Asia's re-emergence" and Asia's economic integration. While contributing to the above research and witnessing the evolution of a prosperous, regionally integrated and globally connected Asia in recent decades, I asked myself the question "How about the historical dimensions, was Asia regionally integrated and globally connected then when it accounted for the largest share of global GDP during the first 18 centuries after the birth of Christ?" Why is this question important? Because if true, it means that the recent rise of Asia is not a revolution and that other regions of the world need not worry because it is simply the restoration of Asia's past glory. And the two centuries of Western domination and colonial rule was just an aberration.

At a conference organized a number of years back to discuss his thought-provoking book — *The New Asian Hemisphere* — Dean Kishore Mahbubani encouraged me to dig further into the historical dimensions of Asian integration. I am very grateful to him for getting me started on this research.

I, therefore, invited prominent scholars on the subject to prepare papers and to present them at a Conference on "Emerging Pan-Asian

Integration: Linking South Asia with East Asia" organized in 2010. Most of the papers are in this book.

I also started to conduct some research on the historical perspectives of South Asia/East Asia linkages. But all that I could do was to survey the works of a few prominent economic historians like Andre Gunder Frank, Ronald Findlay, Kevin O'Rourke, V Shankar, and G Coedes (please see Chapter 2). I discovered that the literature on the subject was huge and that I have barely scratched the surface. I am grateful to Ellen Frost, Anthony Bubalo, and Malcolm Cook for supplementing on the historical perspectives. I am also grateful to Robert Scollay, Douglas Brooks, Barbara Dizon, Biswa Bhattacharyay, Masaaki Amma, Tilak Abeyasinghe, and Ananda Jayawickrama for providing the contemporary perspectives on South Asia's integration with East Asia.

I am very grateful for the support and encouragement of Ambassador Gopinath Pillai, Professor Tan Tai Yong, and other colleagues at the Institute of South Asian Studies with whom I was associated when the Conference was organized.

I would also like to thank the Centre for Multilateralism Studies of the RSIS were I completed the work on the book. I am greatful to Dean Barry Desker, Tan See Seng and Ralf Emmers. Thanks are also due to Samantha Yong, Ruchi Hajela, and Robbie Fay for going over many drafts of the manuscript.

Finally, I am grateful to Neeru, Abhi, and Ayush for their continued inspiration without which the Conference would not have been organized and the book prepared.

About the Authors

Tilak Abeysinghe is an Associate Professor of Economics at the National University of Singapore. He obtained his Ph.D. in Economics/Econometrics from the University of Manitoba and worked for the United States Agency for International Development (Colombo) before joining NUS in 1988. His research interests lie in a range of theoretical and applied econometric topics that include economics of ethnic peace, housing affordability, stress and cancer and quantitative health research. He has published in various reputable international journals like Journal of Econometrics and NBER paper series. A major line of his research has been the econometric modeling of the Singapore economy, forecasting and policy analyses. As the coordinator of the Econometric Studies Unit since 1993, he has built a number of econometric models, one of which appears in the Routledge book, The Singapore Economy: An Econometric Perspective, which he co-authored with Choy Keen Meng. Policy analyses based on these models have appeared in news media frequently. Tilak has also held various important administrative responsibilities at NUS such as Deputy/Acting Headship, Director of Economics Graduate Program, Deputy Director of the Singapore

Centre for Applied and Policy Economics and member of the Faculty Tenure and Promotion Committee.

Massaki Amma has worked for Japan Bank for International Cooperation (JBIC) since 1982 and is currently the Head of Policy & Strategy Department. He also serves the academic circles as Visiting Professor both at Graduate School of Management, Kyoto University and at Graduate School of Economics and Business Administration, Fukui Prefectural University. Education: B.A. in Economics (Kyoto University 1982), Diploma in Economics (LSE, 1987).

Biswa Nath Bhattacharyay is presently the Lead Professional and Advisor to the Dean with Asian Development Bank (ADB) Institute and Lead Professional (Infrastructure) with ADB. He is also the task manager and principal author of ADB/ADBI's Flagship Study on "Infrastructure for a Seamless Asia" and presently undertaking another Flagship Study on "Role of Key Emerging Economies — ASEAN, PRC, and India — for a Balanced, Resilient, and Sustainable Asia".

Previously he worked with ADB's Office of the President, Office of Regional Economic Integration, the Strategy and Policy Department and the Economics Research Department. Prior to joining ADB, he worked in various senior capacities: (i) Chief Researcher and Training Advisor, Institute of Banking Studies, Kuwait Central Bank; (ii) Economic Advisor in the Economic Policy and Research Department, Qatar Central Bank; and (iii) Professor at National Institute of Bank Management of India, National Institute of Industrial Engineering of India, Indian Statistical Institute, University of Missouri-Columbia. He has obtained his Ph.D. from Iowa State University and MS and BS (Hons.) from Indian Statistical Institute. He is a Fellow of CESIfo, a joint initiative of Ifo Institute for Economic Research and University of Munich. He has published several books, many articles and produced many project/consultancy reports, and ADB Board papers in several areas including, (i) regional economic, trade, investment; infrastructure, monetary and financial cooperation and integration; (ii) economic and international development; (iii) international trade and finance; (iv) financial sector and economic and financial surveillance; (v) financial sector reforms and policy; (vi) banking and finance; (vii) infrastructure development-energy transport, telecommunications, water and sanitation; and (viii) governance.

Douglas H. Brooks is the Assistant Chief Economist in the Economics and Research Department at the Asian Development Bank. His research focuses mostly on the areas of international trade and investment. He has also worked as the Acting Director of Research and a Senior Research Fellow at the Asian Development Bank Institute in Tokyo, as Director in the Country Economic Analysis Department of the Export-Import Bank of Japan and the Japan Bank for International Cooperation, and as an economist in the United Nations system, US government and academia.

Anthony Bubalo is the Program Director, West Asia at the Lowy Institute for International Policy in Sydney, Australia. His principal research interest is the politics of the Middle East and Australian Policy in West Asia. Major publications include, with Dr. Greg Fealy, 'Joining the Caravan? The Middle East, Islamism and Indonesia'. Before joining the Lowy Institute, Anthony served in Australian diplomatic missions in Saudi Arabia and Israel and was Senior Middle East Analyst with the Office of National Assessments. He was also director of the Policy and Coordination Unit of the Australian government's Iraq Task Force, and immediately prior to joining the Lowy Institute, Anthony was DFAT's senior speechwriter.

Malcolm Cook is the former Program Director for East Asia at the Lowy Institute. He is now Dean of the School of International Studies at Flinders University. Malcolm completed a Ph.D. in international relations from the Australian National University, and holds an MA in international relations from the International University of Japan and an honors degree from McGill University in Canada. Before joining the Institute in November 2003, Malcolm ran his own consulting practice on Southeast Asian political and economic policy reform and risk analysis.

Barbara M. Dizon is an Economics and Statistics Officer at the Development Indicators and Policy Research Division of the Economics and Research Department of the Asian Development Bank. She oversees several portfolios in the management and implementation of statistics, regional technical assistance, research, and administrative work. Ms. Dizon is a graduate of Economics at the University of the Philippines and holds an MBA from the Ateneo Graduate School of Business.

Ellen L. Frost is a visiting fellow at the Peterson Institute for International Economics and an adjunct research fellow at the National Defense University's Institute of National Strategic Studies. Her most recent book is Asia's New Regionalism (Lynne Rienner Publishers, 2008). She previously served in the US government as Counselor to the US Trade Representative (1993–1995), Deputy Assistant Secretary of Defense for International Economic and Technology Affairs (1977–1981), various positions in the Treasury Department (1974–1977) and the State Department (1963), and as a legislative assistant in the US Senate (1972–1974). During the 1980s, she worked for two multinational corporations. She is a member of the Council on Foreign Relations, the International Institute of Strategic Studies, and the US Committee of CSCAP (Council on Security Cooperation in Asia Pacific). She received her Ph.D. from the Department of Government at Harvard University, where she specialised in the politics and foreign policy of China; an MA from the Fletcher School of Law and Diplomacy; and a BA magna cum laude from Radcliffe College/ Harvard.

Ananda Jayawickrama is a Senior Lecturer in Economics at the University of Peradeniya, Sri Lanka. He obtained his Ph.D. in Economics from the National University of Singapore. His research interests include issues in public finance, government and economic growth, trade in services and service economy, macro-econometric modeling and policy simulation, issues in time series econometrics. He has several research publications in international as well as local journals and in book chapters. He has also served as Development Economist at the International Labor Office in Bangkok and Research Fellow at the Singapore Centre for Applied and Policy Economics.

Pradumna B. Rana is an Associate Professor in International Political Economy at the S. Rajaratnam School of International Studies (RSIS) of the Nanyang Technological University (NTU). He is also the Coordinator of Economic Multilateralism and Regionalism Studies at RSIS's Centre for Multilateralism Studies. He was the Senior Director/Senior Advisor of the Asian Development Bank's (ADB's) Office of Regional Economic Integration, which spearheaded the ADB's support for Asian economic integration. Prior to that, he held various senior positions at the ADB for many years. He has teaching and research experience at the NTU, NUS, and the Tribhuvan University (Nepal). He obtained his Ph.D. from Vanderbilt University where he was a Fulbright Scholar and a Masters in Economics from Michigan State University and Tribhuvan University where he was a gold medalist. He has published widely in the areas of Asian economic development and integration, financial crises, and economic policy reforms in transition economies. These include 15 authored or edited books, over 25 chapters in books, and over 50 articles in international scholarly journals including Review of Economics and Statistics, Journal of International Economics, Journal of Development Economics, Journal of Asian Economics, World Development, Developing Economies, and Singapore Economic Review. Recently, he co-authored books on Asia and the Global Economic Crisis: Challenges in a Financially Integrated World (Palgrave Macmillan) and South Asia: Rising to the Challenge of Globalization (World Scientific Publishers). He co-edited books on Pan-Asian Integration: Linking East and South Asia (Palgrave Macmillan) and National Strategies for Regional Integration: South and East Asian Case Studies (Anthem Press, UK). He was also the Guest Editor of the Singapore Economic Review Special Issue on Asian Economic Integration (Volume 55, Number 1, March 2010).

Introduction and Summary

Pradumna B. Rana

> *Vision without action is a daydream.*
> *Action without vision is a nightmare.*
>
> — Japanese proverb

Recently, there has been much discussion about the economic rise of China and India, and the intensification of regional integration between these two Asian giants and the rest of Asia more generally. Asia's emergence and integration is undoubtedly of contemporary relevance. However, these are not phenomenon without precedent and it would be more appropriate to refer to it as Asia's "re-emergence" and "re-integration" or the "Renaissance of Asia".

By now, it is well-known — thanks to the seminal work of the late Angus Maddison — that during the first 18 centuries after the birth of Christ, Asia (mainly led by China and India) accounted for the largest share of global GDP. The 19th century was of European dominance and the 20th century was of American dominance. However, what is less well-known is that, during the period when Asia dominated in terms of world GDP shares, Asia was also regionally-integrated and globally-connected. Trade on the Northern Silk Road and the Southern Maritime Highway was extensive, and where traders went, religion and culture followed suit.

During the colonial period of the 19th century, and the first half of the 20th century, South Asia strengthened its linkages with its colonial masters and withdrew from the Asian scene. The colonizers also established cartels and monopolies and a new class of elite oriented towards the center instead of their neighbours. Furthermore, after independence in the late 1940s and 1950s, for over four decades, South Asia adopted an inward-looking development strategy and continued its isolation from the rest of Asia and the world. Therefore, the focus was on East Asia (defined as Southeast Asia and Northeast Asia or the ASEAN+3) or what Frost in Chapter 3 and Bubalo and Cook in Chapter 4 of this book refer to as "Maritime Asia" comprising cities energized by trading diasporas.

Since the 1990s, we are witnessing the "Renaissance of Asia"[1] led by the economic dynamism and "re-encountering" between China and India. Asia's integration within itself is also intensifying, driven by market-oriented production networks in East Asia and economic policy reforms including the implementation of "Look East" policies in South Asia and "Look West" policies in East Asia. In 2009, China became the largest trading partner of India in terms of trading goods. Asia is starting to be "re-centred" as trade and investment relations between South Asia and East Asia surge.

---

[1] While this book focuses on the economic aspects of Asian Renaissance, George Yeo, the former Foreign Minister of Singapore, has written on the cultural, social, governance, scientific enquiry, architecture, wellness, and aesthetics aspects of the process. He writes "Asians are rediscovering their own past and deriving inspiration from it for the future… In the same way, as one would identify the origins of Western civilisation in Greece, Rome, and Judeo-Christianity, one could also trace the origins of East Asian civilisation to the influence of Confucianism, Taoism, and Mahayana Buddhism" *The Strait Times*, 14 April 2011. Just as Yeo sees the revival of Nalanda as an icon of Asian Renaissance, in the philosophical, educational and cultural sense, Asia's "re-emergence" and "re-integration" are the economic dimensions of the Asian Renaissance.

The objectives of the book are to (i) review the pattern of economic linkages between South Asia and East Asia[2] from both a historical and contemporary perspective; (ii) analyse the factors underlying the linkages and examine the benefits of greater integration; and (iii) identify the constraints and make recommendations for moving the South Asia–East Asia economic integration process forward.

This book comprises 9 chapters. This chapter consists of the introduction and summary. Chapter 2 by Rana begins with the historical perspectives on the economic relations between South Asia and East Asia. Some of his findings have already been summarised above. Rana then argues that a prosperous and integrated Asia has started to emerge since the end of World War II, led by the economic dynamism of East Asia. Until the early 1990s, South Asia had isolated itself through the adoption of an inward-looking development strategy. With economic reforms, economic linkages between South Asia and East Asia have been surging, and Asia is being "re-centered". Rana also outlines the next steps for deepening East Asian economic integration, linking South Asia with East Asia, and enhancing integration in South Asia.

Going forward, Rana expects East Asian economic integration to follow a "variable geometry, flexible borders" approach with trade (including infrastructure), finance, and monetary tracks, and with new members coming onboard when they feel ready. Chiang Mai Initiative Multilateralisation (CMIM) and the newly-established ASEAN+3 Macroeconomic Research Office (AMRO) have set the stage for institutionalising East Asia regionalism. Hence, new institutions to support Asian integration are expected to emerge. "Bottom-up" integration in East Asia will start being "top down" as well, following the European approach.

---

[2] This book focuses only on economic relations between South Asia and East Asia as it comprises of the second highest component of total inter-regional and intra-regional trade in Asia. In 2006, intra-regional trade among East Asian countries totalled US$2 trillion, while trade between South Asia and East Asia was US$23.8 billion. Inter-regional and intra-regional trade between other Asian sub-regions was much lower (Rana and Dowling, 2009).

On the trade track, efforts should be made to (i) make the Free Trade Agreements (FTAs) compatible with each other (by having similar rules of origin as in Europe); and (ii) consolidate the proliferation of FTAs into a deeper and wider FTA such as the East Asian FTA. Connectivity issues including infrastructure development and trade facilitation are also being addressed.

On the finance track, Asian bond markets should be developed further. With the progress in reforming market infrastructure at the national level, a regional body to promote coordination of capital market rules, regulations and dialogues on financial market vulnerability issues, such as an Asian Financial Stability Board (AFSB), could be established.

The additional steps required in moving from the CMIM to the Asian Monetary Fund (AMF) are (i) strengthening the ASEAN+3 Macroeconomic Research Office (AMRO) as an independent professional secretariat for analytical works and developing independent conditionality; and (ii) delinking the CMIM from the IMF. The deepening regional and financial integration in the region together with the synchronization of business cycles suggests that East Asia should initiate actions to coordinate exchange rate policies using a step-by-step approach.

Rana also recommends a number of policy actions that could be considered to enhance the level of South Asia–East Asia integration. First, the levels of tariffs and non-tariff barriers (NTBs) are already low in many East Asian countries, and South Asia has made encouraging progress in the same direction since the 1990s. However, there is room for further reductions in tariffs and NTBs in both regions (especially NTBs in East Asia because tariffs are already low). Second, in addition to reducing tariffs and NTBs, South Asian countries and several East Asian countries also need to make progress in implementing the remaining reform agenda namely, the so-called second generation reforms to enhance transparency, good governance and the quality of fiscal adjustment. These include, among others, reforms of civil service and of delivery of public goods, creating an environment that is conducive to private sector opportunities (greater competition, better regulations and stronger property rights), and reforms of institutions that create human capital (e.g., health and education). Third, South and East Asian countries need to consolidate their FTAs.

The fourth measure that could have a significant impact on the level of trade between South Asia and East Asia is the reduction of trading costs. This could be brought about through (i) investment in trade-related infrastructure; and (ii) streamlining of cross-border procedures (including customs procedures and logistic costs). Most of the cargo between South Asia and East Asia moves by water and air as there are no land transport services that are operational at the moment. Rapid growth in trade has been accommodated through the introduction of larger container ships. Expansion and diversification of feeder services and bottlenecks, primarily in public ports, remain to be addressed. Land transit through Myanmar is not possible at present. Additional corridors between India and China with Bangladesh, Bhutan and Nepal as "land bridges" will have to be developed. China has plans to extend the recently-opened Qinghai–Tibet railway to Nepal and India.

Fifth, countries should make efforts to reduce transport and logistic constraints to facilitate movement of goods between the two regions. These include delays in customs inspection, cargo handling and transfer, and processing of documents. Customs procedures could be modernised by (i) aligning the customs code to international standards; (ii) simplifying and harmonising procedures; (iii) making tariff structures consistent with the international harmonised tariff classification; and (iv) adopting and implementing the WTO Customs Valuation Agreement. South Asian and East Asian countries have made progress in implementing many of these procedures but much more remains to be done.

In this chapter, Rana also derives several lessons that South Asia could learn from East Asia's successful experience with economic integration. The first is for South Asia to take advantage of the recent positive signs and promote integration within itself by giving primacy to economic issues and not allowing political differences to stand in the way of regional integration efforts. The East Asian countries have not been immune to political conflicts. They have had their fair share.

However, despite these problems, the East Asian leaders have pressed ahead and agreed to keep their political differences aside on the regional cooperation agenda. It is now time for the South Asian leaders to also follow suit and implement on-going integration schemes effectively and deepen them further.

The second is for the South Asian leaders to adopt the East Asian concept of "open regionalism" rather than the failed concept of "closed regionalism". This means extending any preferences granted by a country to its neighbours and eventually to the rest of the world as well or "multilateralising regionalism". Successful implementation of "open regionalism" in East Asia has contributed to the establishment of regional production networks and increased intra-regional trade without trade being diverted from the rest of the world. In fact, East Asia's trade with its three main partner groups (the EU, the US, and the rest of the world) has increased as a percentage of GDP. This, in turn, has had favourable spillover effects on East Asian intra-regional trade and investment. South Asia could also "multilateralise regionalism" by promoting trade with the rest of the world, including East Asia.

The third is for South Asia to adopt the East Asian approach to sequencing integration and not the European one. When the Europeans initiated the integration process in the post-World War II period, there was a strong political will to cooperate and promote peace in order to avoid wars in the future. That is the reason why they went for a customs union and an economic union. Efforts to promote monetary integration began only later in 1979 when the European Monetary System (EMS) was established. The East Asian sequence was different. Given the weakness in the global financial architecture, East Asia initiated cooperation in money and finance by establishing the ASEAN and the ASEAN+3 Finance Ministers Process and the Chiang Mai Initiative. Efforts to promote trade integration started later after 2000 when countries started to promote FTAs. For South Asia too, given the lack of political will, it might be advisable to build up on the various activities of SAARCFINANCE.

In Chapter 3, Frost also begins with a historical perspective. She argues that for several thousand years, relations between South Asia and East Asia were embedded in a much wider pattern of trade, cultural exchange and conquest. These networks stretched all the way from China to the eastern Mediterranean region. Goods, people, culture, religion, money and ideas that nourished the South Asia–East Asia relationship flowed along two great pathways of trade and travel. One route was the branched vein of desert trails and mountain passes known today as the Silk Road, and the other was a network of maritime highways that gradually expanded from the coastline to the open seas. The latter routes linked what the author calls "Maritime Asia," which she defines as the sweep of coastal communities, port cities, towns and inland trading nodes clustered along ocean-destined rivers not far from the sea.

Frost then argues that governments in both South Asia and East Asia are now pursuing closer economic relationships, more cooperative security dialogues, and more frequent cultural exchanges with each other. Some leaders have evoked history to bolster the legitimacy of these initiatives. An example is the Indian Prime Minister Manmohan Singh's suggestion at the 2009 India-ASEAN Summit that his country and ASEAN should jointly plan and execute a "commemorative ship expedition" in 2011–2012. The ship would sail along the sea routes that linked India with Southeast Asia in the 10th–12th centuries, stopping at both ancient and modern ports in ASEAN and other East Asian countries. Frost then explores the validity of this historical claim and reaches three main conclusions:

i. Fully appreciating the history of South Asia–East Asia relations requires us to re-map and re-centre our notions of Asia;
ii. When seen with this revised concept of Asia in mind, the history of South Asia–East Asia relations supplies ample precedent for efforts to restore closer integration between the two regions;
iii. Asia's maritime history provides a stronger rationale for re-integration than the Silk Road or other land-based connections.

In Chapter 4, Bubalo and Cook state that the emergence of the 21st century as an "Asian century" is now conventional wisdom, with power shifting inexorably away from the West to Asia.

They then ask: what do we mean by "Asia"? In the heyday of Western imperialism, "Asia" typically referred to everything from the Suez to Shanghai, with a particular emphasis on those parts of Asia readily accessible to Western navies and merchant ships. But, by the third quarter of the 20th century, a series of events — the War in the Pacific, the rise of a communist regime in China, the Korean and Vietnam Wars, the economic ascent of Japan and the Asian Tigers (South Korea, Taiwan, Hong Kong and Singapore) — both narrowed what we considered to be "Asia" and underlined its growing importance. For most purposes, the north–south coastal region extending from Korea to Indonesia came to be known as Asia. The fact that the West's key strategic interaction with the continent was via the American naval power, reinforced this vertical maritime conception of Asia, as did the late 20th century efforts at regional organisation. Often expressed in the concept of the "Asia Pacific", this particular geostrategic artifice created some odd legacies — Asia's pre-eminent economic and political body, APEC, includes Chile but not India, Mexico but not Mongolia.

Bubalo and Cook then argue that the vertical idea of Asia has now outlived its usefulness. If the rise of Japan and the Asian Tigers, all island or coastal nations closely bound to the United States, accentuated Asia's vertical, maritime identity, then the rise of the great Asian land powers, India and China, and the persisting position and power of Russia, are surely re-defining Asia in more horizontal and continental terms. That will matter enormously for the West. Chinese, Indian and Russian influence will grow in the Persian Gulf and Central Asia; and a less maritime Asia will be, unsurprisingly, less amenable to Western maritime power.

Bubalo and Cook point out that for a good part of the 20th century, economic exchange, or rather the lack of it, had helped to keep Asia divided. The Soviet Union, India and China evinced little interest in international trade. By and large, all three countries had enough critical resources to satisfy their grinding, public sector-dominated economies. The consequence was to paralyse any movement toward transcontinental economic integration. But all of that has changed now as Asia returns to its geostrategic roots by way of new economic networks.

They then note that Asia's growing economic and energy ties are now being reflected in and reinforced by an expanding network of roads, railways and pipelines that are becoming the physical infrastructure of horizontal Asia. Asian oil and gas pipelines used to attract attention due to their failure to get built which is no longer the case.

Chapter 5, by Scollay, focuses on trade relations between South Asia and East Asia in recent years. Scollay argues that until recently, economic integration in East Asia and South Asia were essentially separate processes. The closing decades of the 20th century saw the economies of East Asia getting increasingly integrated through expanding trade and investment linkages and these were important factors both in the region's impressive growth and in its rapid recovery from the deep economic crisis of 1997–1998. South Asia presented a contrasting picture of slow and halting progress in economic integration, impeded by political conflicts and inward-looking economic policies. Trade and investment linkages between the two regions remained at a low level.

Scollay adds that since the turn of the century, preferential trading arrangements between the East Asian economies have been proliferating rapidly, and a proposal to create an East Asian Free Trade Agreement encompassing 13 countries in the region is also under discussion. At the same time, economic liberalisation and the associated emergence of rapid economic growth in India has led to an upsurge of interest in the expansion of economic linkages between East Asia and South Asia. Recognition of India's potential to emulate China as a rapidly-expanding economic giant has been a key factor in this upsurge of interest. The implications for countries in both regions of increasing economic interaction between these two dynamic "growth poles", as well as between India and other East Asian countries, has accordingly commanded growing attention. Reflecting this growing interest, consideration has begun to be given to the potential for, and implications of formally linking East Asia and South Asia together as a single integrated region. Scollay then presents a detailed examination of patterns of trade flows, highlighting varying extents to which the potential for integration exists and has been exploited both between and within the two regions.

In Chapter 6, Brooks and Dizon argue that investment in infrastructure is an important determinant of trade flows across countries as it reduces trading costs. Three types of infrastructure that facilitate trade are: (i) physical or hard infrastructure such as expanding capacities of roads, or improvements and development of ports; (ii) soft infrastructure which refer to streamlining trade operations through improvements in ports rules, reducing tariff and non-tariffs barriers, decreased red tape; and (iii) improvements of logistics and financing arrangements. Available literature suggests that lowering trade costs by 10 percent through infrastructure development can increase exports by over 20 percent. Also the median land-locked country has 55 percent higher transport cost than the median coastal one and transporting goods over land is around seven times costlier for a similar distance by sea.

Brooks and Dizon argue that the changing nature of Asia's trade in favour of declining weight-value ratios and vertical specialisation is stimulating rapid growth in air cargo shipments although a bulk of Asia's trade is still carried by cargo ships. The authors go on to argue that Asia's infrastructure is currently inadequate to meet the task. East Asia as a whole is relatively better than other sub-regions in terms of expenditure on infrastructure development and performance, however comparison with high-income countries still shows significant room for improvement. South Asia is very much behind. For example, China's performance in terms of custom services, infrastructure, logistic quality, and competence in tracking and tracing shipments is much better than that of India. Therefore, actions to improve infrastructure for trade are required in both sub-regions, but especially in South Asia. There are also possibilities for cooperation between South Asia and East Asia in the provision of trade infrastructure. The authors note that bilateral trade costs between China and India fell significantly during the period 1990–2008 contributing significantly to the surging trade flows between the two countries.

Chapter 7 by Bhattacharyay begins by defining connectivity and by identifying the benefits that seamless infrastructure connectivity can bring for Asia. These include facilitating trade and investment, and expanding and deepening regional production networks and supply chains. He then highlights the disparities and shortcomings in infrastructure supply both in South Asia and East Asia. Like Brooks and Dizon, Bhattacharyay also makes the point that improved connectivity can have a significant catalytic impact on South Asia–East Asia trade and investment integration. Myanmar is a key node in connecting South Asia with East Asia and, therefore, needs to be involved. Connectivity through the narrow "chicken neck" corridor separating mainland India and its seven north-eastern states also needs to be improved.

Bhattacharyay then identifies several key projects to link South Asia with East Asia. They are the relevant portions of the Asian Highway and the Trans-Asian Railway project, China–Nepal Second Friendship Bridge project, India–Myanmar–Thailand Highway project, India–Myanmar–Thailand–Vietnam Railway Cooperation, and two energy projects (namely, the Myanmar–Bangladesh–India gas project, and the Myanmar–India hydro power project). He then provides ballpark estimates of infrastructure financing needs of South Asia and East Asia and the total costs of connecting the two sub-regions. Various alternative financing possibilities are considered such as mobilising the region's saving surplus by developing capital markets and through multilateral support.

In Chapter 8, Amma begins by arguing that Japan's economic growth during the period preceding the global economic crisis depended mainly on exports of electrical and electronic goods, automobile and their components, and other high-valued products to consumers in the US and Europe. Therefore, Japan was adversely affected by the global economic crisis of 2007–2009. In the post-crisis period, the Japanese manufacturing industry faces a number of challenges and it needs to diversify export markets to emerging markets, especially those in Asia, by manufacturing new products that meet the demands from this region; enhance the competitive edge of its high value-added exports with new marketing and branding strategies; relocate production activities overseas not only for assembly but also for production of key components; relocate R&D bases closer to markets; and forge closer collaboration with local people in formulating marketing strategies.

Amma presents data and analysis to argue that Japanese manufacturing firms have already established major business presence in the ASEAN countries. Their presence in China and especially in India is, however, still relatively weak. He argues that improved connectivity between ASEAN and South Asia could go a long way in establishing Asia-wide production/distribution networks, thereby, further deepening Asia-wide economic integration and ultimately economic growth.

Chapter 9 by Abeysinghe and Jayawickrama argues that large firms operating in East Asia are aiming to capitalise on the business potential offered by South Asia in terms of lower production costs and mega domestic markets. Although the opening up of India in the early 1990s was a major catalyst for this inter-regional integration process, economic links between East Asia and Sri Lanka have been strengthening since 1977 when Sri Lanka entered a new phase of economic liberalism. Sri Lanka's trade share with the high performing economies in East Asia has increased remarkably over the years. In particular, Singapore has emerged as its sixth largest trading partner.

Abeysinghe and Jayawickrama provide data to show that Singapore is one of the largest foreign investors in Sri Lanka, though the latter is a small recipient of Singapore's total overseas investment. The majority of Singapore's investment in Sri Lanka has been in service industries. As usual, these investments have created many employment opportunities. However, because of high import dependence, Singapore firms in Sri Lanka began to generate trade surpluses only after 1998. Shifting comparative advantages, attractive fiscal incentives and low-cost factors of production indicate that there are large investment opportunities in the manufacturing sector that remain unexploited. The authors argue that the end of the protracted war that deterred the expansion of Sri Lanka's FDI base to its full extent has added the much needed confidence booster to the Sri Lankan economy.

Reference

Rana, P. and J. M. D Dowling (2009). *South Asia: Rising to the Challenge of Globalization.* World Scientific Publishing, Singapore.

Chapter 2

Regional Economic Integration in Asia: Historical and Contemporary Perspectives

Pradumna B. Rana

Introduction

As highlighted in the preceding chapter, rather than Asia's emergence and integration, it is more appropriate to refer to Asia's "re-emergence" and "re-integration" or the "Renaissance of Asia." This chapter argues that (i) during the first 18 centuries after the birth of Christ, Asia not only dominated the world economy but was also a relatively well-integrated region of the world with substantial amounts of trade and labour mobility between each other; (ii) during the 18th and 19th centuries when the industrial revolution occurred in Europe and Asia was colonised, Asia lost its economic dominance to Europe (in the 19th century) and the US (in the 20th century): Asia also became fragmented and intra-Asian economic relations dwindled; (iii) after World War II, East Asia started to "re-emerge" and "re-integrate". South Asia joined the process and Asia started to

13

"re-center" after South Asia started to implement its economic reform program in the 1990s. This chapter also outlines policies to deepen economic integration in East Asia and South Asia and to enhance linkages between the regions.

The chapter begins by focusing on Asia's "re-emergence". It then presents the historical perspectives on economic relations between South Asia and East Asia. The chapter then focuses on contemporary perspectives on Asian economic integration. Although Asian economic integration (especially among the East Asia countries) has started to deepen and linkages between South Asia and East Asia are starting to strengthen, the vision of a prosperous and integrated Asia will certainly take time to be realised and a lot of further thinking and research is required.

Asia's Re-Emergence

India and China were by far the richest countries in the world 2,000 years ago. As far back as 221 BC, China had unified politically and established a centralised political administration. Temperate climate, rapid population growth and alluvial agriculture had led to an early emergence of a commercial society. In terms of innovations, they invented the compass, gunpowder, printing press and paper currency. China was the leader during most of the period from 500 AD–1500 AD. During the Ming Dynasty, China excelled in overseas navigation and conquests. Suddenly in 1433, the emperor suspended all expeditions. Foreign trade and travel were suspended and the per capita GDP declined on a sustained basis.

Also by early 15th century, India had evolved into a sophisticated agrarian economy that sustained a large empire. Textile industry was fairly well-developed, overseas trade was impressive and scholars excelled in Mathematics.

Maddison (1991) estimates that at the beginning of the Christian Era, Asia accounted for nearly 80 percent of the world's GDP, based on the strengths of the Chinese and Indian civilisations. This was true until about the 18th century. Subsequently, for a very long time, the center of economic gravity shifted away from Asia. Europe led after

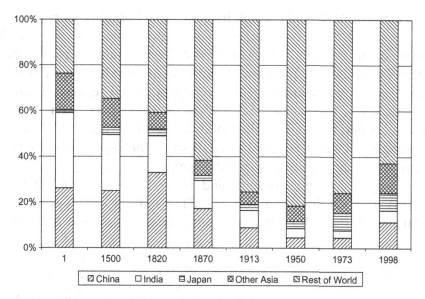

Fig. 2.1: Asia's share of world GDP (1990 international dollars).
Source: Maddison (1991).

the Industrial Revolution in the 19th century and the US led in the 20th century.[1] Therefore, the relative share of Asia declined sharply on a trend basis. It fell to only about 20 percent in 1950 (Fig. 2.1). Since then, led by the dynamism of Japan in the 1960s and the 1970s, China's after the 1980s and India's after the 1990s, Asia's share of world GDP has risen and today it stands at around 40 percent of the world GDP on a purchasing power parity basis. In terms of constant dollars, it is lower at about 21 percent.

The much-quoted 2003 Goldman Sachs study (Wilson and Purushothaman, 2003) had predicted that by 2050, three of the four largest economies in the world would be in Asia in this order: China, the United States, India and Japan. The 2007 Goldman Sachs report (Poddar and Yi, 2007) updated the forecast and noted that India would overtake the United States earlier than expected and be the second largest economy in the world by 2050 after China.

---

[1] Ferguson (2011) argues that western domination in terms of per capita income lasted over 500 years.

A recent ADB study (2009) has noted that India has the potential to overtake the US even earlier. Using a global model to provide a sense of the economic trajectory for different country groups, the ADB has noted that India could accelerate its real GDP growth over the next 30 years to around 9.5 percent per year and become an affluent society in a generation.[2] Therefore, in 2039 India could be the second largest economy in the world, second only to China and surpassing the United States. The ADB study forecasts that in 2039, Asia would once again dominate the world economy.

However, one must bear in mind that the "re-emergence" of Asia discussed so far, is only in terms of GDP and not GDP per capita. Data in Fig. 2.2 show that although Korea, China and India are

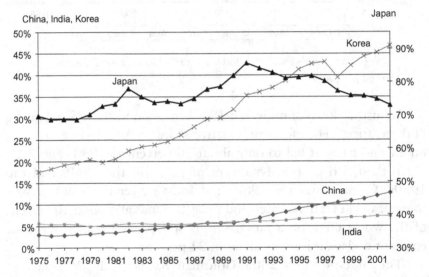

Fig. 2.2:   PPP GDP per capita in US$ (as % of US PPP GDP per capita).

Source: World Bank, World Development Indicators Online.

---

[2] But this requires a formidable set of reforms to (i) tackle disparities among various social groups; (ii) improve the environment; (iii) eliminate pervasive infrastructure bottlenecks; (iv) renew education, technological development and innovation; (v) transform the delivery of public services especially in cities; (vi) revolutionise energy production and consumption; and (vii) foster a prosperous South Asia and become a responsible global power.

catching up with the US, their GDP is much lower than that of the US — 45 percent, 12 percent and 7 percent of the US GDP respectively. Japan's per capita GDP has been declining relative to that of the US. Also, though countries are upgrading their militaries, their combined military spending in 2008 was only about one-third of the US.

South Asia's Economic Relations with East Asia: Historical Perspective

South Asia has a long history of economic ties and cultural and religious exchange with East Asia which date back to the pre-Christian era.

Precolonial years

The first millennium of the Christian era was a period of rapid growth for India and China. Trade ties between these two countries increased and the expansion of trade links between these countries widened localised networks into regional ones.[3] Exports from India comprised of mainly rice, sugar and cotton textiles while imports were more varied and included Indonesian spices, various kinds of woods, Chinese silk, tea, gold and non-precious metals such as tin, copper and vermillion. India and China were in contact with each other through a network of land and sea routes. Land routes started off as localised networks and were gradually linked into long distant trading channels known as the Silk Road. There were two major maritime ports along the east coast of India, namely, the port of Coromandel (near present-day Chennai) and Bengal. There is evidence of extensive trade with Burma and Thailand.

The opening of the Straits of Malacca in the 5th century enabled direct contact with the northwestern edge of the Java Sea region where intra-regional trade was strong and led to the establishment of the Srivijaya Empire (present-day Indonesia). In the 7th century,

---

[3] For a more comprehensive discussion, see Frost (2009), Findlay and O'Rourke (2007), Shankar (2004), Mishap (2001), and Frank (1998).

Persian merchant ships led the navigation to China, but they were supplanted by Arab traders in the 9th century. The emergence of the Chola Empire in South India and the Sung Dynasty in China in the 10th and the 11th centuries as large, unified and prosperous regional powers provided an additional fillip to regional economic trade and exchange. Strategically located on the great maritime route connecting China and the West, Southeast Asia also provided a staging ground for merchants from the East and the West. Various strategic alliances were also made. Rajendra I of the Chola dynasty conducted a naval expedition to Srivijaya to protect trade with China.

By the 12th century, huge Chinese junks had nosed other ships aside. The 15th century voyages of admiral Zheng He were well documented with armadas of up to 300 vessels and 30,000 men. In that century, the expansion of Gujarati commerce and the rise of Western Java shipping also increased the volume of traffic on the Southern Maritime Highway. The end of the 15th century saw the trickle of Western explorers who sought to circumvent Muslim hegemony by sailing to Asia around the Cape of Good Hope. Hence, during the pre-colonial period, in addition to being the dominant region of the world, Asia was one of the most integrated regions of the world. The latter fact is relatively less known.

Together with land and sea-borne commerce, traders, missionaries, priests, adventurers and fortune seekers moved from South Asia to Southeast Asia. The Sanskrit language, Hinduism and Buddhism were like old wine lacing East Asia's culture. Names from the Sanskrit language and various Hindu–Buddhist cults were adopted in East Asia. The common people, too, were influenced by the stories of the Ramayana and various deities became popular.

Findlay and O'Rourke (2007) remark that around 1000 AD, various regions of Asia (namely, Central Asia, South Asia, Southeast Asia and East Asia) had extensive trade and cultural links with each other and also with the Islamic world (now, the Middle East) but little contact with Eastern and Western Europe (Table 2.1). There were two routes for trade — the overland Silk Road and by sea.

Shankar (2004) writes, "Throughout pre-colonial history, Asia has functioned not only as an active participant in the global economy

Table 2.1.   Inter-regional trade flows, ca. 1000 AD.

To From	Western Europe	Eastern Europe	Islamic World	Central Asia	Sub-Saharan Africa	South Asia	Southeast Asia	East Asia
Western Europe	X	Swords	Slaves, swords	—	—	—	—	—
Eastern Europe	Slaves, furs, silver	X	Slaves, furs, silver	Furs, swords	—	—	—	—
Islamic World	Pepper, spices, textiles, silk, silver	Textiles, silver	X	Textiles	Salt, textiles, manufactures, swords, horses	War horses	Gold	Spices
Central Asia	—	Silver	Paper, silver, slaves	X	—	Silver, re-exports from China and Muslim world	—	Horses

(*Continued*)

Table 2.1.   (*Continued*)

To From	Western Europe	Eastern Europe	Islamic World	Central Asia	Sub-Saharan Africa	South Asia	Southeast Asia	East Asia
Sub-Saharan Africa	—	—	Gold, Slaves, ivory, rice	—	X	Timber, iron	—	—
South Asia	—	—	Pepper, spices, silk, teak, textiles	Pepper, textiles	Textiles	X	Textiles, pepper	Textiles
Southeast Asia	—	—	Spices, perfumes	—	—	Silk, spices, teak, rice, rubies	X	Perfumes, spices, sandalwood
East Asia	—	—	Silk, porcelain	Silk, tea	—	Silk, porcelain	Silk, copper, cash	X

Source: Findlay and O'Rourke (2007).

but also, and perhaps much more so, as an integrated region, with close economic ties ... What is perhaps not so well-known is the existence of a complex and thriving network of interaction among the Asian countries. By the 15th century, Asia was integrated into a large and vibrant regional network of exchange, which in turn was linked to the global economy through trade and commerce with the Middle East and Europe".

Frank (1998) provides a comprehensive analysis of global trade during the period 1400–1800. His major thesis is that contrary to widespread doubt and denials, during this period when Asia dominated, there was a single global world economy with a worldwide division of labour and multilateral trade. Using a "Nordic/global" projection of the world, he shows the major trade routes used during that period (Fig. 2.3). As he notes, this map is Euro-centric and Asia appears much smaller than it should and, therefore, has to be "re-oriented". This, he could not do because of a lack of computer software.

On intra-regional trade, Frank writes: "Intra-American trade... was surely less than they were between each of them and one or another part of Europe. Some parts of Europe also had less relations among themselves than they had with people and areas in the US and Asia. On the other hand, perhaps most of the major regions or subregions in the Indian subcontinent or within China probably had denser intra-Indian or intra-Chinese interregional trade than they did with other parts of the world". However, parts of Southeast Asia, especially Manila and Malacca, were entrepôts with extensive trade relations with many parts of the world.

Frank presents several interesting maps (Figs. 2.4 and 2.5), which show the major trade routes used during 1400–1800 and commodities traded on these routes together with the balance of trade which was settled, at that time, through the flow of silver or gold. For example, India at that time, exported silk/textiles, ceramics, slaves, diamonds, rice, iron & steel products and shipping services to Southeast Asia. India, in turn, imported pepper, spices, rice, sugar, elephants, tin, copper, cinnamon, teak and rubies. The balance of trade was generally in Southeast Asia's favour and this was

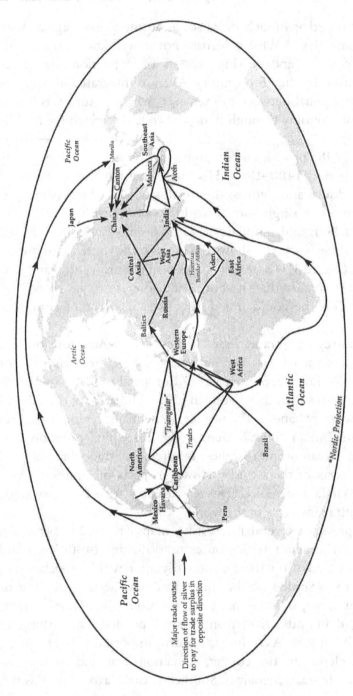

Fig. 2.3:   Major circum-global trade routes, 1400–1800.

Source: Frank (1998).

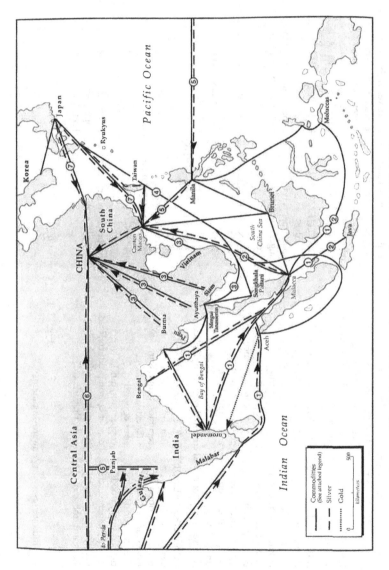

Fig. 2.4: Asian region: Major trade routes 1400–1800.

Source: Frank (1998).

ROUTES
North - Westward | South - Eastward

1. INDIA-SOUTHEAST ASIA

North - Westward	South - Eastward
pepper, spices, rice, sugar, elephants, tin, copper, other metals, cinnamon, teak, rubies, GOLD	cot. textiles, silk textiles, slaves, diamonds, rice, iron & steel/prods., diamonds, shipping/services [SILVER]

2. ARCHIPELLAGAN SOUTHEAST ASIA - CHINA

North - Westward	South - Eastward
pepper, spices, tin, rice, sugar, fish, salt, aromatic woods, resins, lacquer, tortoise shell, pearls, precious stones, amber, jade, birdnests, jaggery, jasper, cutch, tin [SILVER]	silk/textiles, ceramics, tea, cloth, satin, velvet, paper, fruit, drugs, arms & powder, copper & iron products, gold/silver thread, zinc, cupro-nickel

see also route 3 for partial commodity overlap/duplication

3. CONTINENTAL SOUTHEAST ASIA - CHINA
(north)

North - Westward	South - Eastward
rice, sugar, cotton, rubies, amber, jade, deer & tiger skins, timber, ships, woods, jaggery, paper, cutch, beetelnut, birdsnests, shark fins, tobacco,	ceramics, lacquerware, silk/textile, clothing, arms & powder, copper cash, quicksilver, copper & iron products, lead, zinc, cupro-nickel, salt, fruit, rhubarb, tea,

ROUTES
North - Westward | South - Eastward

3. CONTINENTAL SOUTHEAST ASIA - CHINA, cont.

North - Westward	South - Eastward
pepper, sappan wood, tin, lead, salpeter, SILVER	satin, velvet, brocades, thread, paper, dyes, carpets, shoes, stockings, housewares, labor, shipping/services

4. SOUTHEAST ASIA - JAPAN [VIA TAIWAN & RYUKUS]

North - Westward (north)	South - Eastward (south)
spices, pepper, tin, sugar, medicines [cot. textiles]	copper, sulphur, camphor, swords, shipping, SILVER

5. CHINA - MANILA GALLEON - ACAPULCO/ MEXICO

North - Westward	South - Eastward
PERU SILVER	silk/textiles, ceramics, quicksilver

6. CENTRAL ASIA - CHINA

North - Westward	South - Eastward
silk/textiles, tea, arms, clothing, ceramics, medicines, paper money	horses, camels, sheep, jade, medicines [SILVER]

7. JAPAN - CHINA
SILVER

North - Westward	South - Eastward
copper, sulphur, camphor, swords, iron	silk/textiles, cot. textiles, sugar, skins, woods, dyes, tea, lead, manufactures

Fig. 2.4: (*Continued*)

Note: Brackets indicate re-export/onward-shipment.

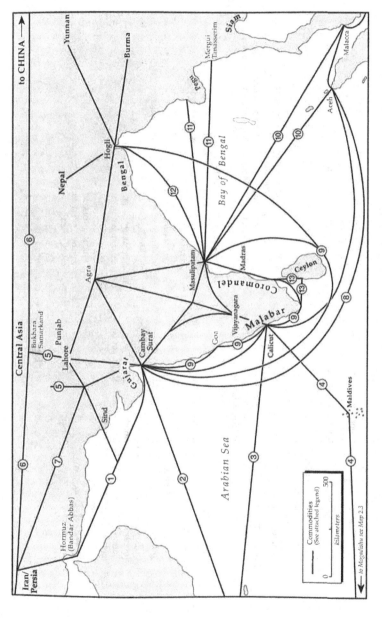

Fig. 2.5: Indian Ocean region: Major trade routes, 1400–1800.

Source: Frank (1998).

ROUTES	Westward	Eastward
1. INDIA-WEST ASIA	cotton textiles, dies, indigo, silk, silk textiles, iron & steel products, housewares, wood & glass prods., rice, pulses, wheat, oil [spices, pepper, ceramics] aromatics, incense, shawls, blankets, paper, gumlace, saltpeter	dye woods, salt, pearls, minerals, metal/prods., copper, lumber, horses, carpets, luxury goods, fruits, dates, arms, coral, rosewater, dye woods SILVER
2. GUJARAT-GULF	same as 1	wine, opium, pearls, aromatics, incense, SILVER, GOLD
3. MALABAR-GULF	pepper, rice [spices]	GOLD
4. MALABAR-EAST AFRICA	rice, cowries	ivory, slaves, fish, GOLD
5. GUJARAT/PUNJAB-CENTRAL ASIA	[northward] cotton & silk textiles, pulses, rice, wheat, indigo, tobacco	[southward] horses, camels, sheep, cotton
6. WEST-CENTRAL-EAST ASIA	silk, tea	horses

ROUTES	Westward	Eastward
7. GUJARAT-SIND-PUNJAB-WEST ASIA	cotton textiles, wheat, indigo	SILVER
8. GUJARAT- SOUTHEAST ASIA	spices, [sugar, silk, ceramics] GOLD	cotton textiles coral, copper, glass [re-exports from Aden/Gulf] SILVER
9. INDIAN INTER-REGIONAL [not fully represented]	exchanges among most major Indian products along maritime and overland trade routes among Punjab, Sind, Gujarat, Malabar, Vijayanagara, Coromandel, Bengal	
10. COROMANDEL - SOUTHEAST ASIA	tin, sugar, metals, elephants, [ceramics, silk] GOLD	cotton textiles, slaves, rice, diamonds, SILVER
11. COROMANDEL - BURMA/SIAM	tin, elephants, woods, SILVER	cotton textiles
12. COROMANDEL - BENGAL	silk, cotton textiles, rice, sugar	
13. CEYLON - INDIA	elephants, cinnamon, jewels, pearls	rice

Fig. 2.5:   (*Continued*)

settled by outflow of silver from India. India obtained silver through its trade with the Middle East and Europe.

India's trade with Southeast Asia was conducted using the sea route from the ports on the Malabar and Coromandel coasts and in Bengal. While ports on the Coromandel coast were used to trade with Burma, Thailand and Malacca onwards to Indonesia, those on Malabar coast and Bengal were used to trade with Malacca and Indonesia.

While there were road links between India and the Central Asian countries on the Silk Road, by which India exported cotton and silk textiles, pulses, rice, etc and imported horses, camels, sheep and cotton, Frank notes that there were no direct trade links between India and China. India exchanged cotton textiles for silk and porcelain and other ceramics with China using the same routes that it used for trade with the South East through ports on the Malabar and Coromandel coasts and Bengal. From ports on Coromandel and Malabar coasts, goods were transported by ships to Burma and Thailand and then they were taken overland to China. From Bengal, goods were taken to Malacca and then to China by ships.

India also traded with China through Nepal. Bengal and Assam exported textiles, indigo, spices, sugar, hides and other goods to Tibet for sale to merchants there, who further sold them in other provinces of China. Payment was in Chinese products, tea and often gold. Frank does not mention trade between India and China through the Nathu La pass in Sikkim.

During the period under review, Malacca was peopled almost entirely by expatriate merchants. Maharasthi merchants from Cambay and Surat were probably the majority in Malacca. Manila counted 30,000 Chinese merchants to support transpacific–China trade. These port cities and others (such as Cambay, Goa, and Macassar) were religiously tolerant, cosmopolitan places, driven by trading diasporas.

Some refer to "Farther India" or "Greater India" to describe Indian influence in Southeast Asia in those days. Coedes (1968) notes that "Farther India" comprised of Indonesia and insular Southeast Asia (except the Philippines) and the Indochinese and Malay peninsula. In the pre-colonial period, India contributed greatly to East Asia's culture and history. Buddhism was perhaps India's greatest gift to East Asia and indeed to the world. Along with Buddhism came the Sanskrit religion and names that we see all over East Asia. Indian merchants, while engaging in trade with East Asia, were also middlemen in East Asia's trade with the rest of the world.

The 19th and early 20th century (The colonial period)

Vasco De Gama sailed around the Cape of Good Hope and reached Calicut in the Malabar Coast of India on 20 May 1498. Eventually, the Dutch, the Spanish, the French and the British also followed suit. Initially, the colonizers did not disrupt intra-Asian trade. They focused on developing coastal towns — Madras (1639), Bombay (1668) and Calcutta (1690) — as trade bases. They gradually established direct rule. For example, in India, the British conquered the Moghul province of Bengal in 1757, took over the province of Madras and Bombay in 1803 and seized Punjab from the Sikhs in 1848. They also succeeded in marginalising their French and Dutch commercial rivals. However, the British government did not establish direct rule in India until after the Indian mutiny in 1857 when the East India Company was disbanded (Maddison, 2007). Eventually, the colonizers divided up most of Asia into spheres of influence and took control of trade & customs and restricted access to inland waterways.[4] They destroyed Asian trading systems and diverted profits to Europe. This distorted centre-periphery relations making Europe stronger while the Asian Empires and kingdoms became weaker. Economic linkages between South Asia and East Asia also weakened as South Asian soldiers were used to quash rebellions in other parts of Asia such as China (the Opium War) and Malaya.

The postcolonial period (1950s onwards)

Under India's first prime minister, Jawaharlal Nehru, India started to re-engage with East Asia. The Asian Relations Conference held in

---

[4] However, trade within the spheres of influence were high. It is estimated that at that time, the level of intra-South Asian was about 25 percent.

New Delhi in 1947 under the leadership of Nehru served as one of the earliest attempts to form a Pan-Asian identity. Forming a common cause with other Asian leaders on decolonization, Western imperialism, equality and developing-world solidarity, Nehru helped forge the "Bandung Spirit" of 1955, which led to the non-aligned movement. However, this phase of India's engagement with East Asia ended with India's border war with China in 1962 and its preoccupation with Pakistan. India turned inward and adopted the Soviet model of development.

Asian Economic Integration

Contemporary Perspectives

During the post-World War II period, Asian economic integration started to deepen especially among the East Asian countries.[5] Initially, this process was market-led due to the close nexus between trade and investment or regional production networks but after the Asian financial crisis, various regional cooperation policies were also adopted. The major factor that ignited the interest of East Asian countries to regional monetary and financial integration was the virulent contagion of the East Asian financial crisis and the policy mistakes made by the IMF in managing it.[6] It was also felt that the resources of the IMF were limited and that might not be enough to handle a capital-account crisis associated with large surges and outflows of short-term private capital. Slow progress in the Doha Round under the auspices of the WTO and the popularity of regionalism elsewhere (e.g., EU and NAFTA) also encouraged East Asian countries to promote regionalism in trade. The on-going global economic

---

[5] East Asia is defined as ASEAN+3.

[6] Given that the Asian financial crisis was a capital account crisis, the IMF should not have required Asian countries to tighten fiscal policy and raise interest rates. It should also not have gone overboard in requiring these countries to meet many structural conditions that were imposed in its program. Its approach to financial and corporate reforms was also inappropriate, at least, in Indonesia. Subsequently, the IMF accepted many of these criticisms.

crisis has further enhanced the case for Asian regionalism by strengthening the case for policy cooperation and rebalancing growth at a regional-level.

East Asian trade integration

On trade integration, East Asia has made encouraging progress with intra-regional trade reaching 57 percent of total trade (up from 43 percent in 1990), which is higher than the level for the North American Free Trade Agreement (NAFTA) at 46 percent but lower than that for the European Union (67 percent). Much of this expansion has been driven by market forces, especially the establishment of production networks in East Asia.

East Asian governments began to use FTAs as instruments of trade policy in the late 1990s. In 2000, only three FTAs were in effect but today there are 47 bilateral and multilateral FTAs in effect with another 64 in the pipeline.[7] FTAs will no doubt proliferate further, if the Doha Round continues to falter. If they are designed properly, FTAs can help countries reap the benefits of their comparative advantage. That is why, FTAs are allowed as exceptions to the antidiscrimination rules of the GATT/WTO. But there is a risk that the proliferation of FTAs could come at the expense of trade with nonmembers, known as trade diversion. It could also create an "Asian noodle bowl" effect and raise administrative costs of trade, especially to small and medium-scale enterprise. Multiplicity of bilateral and plurilateral deals could also hinder the push toward a global trade agreement.

East Asian financial integration

Lack of data makes it difficult to measure the level of financial integration in East Asia but available indicators (both price and quantity) suggest that it is increasing, albeit from low levels. East Asian countries have taken collective actions to develop local currency bond markets as these will reduce the "double mismatch" problem, which

---

[7] ADB's database in www.aric.adb.org.

was at the heart of the crisis and overcome the so-called "original sin" problem.[8] The basic idea is to mobilise the region's vast pool of savings to be intermediated directly to its long-term investment, without going through financial intermediaries outside. Regional financial intermediation through bond markets would diversify the modes of financing in the region and reduce the double mismatch. The initiatives include the EMEAP Asian Bond Fund (ABF) Initiative and the ASEAN+3 Asian Bond Markets Initiative (ABMI).

The ASEAN+3 Finance Ministers' process launched ABMI in August 2003. The ABMI aims to focus on facilitating market access to a diverse issuer and investor base and enhancing a market infrastructure for bond market development, thereby creating robust primary and secondary bond markets in the region. The ABMI initially created six working groups and later reorganised these into four working groups and two support teams (Ad Hoc Support Group and Technical Assistance Coordination Group).

In May 2009, the ASEAN+3 Finance Ministers endorsed the establishment of the Credit Guarantee and Investment Facility (CGIF) as a trust fund of the ADB. The establishment of the CGIF trust fund was approved by the ADB's Board of Directors in April 2010, with an initial capital of $100 million. The CGIF seeks to promote the development of Asian bond markets by providing guarantees for investors that make it easier for firms to issue local-currency bonds with longer maturities.

East Asian macroeconomic policy coordination

Macroeconomic policy coordination is essentially a post-crisis phenomenon in East Asia. There is an ascending order of intensity

---

[8] The "double mismatch" problem refers to borrowing unhedged foreign funds to lend long-term in domestic currency and borrowing short-term to lend long-term. The "original sin" is a situation where emerging economy residents cannot borrow abroad in domestic currency nor borrow long-term, even domestically. Hence domestic banks and corporations tend to face a currency or maturity mismatch or both, thus facing balance-sheet vulnerabilities to sharp changes in exchange rates and/or interest rates.

of these efforts, in the sense that they involve progressively, increasing constraints on the amount of discretion that individual countries can exercise in the design of macroeconomic policies. By level of intensity, these efforts have ranged from economic review and policy dialogue to establishing regional financing arrangements and eventually toward coordinating exchange rate policies.

(i) *Economic review and policy dialogue*

In the area of economic review and policy dialogue, there are three major ongoing initiatives. First, the ASEAN Surveillance Process was established in October 1998 to strengthen the policy-making capacity within the group. Based on the principles of peer review and mutual interest, this process reviews global, regional, and individual country developments and monitors exchange rate and macroeconomic aggregates, as well as sectoral and social policies. Under this Process, the ASEAN Finance Ministers meet annually and the ministries of finance and central bank deputies meet semiannually to discuss issues of common interest.

Second, with the formation of the ASEAN+3 Finance Ministers Process in November 1999, the ASEAN+3 Economic Review and Policy Dialogue (ERPD) process was introduced in May 2000. Under the ERPD, ASEAN+3 finance ministers meet annually and their deputies meet semiannually. Initially, deputies would meet for a couple of hours but now their meeting lasts two days and discussions focus on (i) assessing global, regional and national conditions and risks; (ii) reviewing financial sector (including bond market) developments and vulnerabilities; and (iii) other topics of interest. The value-added of regional surveillance is that countries tend to be more frank with each other in a regional forum as they focus on issues of common interest (such as high oil prices, avian flu, global payments imbalances and capital inflows). However, so far, the ERPD is in transition from the simple "information sharing" stage to "peer reviews" among the member countries. Currently, the ADB and till more recently, the IMF provided assessments of regional economic and financial conditions and risks and individual countries provide self-assessments of their respective economic situations. With a move toward "peer reviews", the participating members are expected to conduct more active discussions of other countries' policy making.

Steps have been taken to monitor short-term capital flows and develop early warning systems of currency and banking crises. National Surveillance Units have been established in many ASEAN+3 countries for economic and financial monitoring with ADB support in addition to a Technical Working Group on Economic and Financial Monitoring. A group of experts has also been appointed. But the ASEAN+3 does not have a technical secretariat, which prepares a comprehensive assessment of member countries' economic and financial outlook and risks.

Third, central bank governors in the region have also developed their own forums such as the Executives Meeting of Asia-Pacific Central Banks (EMEAP), South East Asian Central Banks (SEA-CEN), Southeast Asia, New Zealand and Australia (SEANZA) for regional economic information exchange, analysis and policy dialogues. EMEAP is the most prominent and was organised in February 1991 with the leadership of the Bank of Japan and the Reserve Bank of Australia. Its major objectives include enhanced regional surveillance, exchange of information and views, and the promotion of financial market development. Its activities include annual meetings of EMEAP central bank governors, semiannual meetings of the deputy governors and three working groups concerned with bank supervision, financial markets and payments and settlement systems. Like the ASEAN+3 finance ministers' process, EMEAP has no secretariat.

Until its dissolution in December 2005, the Manila Framework Group was another forum that brought together deputies from a wider range of countries for policy dialogue. There are trans-regional forums such as the Asia-Pacific Economic Cooperation (APEC) finance ministers and the Asia-Europe Meeting (ASEM) finance ministers for trans-regional processes.

(ii) *Regional financing arrangement*

Progress has also been made in establishing regional financing arrangements. They are designed to address short-term liquidity needs in the event of a crisis or contagion and to supplement the existing international financial arrangements. At their May 2000 meeting in Chiang Mai, the ASEAN+3 Finance Ministers agreed on the Chiang Mai Initiative (CMI) to expand the ASEAN Swap Arrangement (ASA) to all ASEAN members and to set up a network of bilateral swap arrangements (BSAs) among ASEAN+3 countries. The ASA expansion was done in November 2000 and its size increased from US$200 million–US$1 billion. In April 2005, the ASA size was again increased to US$2 billion. A network of BSAs has been signed among the plus-3 countries (China, Japan and Korea) and between a plus-3 country and a selected ASEAN country. Eight ASEAN+3 members have signed 16 BSAs amounting to US$84 billion.

One of the important features of CMI BSA was that, members requesting liquidity support could immediately obtain short-term financial assistance for the first 20 percent (originally 10 percent) of the committed amount. The remaining 80 percent was provided to the requesting member under an IMF program. Linking the CMI liquidity facility to an IMF program — and hence its conditionality — was designed to address the concern that the liquidity shortage of a requesting country may be due to fundamental problems rather than mere panic and herd behaviour by investors and that the potential moral hazard problem could be non-negligible in the absence of tough IMF conditionality. The general view was that with the region's currently limited capacity to produce and enforce effective adjustment programs in times of crisis, linking CMI to IMF programs was prudent, at least for the time being.

Substantial progress has been made on CMI Multilateralisation (CMIM). Some of the major developments over the last few years include:

1. Integration and enhancement of ASEAN+3 ERPD into the CMI framework (May, 2005);

2. Increasing the ceiling for withdrawal without an IMF program in place from 10 percent to 20 percent of the total (May, 2005);
3. Adoption of the collective decision-making procedure for CMI swap activation, as a step toward multilateralising the CMI (May, 2006);
4. Agreement in principle on a self-managed reserve pooling arrangement governed by a single contractual agreement as an appropriate form of CMI multilateralisation (May, 2007);
5. Agreement that the total size of the multilateralised CMI would be at least US$80 billion (May, 2008);
6. The size of the multilateralised CMI increased to US$120 billion (February, 2009); and
7. CMIM came into effect on 24th March 2010 and a consensus was reached on the key elements of the ASEAN+3 Macroeconomic Research Office (AMRO) (May, 2010).

On CMIM, at their meeting in Hyderabad in 2006, the ASEAN+3 Finance Ministers decided that "all swap providing countries can simultaneously and promptly provide liquidity support to any parties involved in bilateral swap arrangements at times of emergency". At their Kyoto meeting in 2007, the Ministers decided to establish a "self-managed reserve pooling arrangement". At their May 2008 meeting in Madrid, the Ministers "agreed that the total size of the multilateralised CMI would be at least US$80 billion". In response to the global economic crisis at the Special ASEAN+3 Finance Ministers' meeting in Phuket in February 2009, the amount was subsequently increased to US$120 billion. At their May 2009 meeting, the Ministers announced that they had agreed to implement CMIM before the end of 2009. In their May 2010 statement, the ministers announced that the CMIM agreement with US$120 billion crisis fund came into effect on 24 March 2010. They also reached a consensus on all the key elements of the regional macroeconomic surveillance unit of the CMIM called the AMRO.

The AMRO was eventually established in May 2011 in Singapore. The AMRO will (i) conduct regional surveillance of macroeconomic and financial vulnerabilities of the region and individual countries, and (ii) assist in the activation of the CMIM. The AMRO is not intended to be a substitute for the IMF. It is intended to enhance objective monitoring by supplementing the IMF especially its new Short-term Liquidity Facility, which enables certain countries to borrow without conditions.

Next steps in East Asian financial integration

East Asia's market-led integration, which now is also being driven by various policy actions, is expected to deepen further. One reason for optimism is that the increasing level of trade integration has led to a greater synchronisation of output and business cycles in the region. This means that symmetric shocks are expected to prevail, enhancing the case for cooperation and coordination of macroeconomic policies (Rana, 2008).

Going forward, East Asian economic integration is expected to follow what Senior Minister Goh Chok Tong (2006) once referred to as the "variable geometry, flexible borders" approach. The process will be multi-track with a trade (including infrastructure), finance, and monetary tracks and with new members coming on board when they feel ready. The CMIM and AMRO have set the stage for institutionalising East Asia regionalism. Hence, new institutions to support Asian integration are also expected to emerge. "Bottom-up" integration in East Asia is starting to be "top down" as well, following the European approach.

On the trade track, efforts should be made to (i) make the FTAs compatible with each other (by having similar rules of origin as in Europe); and (ii) consolidate the proliferation of FTAs into a deeper and wider FTA such as the East Asian FTA (including India). Kawai and Wignaraja (2009) have shown that an ASEAN+6 FTA would provide more gains than an ASEAN+3 FTA. Connectivity issues including infrastructure development and trade facilitation are also being addressed.

On the finance track, Asian bond markets should be developed further. With the progress in reforming market infrastructure at the national-levels, a regional body that promotes coordination of capital market rules, regulations and dialogues on financial market vulnerability issues such as an Asian Financial Stability Board (AFSB) could be established. In addition to micro-prudential monitoring, the AFSB could conduct macro-prudential monitoring to reduce systemic risks at the regional-level. The AFSB could also focus on long-term financial market development and integration issues in the region.

The additional steps required in moving from the CMIM to the AMF are (i) strengthening the AMRO for analytical works and developing independent conditionality; and (ii) delinking the CMIM regional surveillance from the IMF — this can be done after the AMRO is strengthened.

The deepening regional and financial integration in the region together with the synchronisation of business cycles suggests that East Asia should initiate actions to coordinate exchange rate policies using a step-by-step approach. The first step could be to promote a greater exchange rate flexibility while maintaining a certain amount of intra-regional stability by monitoring deviations from an Asian Currency Unit (ACU) basket (Kawai and Rana, 2009).

Some commentators see recent trends in the region as heralding the eventual adoption of a single currency or the establishment of an East Asian monetary union. Europe's experience shows that a monetary union imposes stringent demands on policy coordination and institution building that needs strong political will and a strong sense of common purpose, which East Asia lacks at the present.

In addition to being multi-track, East Asian regionalism is also expected to be multi-speed — with the pace of progress for different aspects of regional cooperation and integration varying and with members, from other Asian regions as well, joining as and when they feel that they are ready to do so. It will also be a bottom-up approach as compared to the European institution-led approach.

Economic Relations between South Asia and East Asia[9]

In addition, to deepening, East Asian economic integration is also broadening to become Pan-Asian as many East Asian countries have seen economic opportunities in South Asia especially India.

---

[9] Updated based on Rana and Dowling (2009).

India started to enhance its linkages with East Asia only in 1992 in the aftermath of the Cold War and the start of its economic liberalisation policies when it launched its "Look East" policy. Under the Congress government of Manmohan Singh, the "Look East" policy has been re-energised with a renewed focus on India's place in the global economy. Other South Asian countries have also followed suit. "Look East" policies in South Asia have sought to establish trade and investment links with the dynamic ASEAN and now the East Asian countries. India's engagement with ASEAN began as a sectoral dialogue partnership in 1992, which was upgraded into a full dialogue partnership in 1995 and membership in the ASEAN Regional Forum in 1996. The first summit-level interaction began in November 2002. A long-term vision 2020 paper for the ASEAN–India partnership has been prepared and is under implementation. Since 1995, India has also participated in the East Asia Summit that brings together the heads of states and governments of ASEAN+3 plus Australia, New Zealand and India. At the Summit in Singapore in 2007, it was decided to revive the 3000-year old Nalanda University in India as a Pan-Asian centre of excellence. The recent observer status given to China and Japan in the SAARC also portends well for South Asia–East Asia economic relations. Observer status to Korea and ASEAN is also being considered. At the 2006 Asia-Europe Finance Ministers' meeting, a decision was made to expand membership to include India, Pakistan, Mongolia and the ASEAN Secretariat from the Asian side, and Rumania and Bulgaria from the European side.

South Asia's total merchandise trade with East Asia has grown significantly in absolute terms albeit from a low base. It increased twelve-fold during 1990–2007, from US$12.4 billion–US$148.2 billion (Rana and Dowling, 2009). The annual growth rate was relatively moderate until 2000 but it has surged after that growing by over 25 percent per annum. As expected, a large part of the increase (roughly one-third) in South Asia–East Asia trade is accounted for by the bilateral trade between the two giant economies of India and China.

However, in relative terms the level of South Asia–East Asia trade accounted for 18.9 percent of South Asia's total trade in 1990 and is now about 25 percent. On the other hand, South Asia accounted for a mere 1.3 percent of East Asia's trade and a slightly higher 2.0 percent in 2007. Hence, East Asia is a more important trading partner for South Asia than *vice versa*.

The absence of comparable data on FDI by source limits an analysis of investment relationships between South Asia and East Asia. The data available from national sources and the ASEAN Secretariat shows that investment relations between the two regions, although starting to increase in recent years, is still limited.

Calculation of revealed comparative advantage indices shows that there is potential for enhancing trade between the two regions. South Asia has comparative advantage mainly in primary goods and labour-intensive manufactures and IT services, while East Asia has comparative advantage across a much wider range of products. These include primary goods such as crude rubber and fish, labour-intensive manufactures such as textiles, travel goods and footwear and more capital and knowledge-intensive items such as office machines and telecommunications equipments.

More recently, as in other parts of the world, there has been a proliferation of FTAs between South Asia and East Asia. In 1975, there was only the Bangkok Agreement. Now 7 FTAs are already in effect and 12 are either under negotiation or have been proposed (Table 2.2). The most significant of these, so far, is the signing of the India–Singapore Comprehensive Economic Cooperation Agreement (CECA) in June 2005. The CECA became effective in August 2005 and covers not only trade in goods but also services, investments and cooperation in technology, education, air services and human resources. The Asia Pacific Trade Agreement went into effect in 1976, the Group of eight FTA in 2006, the China–Pakistan FTA in 2007 and the Malaysia–Pakistan FTA — Malaysia's first with a South Asian country — in 2008. Two year ago, the India–ASEAN and the India–Korea FTAs became effective. Although comprehensive in terms of trade liberalisation, the former allows India to protect its agriculture and services sector for some time. The India–Korea FTA has the potential of attracting Korean investment into India for export to third country markets.

Table 2.2. FTAs involving South and East Asian countries.

___

FTAs in Effect

- Asia-Pacific Trade Agreement (APTA, formerly known as the Bangkok Agreement), signed in 1975 and in effect since 1976.
- India–Singapore Comprehensive Economic Cooperation Agreement (CECA), signed in June 2005 and effective since August 2005.
- Preferential Tariff Arrangement-Group of Eight Developing Countries (D-8 PTA),[10] signed in 2006.
- China–Pakistan Free Trade Agreement, signed on 24 November 2006 and in effect as of 1 July 2007 [agreement on Early Harvest Program (EHP) was also signed].
- Malaysia–Pakistan Closer Economic Partnership, signed in November 2007 and took effect in January 2008.
- Association of Southeast Asian Nations (ASEAN)-India Free Trade Agreement, signed in August 2009.
- India–Korea Comprehensive Economic Partnership Agreement (CEPA), signed in August 2009.

FTAs Under Negotiation

- India–Thailand Free Trade Area.
- Bay of Bengal Initiative for Multi-Sectoral Technical and Economic Cooperation (BIMSTEC) Free Trade Area.
- Pakistan–Singapore Free Trade Agreement.
- Pakistan–Indonesia Free Trade Agreement.
- Trade Preferential System of the Organisation of the Islamic Conference (TPS-OIC).

FTAs Proposed

- Pakistan–Brunei Darussalam Free Trade Agreement.
- China–India Regional Trading Arrangement.
- India–Indonesia Comprehensive Economic Cooperation Arrangement.
- Japan–India Economic Partnership Agreement.
- Pakistan–Philippines Free Trade Agreement.
- Pakistan–Thailand Free Trade Agreement.
- Singapore–Sri Lanka Comprehensive Economic Partnership Agreement.

___

Source: ADB FTA Database (www.aric.adb.org).

___

[10] D-8 PTA members are Bangladesh, Egypt, Iran, Malaysia, Nigeria, Pakistan, Indonesia, and Turkey.

Table 2.3 presents some landmarks in South Asia's evolving linkages with East Asia including the signing of various FTAs and Comprehensive Economic Cooperation Agreements. India's engagement with ASEAN first as a sectoral dialogue partner is also highlighted.

Table 2.3. South Asia–East Asia economic relations: Some landmarks.

1975	• Signing of Bangkok Agreement by Bangladesh, India, Laos, Republic of Korea, Sri Lanka, and China.
1985	• Formation of the South Asian Association for Regional Cooperation (SAARC) by Bangladesh, Bhutan, India, Maldives, Nepal, Pakistan, and Sri Lanka. Afghanistan joined in 2007.
1991	• India adopted "Look East" Policy to strengthen economic relationships with East Asian countries.
1992	• Signing of the Association of Southeast Asian Nations (ASEAN) Free Trade Area (AFTA) by Brunei Darussalam, Indonesia, Malaysia, Philippines, Singapore, and Thailand. Other Southeast Asian countries joined later: Vietnam (1995), Lao PDR and Myanmar (1997), and Cambodia (1999). AFTA became fully operational in 2003. • India became a sectoral dialogue partner of ASEAN.
1993	• Signing of Agreement on SAARC Preferential Trading Arrangement (SAPTA) by eight SAARC members. SAPTA entered into force in 1997.
1996	• India became a full dialogue partner of ASEAN.
1997	• East Asian financial crisis, which highlighted the importance of regional cooperation among East Asian economies.
1998	• Signing of Indo–Sri Lanka Free Trade Agreement, which came into force in 2000.
2000	• China joined the World Trade Organisation (WTO), starting with an early harvest program that liberalised 600 farm products. An agreement to trade in goods was signed in 2005, liberalising 7,000 trading goods.
2002	• India–ASEAN partnership was upgraded to summit-level dialogue. • Signing of Framework Agreement between the China and ASEAN. Early Harvest Scheme came into force in 2005.
2003	• Signing of a Framework Agreement on Comprehensive Economic Cooperation between India and ASEAN, incorporating free trade agreement (FTA), at the Bali Summit.

(*Continued*)

Table 2.3.   (*Continued*)

2004	• Signing of an Agreement on South Asian Free Trade Area (SAFTA) during the 12th SAARC Summit in Islamabad. SAFTA came into force in 2006.
	• Signing of a Long-Term Partnership for Peace, Progress and Shared Prosperity by India and ASEAN at the Laos PDR Summit.
	• Signing of Early Harvest Scheme for the India–Thailand Free Trade Framework Agreement under which preferential concessions have been exchanged on a specified set of commodities.
	• Signing of a Framework Agreement under the Bay of Bengal Initiative for Multi-Sectoral Technical and Economic Cooperation (BIMSTEC) by Bangladesh, Bhutan, India, Myanmar, Nepal, Sri Lanka, and Thailand.
2005	• Signing of a Comprehensive Economic Cooperation Agreement (CECA) between India and Singapore.
	• Renaming of the Bangkok Agreement as the Asia-Pacific Trade Agreement (APTA), which would offer up to 4,000 tariff concessions to members.
	• Signing of a Comprehensive Economic Framework Agreement between Pakistan and Indonesia.
2006	• China became an observer of SAARC.
	• Ongoing Japanese proposal for a comprehensive agreement covering ASEAN+3, India, Australia, and New Zealand.
	• Signing of an FTA between the China and Pakistan.
2007	• Signing of Pakistan–Malaysia Free Trade Agreement — Pakistan's first comprehensive FTA and Malaysia's first bilateral FTA with a South Asian country.
2009	• Signing of the ASEAN–India FTA in August 2009.
	• Signing of the India–Korea Comprehensive Economic Partnership Agreement in August 2009.

Source: Author.

Looking forward, a number of policy actions could be taken to increase the level of South Asia–East Asia integration. First, the levels of tariffs and non-tariff barriers (NTBs) are already low in many East Asian countries and South Asia has made encouraging progress in the same direction since the 1990s. However, there is room for further reductions in tariffs and NTBs in both regions (especially NTBs in East Asia because tariffs are already low). Second, in addition to reducing tariffs and NTBs, South Asian countries and several East Asian countries also need to make progress in implementing the so-called second generation reforms to make markets work better by enhancing transparency, good governance, and the quality of fiscal adjustment. These include, among others, reforms of civil service and delivery of public goods, creating an environment that is conducive to private sector opportunities (greater competition, better regulations and stronger property rights), and reforms of institutions that create human capital (e.g., health and education).

Third, South and East Asian countries need to consolidate their FTAs. Quantitative estimates using the computable general equilibrium (CGE) model and the Global Trade Analysis Project (GTAP) database suggest that a broader regional approach will have a large beneficial impact. The estimated impact on national income of an ASEAN+3 and South Asia FTA is much higher than that of an ASEAN+3 and India FTA, which in turn is higher than that of an ASEAN FTA. While India benefits from an ASEAN+3 and India FTA, other South Asian countries lose. However, a broader ASEAN+3 and South Asian FTA is a win-win for all. Countries should also deepen FTAs — extend coverage beyond trade in good into services, investment, technology etc. The Comprehensive Economic Partnership Agreement for East Asia, which is an FTA that includes all East Asia Summit countries, is being established and the Economic Research Institute for ASEAN and East Asia has been established to sensitise and support the process.

The fourth measure that could impact significantly on the level of trade between South Asia and East Asia is the reduction of trading costs. This could be brought about through (i) investment in trade-related infrastructure; and (ii) streamlining of cross-border procedures (including customs procedures and logistic costs). Most cargo between South Asia and East Asia moves by water and air as there are no land transport services that are operational at the moment. Rapid growth in trade has been accommodated through the introduction of larger container ships. Expansion and diversification of feeder services and bottlenecks, primarily in public ports, remain to be addressed. Land transit through Myanmar is not possible at present. Additional corridors between India and China with Bangladesh, Bhutan and Nepal as "land bridges" will have to be developed. China has plans to extend the recently-opened Qinghai–Tibet railway to

Nepal and India. The proposed Asian Highway and Asian railway have missing links and are not fully operational. The proposal to establish an Asian Infrastructure Fund (AIF) with financing from various multilateral agencies and private-public partnership is making progress. The Pan-Asian Infrastructure Forum (PAIF) to sensitise issues related to promoting greater connectivity in Asia is in the process of being established. The ADB has identified 21 high ticket infrastructure projects to connect Asia.

Fifth, countries should make efforts to reduce transport and logistic constraints to facilitate movement of goods between the two regions. These include delays in customs inspection, cargo handling and transfer, and processing of documents. Customs procedures could be modernised by (i) aligning the customs code to international standards; (ii) simplifying and harmonising procedures; (iii) making tariff structures consistent with the international harmonised tariff classification; and (iv) adopting and implementing the WTO Customs Valuation Agreement. South Asian and East Asian countries have made progress in implementing many of these procedures but much more remains to be done.

Finally, trade promotion efforts through skillful economic diplomacy, regular exchange of business delegations and civil society could be encouraged a lot more. People-to-people contacts can go a long way in enhancing the level of trade and investment across countries.

Economic Integration in South Asia

The World Bank (2004) has estimated that the volume of trade among South Asian countries before the Partition of India and Pakistan in 1947 was around 20 percent of their total trade. This fell to about 4 percent by the 1950s and to 2 percent in 1967 mainly because of mutual mistrusts and political conflicts in the region. Also for four decades after independence, South Asian countries had adopted inward-looking development strategies with high barriers to trade and investment. The two landlocked countries, Nepal and Bhutan, had maintained close trade links with India but not with other South Asian countries and the rest of the world.

This trend of declining intra-regional trade in South Asia started to reverse only in the late 1980s and the 1990s when South Asia started to abandon import-substituting policies and began to adopt market-oriented reforms including trade liberalisation. Nevertheless, the level of intra-regional trade presently stands at only a dismal 5 percent of total trade. The comparative figures for East Asia are about 25 percent in the case of ASEAN and 55 percent in the case of ASEAN+3.

The lackluster performance of South Asian integration can be explained by several factors. First, the deep mistrusts and political conflicts of the past continue. Second, the presence of India as a large country arouses fear of hegemony and economic dominance among the smaller neighbouring countries. Third, complementarities that existed in the 1940s may have lessened considerably as countries have developed similar types of industries. However, a recent ADB/UNCTAD (2008) study finds enormous potential for intra-regional trade among the South Asian countries.

With the view of promoting intra-regional trade, the SAARC initiated the South Asian Preferential Trading Arrangement (SAPTA) in 1995. But SAPTA's progress was painstakingly slow because of the product by product approach to tariff concessions, low product coverage, and stringent rules of origin. One study found that many trade restrictions maintained by South Asian countries were designed not to restrict imports from outside the region but to keep out exports of neighbouring countries, particularly from India (Weerakoon, 2008).

In a sense, the South Asian Free Trade Area (SAFTA) of 2004 was a leap forward. It was formally launched on 1 July 2006, six months late because of Pakistan's failure to ratify it on time. Unfortunately, the SAFTA also had its own weaknesses. Among others, services trade, which is emerging as a major export item from South Asia especially India, was excluded. So was the issue of non-tariff barriers. Despite this, a recent model-based study by the ADB/UNCTAD (2008) finds that the successful implementation of the SAFTA would provide significant trade and income gains for both the larger and the smaller countries in the region.

On money and finance, the SAARCFINANCE, which is a network of central bank governors and finance secretaries set up following the 1998 Colombo SAARC Summit, has achieved some success in forging closer cooperation on macroeconomic policies. The SAARC has also decided to hold regular meetings of the South Asian Finance Ministers modeled after the ASEAN and ASEAN+3 Finance Ministers' meetings. However, the more recently announced goal of attaining a South Asian Economic Union and the expressed desire of a common currency will have to wait for some time in the future as they can be feasible only in the longer term as economic convergence is achieved in the region.

In the area of cross-border infrastructure development, the South Asia Subregional Economic Cooperation (SASEC) program initiated by four members of the SAARC (Bangladesh, Bhutan, India, and Nepal) has made notable progress in identifying projects in the six priority sectors (transport, energy and power, tourism, environment, trade and investment, private sector cooperation). But then again the implementation of the SASEC initiatives has been modest.

More recently, there have been signs which suggest that the region's mindset on regional integration agenda is perhaps starting to change a bit. The recent elections in Bangladesh, Pakistan, and India and decision by Sri Lanka and Pakistan to deal with insurgencies may have created an environment which is more favourable to inter-country cooperation. India, in particular, appears to have adopted a more positive stance on South Asia befitting its rapid emergence in the global economy. The Asian Development Bank's India 2039 study notes that India has the potential of achieving an average of 9.5 percent growth per annum over the next 30 years provided it continues its economic reform programs.[11] By that time, India could be the second largest in the world, second only to China surpassing the

---

[11] This requires a formidable set of reforms to: (i) tackle disparities among various social groups; (ii) improve the environment; (iii) eliminate pervasive infrastructure bottlenecks; (iv) renew education, technological development and innovation; (v) transform the delivery of public services especially in cities; (vi) revolutionise energy production and consumption; and (vii) foster a prosperous South Asia and become a responsible global power.

United States. A prosperous South Asia would be beneficial for all. In 2009, India announced that it would provide free market access to imports from its least-developed neighbours and signed a FTA with Sri Lanka. It also made commitments to reduce its negative list and to promote regional connectivity. More recently, India has also proposed a Dhaka–Delhi–Lahore railway line to connect to the proposed Islamabad–Tehran–Istanbul service. In January 2010, India and Bangladesh signed a series of new agreements to address some of the barriers to bilateral trade through new trade and transit provisions.

Positive signs are not confined to India alone. Despite the terrorist attacks, India–Pakistan relations appear to have thawed a bit. Pakistan has also increased the list of items in its positive list resulting in rapid growth of its imports from India. The new regime in Nepal has made progress in advancing discussions on a number of hydro-electric projects.

In this changing context and based on East Asia's successful experience with regional integration, South Asia needs to learn lessons from East Asia's successful experience with economic integration. The need for further cooperation in South Asia is clear. Burki (2009) argues "South Asia has two options — it could pursue national interests or it could work as a region with the countries in the area prepared to step back a little from including only national interests in their economic strategies (in addressing regional and global issues). South Asia could do so much better by adopting a regional approach". Three lessons are particularly relevant for South Asia.

The first is for South Asia to take advantage of the recent positive signs and promote integration within itself by giving primacy to economic issues and not allowing political differences to stand in the way of regional integration efforts. The East Asian countries have not been immune to political conflicts. They have had their fair share. However, despite these problems the East Asian leaders have pressed ahead and agreed to keep their political differences aside on the regional cooperation agenda. It is now time for South Asia leaders to also follow suit and implement on-going integration schemes effectively and deepen them further. The most likely and faster way to increase South Asian integration would be to do so by expanding bilateral trade and investment relations among the members with the eventual goal of region-wide integration. This is because SAFTA is having difficulty in producing results because of political and economic constraints. However, at the bilateral level the pace of liberalisation can be much quicker and can build confidence.

The second is for the South Asian leaders to adopt the East Asian concept of "open regionalism" rather than the failed concept of "closed regionalism". This means extending any preferences granted by a country to neighbours and eventually to the rest of the world as well or "multilateralising regionalism". Successful implementation of "open regionalism" in East Asia has contributed to the establishment of regional production networks and increased intra-regional trade without trade being diverted from the rest of the world. In fact, East Asia's trade with its three main partner groups (the EU, the US, and the rest of the world) has increased. This, in turn, has had favourable spillover effects on East Asian intra-regional trade and investment. South Asia could also "multilateralise regionalism" by promoting trade with the rest of the world, specially East Asia, which has become its fastest growing trading partner. Such trade would be complementary to and have a catalytic impact on trade within South Asia. Policies that could promote trade between South Asia and East Asia have already been discussed above. Beyond the static analysis presented by comparisons of complementarity and revealed comparative advantage, there is much potential for South Asia to link itself to East Asia and global production networks for goods and services by driving down real trade costs and trade and logistic barriers.

The third is for South Asia to adopt the East Asian approach to sequencing integration and not the European one. When the Europeans initiated the integration process in the post-World War II period, there was a strong political will to cooperate and promote peace in order to avoid wars in the future. That is the reason why they went for a customs union and an economic union. Efforts to promote monetary integration began only later in 1979 when the European Monetary System (EMS) was established. The East Asian sequence was different. Given the weakness in the global financial architecture, East Asia initiated cooperation by establishing the ASEAN and the ASEAN+3 Finance Ministers' Process. Efforts to promote trade integration started later after 2000 when countries started to promote FTAs. For South Asia too, given the lack of political will, it might be advisable to build up on the various activities of SAARCFINANCE, and may even establish an EMS-type system of fixed but adjustable exchange rates before trade integration. The increased level of intra-regional trade brought by such an exchange rate regime could play a catalytic role in encouraging cooperation on trade.

References

ADB (2009). India 2039: An Affluent Society in One Generation.

ADB/UNCTAD (2008). *Quantification of Benefits from Economic Cooperation in South Asia*. Macmillan, New York.

ADBI (2009). Infrastucture for a Seamless Asia.

Angus M. (2001). The World Economy: A Millennial Perspective. OECD.

Burki, S. (2009). South Asia Choices in a Fluid World. Institute of South Asian Studies, *Working Paper No. 83*.

Coedes, G. (1968). The Indianized States of Southeast Asia. In *Suan Brown Cowing trans.*, W. F. Vella (ed.) University of Malaya Press.

Ferguson, N. (2011). *Civilization: The West and the Rest*. Allen Lane, UK.

Findlay, R. and K. O'Rourke (2007). *Power and Plenty*. Princeton University Press, New Jerssey, US.

Frank, A. G. (1998). *ReOrient: Global Economy in the Asian Age*. University of California Press, US.

Frost, E. L. (2009). India's Role in East Asia: Lessons from Cultural and Historical Linkages. RIS Discussion Papers #147.

Goh Chok Tong (2006). "Towards an East Asian Renaissance". Address at the opening session of the 4th Asia-Pacific Roundtable organised by the Global Foundation, the World Bank, and the Institute of Southeast Asian Studies.

Kawai, M. and P. B. Rana (2009). The Asian Financial Crisis Revisited: Lessons, Responses, and New Challenges. In *Lessons from the Asian Financial Crisis*. R. Carney (ed.) Routledge.

Kawai, M. and G. Wignaraja (2009). "Asian FTAs: Trends and Challenges". ADBI Discussion Working Paper Series No. 144.

Maddison, A (2007). Contours of the World Economy, 1-2030. Oxford University Press, UK.

Mishap, P. P. (2001). India-Southeast Asian relations: An overview. *Teaching South Asia*, Vol. 1(1).

Poddar, T. and E. Yi (2007). India's Rising Growth Potential. *Global Economics Paper 152*. Goldman Sachs.

Rana, P. (2008). Trade intensity and business cycle synchronization. The case of Esat Asian countries. *Singapore Economic Review*, Vol. 53(2), 279–292.

Rana, P. and J. M. D Dowling (2009). *South Asia: Rising to the Challenge of Globalization*. World Scientific Publishing Co., Singapore.

Shankar, V. (2004). Towards an Asian Economic Community: Exploring the Past. In *Towards an Asian Economic Community: Vision of a New Asia*, N. Kumar (ed.), RIS and ISEAS.

Weerakoon, D. (2008). "SAFTA: Current Status and Prospects". Institute of Policy Studies of Sri Lanka, Colombo.

Wilson, D. and R. Purushothaman (2003). Dreaming with BRICs: The Path to 2050. *Global Economics Paper 99*. Goldman Sachs.

World Bank (2004). Trade Policies in South Asia: An Overview. *Report No. 29929*. Washington D.C.

Chapter 3

Restoring the Links: Historical Perspectives on South Asia–East Asia Relations

Ellen L. Frost

Introduction: Sailing through History

At the 2009 India–ASEAN summit, India's Prime Minister Manmohan Singh suggested that his country and ASEAN could jointly plan and execute a "commemorative ship expedition" in 2011–2012. The ship would sail along the sea routes that linked India with Southeast Asia in the 10th–12th centuries, stopping at both ancient and modern ports in ASEAN and other East Asian countries.[1]

Highlighting the rich legacy of cross-regional maritime connections is constructive, imaginative and long overdue. The proposal symbolises India's "Look East" policy and sets up a maritime equivalent of the

---

[1] "Prime Minister's Statement at the 7th India–ASEAN Summit", available at http://pib.nic.in/release/release.asp?relid=53420.

land-based Nalanda initiative.[2] The voyage would coincide with the 500th anniversary of the Portuguese conquest of Malacca, which together with the Portuguese conquest of Goa in the previous year, inaugurated Western imperial expansion. Entirely planned and manned by Asians, it would be a fitting symbol of the death of colonialism.

But the proposal glosses over three inconvenient facts. First, "India" as we know it today did not exist in the 10th–12th centuries. Named after the Indus River, the lands we know as "India" were not united until Mogul and later British forces subjugated them. Those who boast that today's India will recapture its past glory are probably thinking about kingdoms such as the Maurya, the Gupta, the Chola, the Delhi Sultanate and the early Moguls, but only the latter, later supplemented by the British, fully and effectively unified the territory now known as India and Pakistan.[3] Substituting "South Asia" for "India" would be more historically accurate, but doing so would involve sharing the commemorative voyage with Pakistan (among others). Neither ASEAN nor the Indian foreign policy establishment would favour bringing Pakistan into the expanding India–ASEAN relationship.

This chapter refers to "India" in a pre-Mogul context, meaning the territory united under various Hindu and Muslim rulers including today's Pakistan, which or through which many rulers of the subcontinent came from. One should also include Sri Lanka, an important centre of religion and trade, as well as the Maldives and

---

[2] Nalanda, located in Bihar, was once a monastery and a great Buddhist centre of learning. Scholars at Nalanda studied and taught not only religion but also astronomy, mathematics, philosophy and other subjects. A new university, to be built near the site of the ruins, will offer the modern equivalent of the same subjects, a centre for religious study and interfaith understanding, and more. The Nalanda project underscores India's great tradition of learning and scholarship and reminds the rest of Asia where Buddhism came from. It signifies that India is prepared to engage in the subtle diplomatic competition for influence in Asia. Major funding will come from the governments of Japan and Singapore, both of which are keeping a watchful eye on China's resurgence.

[3] The Director General of India's Council of Scientific and Industrial Research predicted that India will become "a unique intellectual powerhouse…capturing all its glory which it had in millennia gone by". *Financial Times*, 30 December 2009, p. 5. Such comments are not unusual.

the Himalayan mountain kingdoms. This chapter alas, omits them. It also fails to do justice to the history of East Asia and limits that part of the discussion to the role of China alone.

Second, the historical period to be highlighted by the proposed commemorative voyage (the 10th–12th centuries) is somewhat self-serving. This period was precisely the era when the Chola Dynasty's naval power was surging and its regional influence was at its peak. Not until the 13th century did the Mongols sweep across Asia, pacifying and unifying the Silk Road. Another century and a half would pass before the Chinese admiral Zheng He led his famous naval expeditions.

Finally, the proposal masks a pressing diplomatic challenge: officials in New Delhi are struggling to compete with China's manifold cultural and history-related initiatives. The Chinese government has set up numerous "Confucian Institutes" where the Chinese language and culture are taught. Beijing has also funded museum exhibitions featuring the voyages of Zheng He, the tomb-warriors of the emperor Qin Shi Huang and other highlights of Chinese history. The Indian government cannot match China's expenditures but it can advance a few good initiatives to help balance presentations of the historical record. The challenge is that it must avoid appearing to be either seeking great-power hegemony or competing in any hostile way with China.

These three observations on the proposed voyage expose the risks inherent in writing about South Asia–East Asia relations from a historical perspective. The word "perspective" comes from Latin, which means "to see clearly". Yet the swirl of history is never clear. To write about history is to impose a pattern and meaning on people whose experiences may have seemed random and even chaotic at the time. Most of the people, who walked, rode or sailed between South Asia and East Asia left no records. They did not think of themselves as "Asians". Moreover, the markers and labels that we adopt, such as "pre-colonial" or the now-obsolete "Far East", may implicitly demean indigenous trends and exaggerate the role of the West (Lieberman, 2003). Finally, glorifying history can become a tool of political leaders, who may evoke a semi-mythical "golden age" in order to instill certain values or legitimise certain actions. Those of us who draw on history to justify and promote the re-integration of South Asia and East Asia must guard against all these risks.

With these caveats in mind, I draw three conclusions from the history of South Asia–East Asia relations:

1. Fully appreciating the history of South Asia–East Asia relations requires us to re-map and re-centre our notions of Asia;
2. When seen with this revised concept of Asia in mind, the history of South Asia–East Asia relations, supplies ample precedent for efforts to restore closer integration between the two regions;
3. Asia's maritime history provides a stronger rationale for re-integration than the Silk Road or other land-based connections.

The next three sections develop these three arguments in turn. The final section analyses why connections between South Asia and East Asia ossified and shrank, looks briefly at an earlier version of pan-Asianism and suggests two broad lessons and five corresponding policy initiatives drawn from Asia's maritime history.

Re-Mapping and Re-Centering South Asia–East Asia Relations

"Re-mapping" means redesigning the spatial structures through which we filter and organise our knowledge of the world's continents and regions. All of us possess such structures or else we would be overwhelmed by waves of random information. The way we apply such structures to continents and regions shapes our understanding of them. Maps and their labels reflect our political assumptions, reveal our priorities, influence the way we sort out facts and mold the frame-work of our actions. These spatial structures can shift rapidly in response to a changing world. The resurgence of Asia, and of China and India in particular, justifies adjusting these mental maps.

In their book *The Myth of Continents*, geographer Martin Lewis and Karen Wigen present re-mapping as a blend of physical geography and human interaction. Stressing the diminishing importance of distance, they assert that "regions" can take a variety of spatial forms, not necessarily limited to contiguous blocs. Regions can be sprawling and complex, shaded by borderlands and etched by multiple corridors and crossing points. They reflect historical processes, interactions with others, clusters of ideas, practices, and social institutions. They can contain not only dominant populations but also vast diasporas, cultural archipelagos and populations whose religion, language, and material culture endow them with various mixed or "matrix" identities (Lewis and Wigen, 1997).

Scholars applying the concept of re-mapping to contemporary East Asia have pointed to emerging "webs of interconnectedness", ranging from transnational investment to civil action groups (Pempel, 2005). In the millennia leading up to the colonial period, these webs encompassed trade, religion, culture, warfare and virtually every other form of contact known to mankind. South Asia, or at least large parts of South Asia, participated fully in these linkages.

Among many other features of Asia's geography, an alien viewer would be initially struck by how huge the Deccan is and how dramatically it juts out into the Indian Ocean. She or he would also notice how much of that part of the globe, consists of water. These observations are the subject of the following two sections, respectively.

Re-centering "Asia"

One difficulty with locating the centre of Asia is that the concept of "Asia" is a Western invention. The ancient Greeks envisaged the known world as three regions: Europe, Libya (Africa) and Asia. But Greek and Roman notions of Asia were very limited. When St. Paul described his sufferings in "the province of Asia", he meant Anatolia, what we now call Asia Minor (Turkey). Scholars believe that the name "Asia" probably came from the name of an ancient kingdom in that region.

As the centuries went by and knowledge of more distant territories grew, European notions of "Asia" rolled farther east. Fueled by what eventually became a colonial scramble, maps became increasingly comprehensive and accurate. In the late 18th and 19th centuries, colonial rule became more forceful and exclusive. The imperial powers divided up most of Asia into spheres of influence, drew firm boundary lines, took direct or indirect control of trade and customs and restricted access to inland waterways.

At the same time, Western colonialists facilitated trade and transportation between South Asia and East Asia by building roads, railroads and ports and by imposing their mother tongue within their respective empires. Converting subsistence farming into large plantations and wresting extraterritorial concessions from China after each defeat or failed rebellion, they greatly expanded trade. One of the unsavoury links between British India and China was the sale of large quantities of opium to the Chinese, over the strong objections of the Chinese government.

By the second half of the 20th century, notions of "Asia" had rolled too far east. Thanks in part to dynamic economic growth in East Asia and in part to India's economic insularity, "Asia" became strongly identified with China, Japan and Korea. Maps featuring the United States at the centre sliced the Eurasian continent in two, grouping India with the Middle East. The U.S. State Department, for example, assigned India to the (now-defunct) Bureau of Near East and South Asian Affairs.

Now that India has turned outward again, abandoned autarkic economic policies, developed a blue-water naval capability and sought closer ties with its Asian neighbours, it is time to tug "Asia" back from its extreme eastern edge and acknowledge South Asia's close historical and cultural ties in the region.

Appreciating the oceans

Oceans divide people but they also define and unite them. The great French historian Fernand Braudel named a whole cultural region after a body of water — the Mediterranean (Braudel, 1972–73). There is no better way to begin understanding the history of South Asia–East Asia relations than to recognise the shaping influence of the ocean.

People who live along the coast look outward toward the sea and other coastal communities. As Kenneth McPherson observes, they tend to be more cosmopolitan and pluralistic (McPherson, 1998). Races and nationalities vary widely, mingling more easily and freely than they do in more isolated communities (Wolters, 1999).[4] People who live along coastal routes and ocean-accessible waterways often buy goods of the same brand, adopt the same technology, enjoy the same music and become aware of the same ideas.

Nowhere is this unifying and defining power of the sea more manifest than in the history of Asia. The Indian Ocean, the Bay of Bengal, the East China Sea, the South China Sea, the Banda Sea and major straits and river deltas in between were the watery arms of a great Asia-wide system. The sea defined and bound its parts. The Chinese name for Southeast Asia was *nan yang* — [the region of] the southern oceans. Many scholars have concluded that we should pay more attention to the role of the oceans. The historian Takeshi Hamashita believes that we must study Asian regional history as the history of Asian seas (Hamashita, 1997). The late maritime historian Ashin Das Gupta discerned a creative power at work in the Indian Ocean. He went so far as to say that it was not that the continental state upheld port cities but rather that the Indian Ocean itself created them (Das Gupta, 2001). Assessing today's Asia, former Indian diplomat Sudhir Devare views seas as natural integrators and cites the "strategic homogeneity" of the whole maritime region stretching from India to Southeast Asia to China (Devare, 2006).

A Brief History of South Asia–East Asia Relations

For several thousand years, relations between South Asia and East Asia were embedded in a much wider pattern of trade, cultural exchange and conquest. These networks stretched all the way from China to the eastern Mediterranean region. In a book entitled *Bound Together: How Traders, Preachers, Adventurers and Warriors Shaped Civilization*, Nayan Chanda demonstrates that such contacts date back to the end of the Ice Age (Chanda, 2007).

Goods, people, culture, religion, money and ideas that nourished the South Asia–East Asia relationship flowed along two great

---

[4] Wolters argued that these traits are characteristic of seagoing communities generally.

pathways of trade and travel. One route was the branched vein of desert trails and mountain passes known today as the Silk Road, and the other was a network of maritime highways that gradually expanded from the coastline to the open seas. The latter routes linked what I call "Maritime Asia", which I define as the sweep of coastal communities, port cities, towns and inland trading nodes clustered along ocean-destined rivers not far from the sea. China and South Asia, particularly what is now India, contributed substantially to the flows that nourished and sustained both routes. Their contributions are sketched separately below.

The Silk Road

Camel caravans trudging through wind-swept deserts and frigid mountain passes stopped at Bokhara, Samarkand, Kashgar, Dunhuang and many lesser-known crossways. Although traders and other travelers rarely traveled the whole length of the Silk Road, the route was essentially open. But after the final collapse of the Roman Empire and the rise of warring kingdoms to the East, the Silk Road was beset by bandits and its unity was frequently disrupted. It was reopened and safeguarded by the tribes collectively known as Mongols, who introduced remarkably modern long-distance commercial practices (Weatherford, 2004).

As Genghis Khan's descendants assimilated into other cultures, converted to different religions, or launched wars with one another, the Silk Road crumbled into discontinuous segments once again. The imposition of national borders sealed its fragmentation.

A central argument of this chapter is that, with one big exception (Buddhism), maritime history provides a more promising historical foundation for closer South Asia–East Asia relations than the history of land-based ties. For most of the last millennium, travel by sea was easier and cheaper than travel by land and it remains so even today. The great Himalayan mountain range and other geographic barriers continue to restrict overland travel between China and India. The nations of the Silk Road are nominally at peace, but a traveller is too often met by gun-toting border guards blocking borders or demanding bribes (Bernstein, 2001). It is hard to imagine what or who will move along the Silk Road in large quantities except energy, tourists, cultural entrepreneurs and illegal traffickers. That is why this chapter describes the maritime connection in more detail.

Maritime Asia

The other route connecting South Asia and East Asia was a vast maritime system. Maritime Asia rims the world's largest and third-largest oceans, the Pacific and the Indian. It is fed by three of the world's longest rivers — the Yangtze and the Huang Ho (Yellow River) in China and the Mekong, which runs from China through or along mainland Southeast Asia. The Straits of Malacca and Sunda are located there.

Sea-based trade stretched from the eastern Mediterranean down the Red Sea and the Persian Gulf to Yemen and eastern Africa, coastal India, Sri Lanka, the northern edge of the Bay of Bengal, Sumatra, Java, the southern Philippines, Southern China and from there to northern China, Korea and Japan. Voyages along these routes also date back to the ancient times. In the 2nd century A.D., for example, trade officials in Alexandria imposed a duty on pepper imported from the Malabar Coast.

Not for centuries did traders and other travellers stray far from the coast. As knowledge of navigation grew and the technology of sailing vessels improved, trading vessels struck out for open water and crossed the Indian Ocean and the South China Sea. Until the age of steam navigation, travel by ship was slow and often dangerous. Travelling across the water depended on the wind. Asia experiences a seasonal reversal of winds and rains (the "monsoon effect") stronger than anywhere else. Voyages were timed in accordance with the monsoon, which confined sailors and merchants to long stays at the ports. These lengthy sojourns facilitated the spread of technology, culture and religion.

In contrast to the Silk Road, maritime routes bypassed local wars and political interference and flourished without serious interruption.

If skirmishes closed a trading hub or if a port silted up, ship captains found new routes. This mingling branched out unevenly; for example, it largely bypassed Cambodia and Vietnam.

In this maritime system, the great civilisations of Asia rippled and overlapped. Maritime Asia was open, diverse, tolerant and cosmopolitan. Residents and travellers shared knowledge, innovations, religion and ideas as well as goods. There was neither a single hegemon nor a single "golden age". Local rulers launched wars over land but did not try to control the seas. Various traders came and went but no single political authority dominated the full sweep of Asia's pre-colonial maritime trade.[5]

As kingdoms rose and fell, ownership of major shipping fleets fluctuated. The success of each group of ship owners and merchants stimulated the others to compete. In the 7th century, Persian merchant ships led navigation to and from China, but by the 9th century, Arab traders had largely supplanted them. The Burmese were also active at this time.

In the 10th and 11th centuries, the Cholas of South India arose, looked to the East and eclipsed their rivals. The Cholas conquered Sri Lanka and the Maldives, established contact with Song China and launched naval expeditions against 14 port cities in Southeast Asia (Kulke *et al.*, 2009). Their influence reached a peak in the mid 11th century (Fig. 3.1).

By the 12th century, huge Chinese junks had nosed other ships aside. In the 15th century, the expansion of Gujurati commerce and the rise of western Javanese shipping swelled the sea routes. At the western tip of Sumatra, Aceh became a thriving power and still retains the mixed cultures and cuisines of a former trading centre.

Meanwhile, Islam spread peacefully along the coasts and from there to the interior. Like others arriving by sea, Muslim merchants arriving in Southeast Asia from South Asia had to wait for the prevailing monsoon before returning home. This delay gave them ample time to settle in the local society; many married the daughters

---

[5] A partial exception was the kingdom of Srivijaya, which controlled both sides of the Straits of Malacca and became an intermediary in trade between South Asia and China.

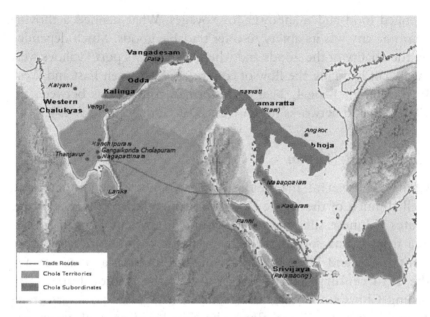

Fig. 3.1: Chola Empire's influence at the height of its power, ca. 1050 A.D.

of local families, who adopted the new faith. Wide-spread conversion to Islam boosted demand for voyages to Mecca. As Chinese ships withdrew, Muslim traders gradually came to dominate major sea routes, blocking unfettered access to South Asia from Europe. The end of the 15th century saw the first trickle of Western explorers who sought to circumvent Muslim hegemony by sailing to Asia around the Cape of Good Hope.

Except for the area bordering the Straits of Malacca, there was little continuity in the exact location of prosperous port towns. In Gujarat, the home of many great Indian merchant shipping families, ascendancy passed from Broach to Cambay, Surat and eventually Bombay (Mumbai). The town of Masulipatam had once been the principal trade depot of India's Coromandel Coast, linking the Golconda kingdom with the outside world. But by 1800, it was a "small, ramshackle place with a crumbling fort, a newly rebuilt English church and a graveyard" (Dalrymple, 2002).

Wherever they were, maritime cities would contain a customs house, a shipyard and a place to do business. Neighbouring villages supplied food and manpower for voyages. What defined a thriving maritime city was its ability to offer tradable goods. Much depended on the quality of the goods and whether the city's port facilities were capable of handling the flow of commodities between East and West. In the Bay of Bengal, Thai ports formed connections between the China Sea and networks to the West (Das Gupta, 2001; p. 49).

China's contribution

China, a powerful magnet for traders since time immemorial, fuelled much of the traffic along both the Silk Road and maritime routes. Chinese silks have been found in ancient Roman tombs. Tea from China spread through monastic communities to Japan, Central Asia and Tibet before arriving in Europe as a luxury item in the 17th century. Traffic was two-way: the rugged horses propelling China's infantry came from Central Asia. Tributary states brought gifts to China along the Silk Road as well as by sea. Persian cobalt was sent to Chinese kilns to colour the famous "Ming blue" porcelain.

Over the centuries, traders from many regions sailed the seas carrying monks, adventurers and others with them. Chinese merchants were prominent among them. The famous 15th century voyages of the Chinese Muslim admiral Zheng He, who ploughed the seas with armadas of up to 300 vessels and 30,000 men, reached Hormuz, Aden, and the east coast of Africa as well as Southeast Asia.

However, during the Ming Dynasty (1368–1644) trade was restricted to tributary states and the consumption of foreign goods was discouraged or forbidden. In 1394, for example, ordinary Chinese were prohibited from using foreign perfumes and other foreign goods (Mungello, 1999). Despite Zheng He's achievement, the goals of Ming emperor Yung-lo were not to conquer territory or establish beachheads for commercial expansion but to assert China's presence in the Indian Ocean, encourage the states there to come to China to trade and discipline Chinese merchants engaging in piracy. In the late 1420s, Ming rulers turned inward and these voyages ceased (Das Gupta, 2001; pp. 61–62).

As the Chinese government turned its attention to meeting the Mongol threat from the north and subduing unruly "barbarians" in the west, the imperial capital moved from Nanking to Peking, which was not a commercial city. Not until 1567 did the Ming government finally revoke its prohibition on maritime trade. Even then, Confucian rulers could not understand why Western governments would subordinate statecraft to the dictates of mere merchants and elevate trade to a national goal.

As the Chinese navy continued to fall into disuse, pirates operating from Japan and Taiwan repeatedly raided China's southern and eastern coastline. Henceforth, Chinese merchants confined themselves to Malacca and points east. Even in the 19th century, when the importance of maritime power was glaringly obvious, the Qing (Ch'ing) government failed to appreciate the importance of a navy and was thrown on the defensive as sea-borne Westerners demanded one concession after another.

Thus, in Wang Gungwu's wonderful prose, China remained "earthbound"; the great "seaward sweep" of Chinese sojourners settling elsewhere in Asia did not begin until the 19th century (Wang, 2000). Despite Zheng He's achievements, China never became a maritime power and its leaders consistently underestimated the threat from the sea.

South Asia's contribution

(i) South Asians and trade

India was literally central to the pre-colonial trading network. It was a huge, U-shaped anchor of trade — "on the way to everywhere", as one scholar put it (Abu-Lughod, 1989). Indian, Chinese, Malay, Arab and eventually Western merchants took advantage of India's central location. South Asian merchants were active throughout the entire trading system and were the first outsiders to seek out Southeast Asia's wealth (Wheatley, 1961). In an early example of what we now call "the export of services", several thousand men from India travelled with the ships and took care of all their commercial needs while in port. When the Indian merchant fleet dwindled and disappeared, their successors accommodated themselves to ship-owners of other nationalities (Das Gupta, 2001; pp. 25–26).

South Asians were avid traders. For centuries, Indian ships from both western and eastern ports crisscrossed the ocean. They were familiar with the Straits of Malacca and docked regularly in Vietnamese, Burmese and Chinese ports. They knew their way to the islands of present-day Indonesia. Their contacts with the Srivijaya and Majapahit in Sumatra and Java are well documented. They docked in what is now southern Thailand, where South Asian goods would be carried across the narrowest part of the Kra peninsula on their way to China. South Asian merchants may also have visited Korea.

(ii) *The spread of hindu culture*

Like China, South Asia was a rich source of culture for the rest of Asia. Hindu stories and symbols reached far beyond their homeland and blended with indigenous cultures. Wolters has highlighted the concept of mandalas (circles of kings) to describe the overlapping kingdoms and diffuse political power characteristic of early Southeast Asia (Wolters, 1999; Derrett, 1975; pp. 131–135). Anyone who has wandered through the great temple complexes of Asia sees carvings and inscriptions reflecting the vast sweep of Hindu influence. Panoramic battle scenes from the Ramayana enliven the walls of Cambodia's Angkor Wat.

Another legacy from South Asia's Hindu tradition is the Sanskrit element in many Southeast Asian languages and alphabets. By 500 A.D., Sanskrit had become the hallmark of civilisation in much of Southeast Asia and was frequently the official language of the court. Once again, this form of Indian influence arrived in the form of culture and religion, not by the sword. Possibly for this reason, language expert Nicholas Ostler observes that nowhere did contact with Sanskrit lead to the loss or replacement of other linguistic traditions. This was not the case with the languages of what Ostler calls "large-scale campaigning civilisations", such as Greek, Latin, Arabic, Spanish, French, and English (Ostler, 2005).

Even today, many local cultures retain myths of Indian origin. Indonesia's shadow-puppet theatre features all-night performances of Hindu epics. Many modern places and institutions preserve Indian names and symbols. The name "Singapore", for example, comes from the Sanskrit simha (lion) and pura (city); according to legend, a 14th century Sumatran Malay prince travelling there, named it so because, he spotted a beast that he assumed was a lion. (Since no lions ever lived there, the creature was probably a tiger.) Names like Indochina and Indonesia incorporate an Indian root. Indonesia's national airline is named for Garuda, the sacred bird that carried the god Vishnu.

(iii) *Buddhism*

Perhaps South Asia's greatest gift to the rest of Asia was Buddhism. Siddhartha Gautama (the Buddha or "Enlightened One"), was born to a wealthy Nepalese family at the end of the 5th century B.C. but left home in search of an end to human suffering. He taught widely in what is now Uttar Pradesh, Bihar and southern Nepal. He probably spoke Prakrit, a colloquial dialect of Sanskrit. In the 3rd century B.C., his teachings gained favour with Ashoka, the great Maurya emperor.

For at least a thousand years, monks and scholars carried Buddhism along the Silk Road, into mainland Southeast Asia and across the water to Sri Lanka and other destinations. The earliest evidence of Buddhism at the court of a Chinese prince, who also practiced Taoism, dates from 65 A.D., but the long process of absorbing Buddhism into Chinese culture did not begin till the third century.[6] As Buddhism spread, the Chinese adapted Buddhist art and iconography to their own ideals; to cite just one example, South Asia's Avalokiteshvara, the bodhisattva of compassion, became China's Kuan Yin. By the Tang Dynasty (618–907 A.D.), Buddhism had acquired such political strength that Tang rulers engaged in a selective revival of Confucianism to control it. Under the Yuan

---

[6] For a concise and thoughtful history of the spread of Buddhism in China, see Wright, *Buddhism in Chinese History.*

(Mongol) dynasty, Buddhism enjoyed a renaissance (Wales, 1967). It took root and acquired royal patronage in Tibet, Bhutan, Nepal, Korea, Japan, Sri Lanka and mainland Southeast Asia.

Vivid scenes from the life of the Buddha ring Indonesia's great temple-mountain complex, Borobodur. Monks from China, Japan and elsewhere made pilgrimages to India to visit holy sites associated with the life of Buddha. Travelling by foot, horse, camel and elephant, the 7th century Chinese Buddhist monk Xuan Zang (Hsuan Tsang) crossed 5000 miles of forbidden territory to seek the original classics of Buddhist thought from its source in India.[7] Ironically, Buddhism lost vitality in its homeland and sank into the vastness of Hindu culture.[8]

Characteristics of Maritime Asia

From a 21st century perspective, four aspects of Maritime Asia's economic, social, and political history lend themselves nicely to efforts to bring about closer relations between South Asia and East Asia. Because of the relative ease of ocean voyages compared to overland travel, these four features provide a stronger rationale for re-integration than land-based connections (important as they were).

First, the free movement of goods was the norm; the main obstacle was the weather. Although China's tributary system defined the formal architecture, unofficial trade flourished. As long as tribute rituals were observed, China did not interfere with either the independence of tributary states or their ability to trade with each other. Restrictions on trade, such as embargoes, discriminatory taxes and exorbitant tariffs, prompted merchants to find ways of circumventing them and to make money in the process. The closure of Tokugawa Japan encouraged smuggling, as did the prior clampdown by Ming authorities. Forbidding trade simply gave Ryukyu Islanders, the Portuguese, and others a chance to serve as middlemen. When authorities banned the sale of certain goods, merchants made profits

---

[7] For a near-recreation of this journey in our time, see Bernstein, Ultimate Journey.

[8] This complex process is described in Wendy Doniger, *The Hindus: An Alternative History*. Today, fewer than 1 percent of Indians are Buddhists.

in the black market. When they imposed price controls, sellers sought other markets even if forbidden to do so.

Second, except for certain caste restrictions in South Asia and occasional bans on emigration imposed by the Chinese and Japanese governments, Maritime Asia gave free rein to the movement of people. Merchants, sailors, artisans and other travellers moved easily among maritime cities and often resettled in one of them. Penang, on the Straits of Malacca, attracted Chinese and South Asian merchants and labourers, along with Thais, Burmese, and others (McPherson, 1998; p. 239). In Southeast Asia, it was customary for rulers to counter a naval attack by employing Gujurati, Malay and/or Chinese vessels and their crew (Reid, 1988).

Third, merchants in major maritime cities enjoyed considerable local autonomy. They developed numerous means of conducting long-distance business largely on their own, including long-distant banking and letters of credit unencumbered by government intervention. Each of the major trading groups was allowed to have a local manager who took care of the community's needs without interference from local authorities. Merchants also banded together in associations for protection and the promotion of mutual interests.

Finally, a well-developed maritime infrastructure and attractiveness to traders were keys to wealth and power. Adequate ports, up-to-date shipping technology and the absence of burdensome restrictions characterised a successful maritime hub. This also reduced transport costs and enriched those who controlled it.

Restoring Asian Unity: Suggestions for Policy

Causes of the great divide

Given the richness and intensity of these connections, why did South Asia and East Asia drift into different spheres? Western Colonialism is only partly to blame. As early as the 12th century, high-caste Hindus were told that "crossing the water" would cause them to lose caste; in a sub-region boasting more than 7000 kilometers of coastline, this was a disastrous idea. The Ming Dynasty turned inward and imposed certain restrictions on trade and travel. Tokugawa Japan largely closed itself off to all but a handful of Dutch and Chinese at Nagasaki.[9]

Then came the colonial powers, who divided up Maritime Asia, hardening old boundaries and creating new and often artificial ones. They also crystallised social structures, established cartels and monopolies, and created a new class of elites oriented to the metropolis instead of to their neighbours. At the same time, the physical infrastructure, technology, education systems and ideas built or imported by the colonial powers connected East Asians and South Asians as never before.

Following colonial-era partition came a string of calamities: the Sino–Japanese War, the Russo–Japanese War, World War I, Japan's military expansion, the Great Depression, World War II, the anti-colonial struggle, local communist insurgencies, the Cold War, the Vietnam War, the ravages of Maoist dictatorship in China, the genocide in Cambodia and wars of national liberation in Southeast Asia to name only the major ones.

Once South Asian and East Asian leaders shook off these traumas, they clung tightly to borders that were often artificial. Their economic policies also worked against the revival of Maritime Asia. Many governments embraced protectionism, central planning, socialist ownership schemes and a quest for autarky. Only in the last two decades of the 20th century, as globalisation blazed up and the Cold War spluttered out, did the natural flow and equilibrium of Maritime Asia revive in modern form.

Pan-Asianism and anti-colonialism

For Asian intellectuals struggling against colonialism, the idea of a united "Asia" was an antidote to the sense of weakness and humiliation stemming from colonial occupation and control. Disseminating this idea posed a huge challenge because the people of the region did not think of themselves as "Asians". The Chinese defined themselves and their neighbours in terms of concentric circles; people who lived beyond inner Asia were "outer barbarians". (Today's Chinese still use the term "Western Regions" to describe western and central Asia, the

---

[9] For a description of this presence, see Jansen (1992).

Caucasus and parts of South Asia.) South Asians tended to define themselves as members of an ethnic group, caste, community or religion. Malay traders, who timed their voyages in accordance with seasonal monsoons called their region "the land below the winds". Persians, Chinese, Arabs and others came from "above the winds (Reid, 1988)". Their neighbours also lacked a common identity; the term "Southeast Asia" came into common use only during the Pacific War as a way of delineating Mountbatten's theatre of command.

Japan's victory over Russia in 1905 stimulated pan-Asianism and anti-colonialism because it demonstrated that an Asian country could defeat a "white" country. Although most reformers stuck to their own country, a few argued that if Asians could only unite, they could shake off the colonial yoke. At the core of their thinking was the notion of moral superiority or at least a distinctive set of moral virtues. The West might have superior weapons but Asians had superior values.[10] Western technology and wealth hid a profound moral weakness. Asians were spiritual, devoted to the communal good whereas Westerners were materialistic, grasping individual rights. Since Asians were morally superior, there was no need to emphasise such "Western" ideas as individual rights and the rule of law.

In a book published in 1904, for example, the Japanese pan-Asianist Okakura Kakuzo coined the phrase "Asia is One". "The common thought-inheritance of every Asiatic race", he wrote, was the "broad expanse of love for the Ultimate and Universal". Westerners, by contrast, were bogged down in "the Particular", fixated by the means, not the end, of life.[11]

For Sun Yat-sen, Asia represented "benevolence, justice, and morality", which he called the Rule of Right. Westerners, by contrast, relied on the Rule of Might.[12] Visiting China in 1924, the Indian

---

[10] One could detect a whiff of this legacy in the "Asian values" championed by Lee Kuan Yew, Mohamad Mahathir, and Kishore Mahbubani in the 1980s.

[11] Quoted in "Pan-Asianism", http://en.wikipedia.org/wiki/Pan-Asianism, p. 1. The Bengali artist Abanindranath Tagore, brother of the famous poet and philosopher Rabindranath Tagore, applied the notion that "Asia is One" to the world of art.

[12] "Sun Yat-sen's Speech on Pan-Asianism", http://en.wikipedia.org/wiki/Sun_Yat_Sen%27s_speech_on_Pan-Asianism, p. 3.

poet and philosopher Rabindranath Tagore hailed the dawning of a "new age" in the East — "No people in Asia can be wholly given to materialism", he said, adding approvingly, "You are not individualists in China (Tagore, 1961)".

As international tensions mounted in the 1920s and 1930s, this conviction of moral superiority slid easily into racism. To rationalise their military aggression, Japanese leaders drew on race to promote the virtues of the "Greater East Asia Co-Prosperity Sphere". They also played an anti-colonialist card, joining with Asian nationalists to throw off the colonial yoke. This took some doing, since Japan had colonized Korea and Taiwan and set up a puppet kingdom in Manchukuo (Manchuria), but Japan's message attracted a number of nationalist leaders, including Subhas Chandra Bose.

This brief sketch of the Pan-Asia movement raises important questions. To what extent, if any, does the effort to re-integrate South Asia and East Asia run the risk of trumpeting moral superiority and anti-Western ideas to compensate for the ongoing Western hegemony? And to what extent should political efforts to re-integrate South Asia and East Asia simultaneously promote values associated with "modernity", such as free-market economics and the rule of law? (Mahbubani, 2008).[13] These topics are largely missing from public debates about Asian regionalism.

Suggested policy lessons

Integration among the coastal communities and ocean-oriented trading nodes of today's Asia already exceeds integration with or within any other major region except Europe. The aforementioned observer from outer space would be struck by the spontaneous resurgence and reintegration of Maritime Asia and by the relatively empty and pockmarked landscape of the Silk Road.

In order to deepen and expand these connections, champions of closer South Asian–East Asian relations might usefully adapt two

---

[13] Kishore Mahbubani lists these two values and five others as worthy of adoption by developing countries in their "Modernity".

broad lessons from Maritime Asia's history to the current policy framework of Asian regionalism. First, recognising the unifying power of the ocean, Asian leaders should explicitly build Maritime Asia into their vision of integration and devise corresponding roadmaps and action plans. Second, since residents of Maritime Asia are natural re-integrators, governments should remove as many barriers to their spontaneous interaction as possible.

Policies that build on the region's most dynamic shared asset — Maritime Asia — will not come easily. Locked in a nation-state mindset and still preoccupied with consolidating national unity within their unwieldy territories, Asian governments have not focused on Maritime Asia as such. Instead, they are pursuing land-based integration among a group of nation-states. They are slow to recognise, let alone correct, the partial mismatch between what is transpiring in official meeting rooms and scholarly conference halls on one hand and what is happening on the street, in ports, airports, and on computers and mobile phones on the other. All but the most specialised maps and statistical handbooks focus on the land, leaving the seas blue and blank.

The agenda adopted by the leaders of the Asian integration movement overlaps with, but does not fully correspond to the needs of individual integrators in coastal zones or ocean-accessible cities. It devotes insufficient attention to the overlap between land and sea and thus understates the richness and unifying pull of Asia's maritime legacies, livelihoods and resources.

South Asian and East Asian governments alike need to assign higher priority to initiatives that facilitate maritime connections for at least two pragmatic reasons. One stems from the global economy. Like the cultures of other maritime regions, Maritime Asia's culture was cosmopolitan and adaptable. The region inherits a rich legacy of trading networks, long-distance banking and credit mechanisms. These assets greatly facilitate local adaptation to globalisation.

The second reason why maritime initiatives are so promising is that, they make full use of traders, investors, inventors and other entrepreneurs, who are the true source of long-term economic growth. The "integrators" of Maritime Asia were private individuals clustered along major bodies of water. For most of its history, the region permitted the free movement of persons and a certain degree of local autonomy. Today's re-integration is driven far more quickly and dynamically by private actors than by governments. Taking advantage of globalisation, new technology, regional peace and stability, and China's rocketing economy, these "re-integrators" form a newly wealthy and highly-cosmopolitan middle class.[14] An overwhelming majority of them are located in Maritime Asia.

Selected maritime initiatives are in place, but they are limited in number and lack both a detailed, regionally endorsed "vision" and a high-level political momentum. Individual governments promote maritime free-trade zones and other special arrangements in their own territory but, to my knowledge, no one in power has acknowledged that Maritime Asia has a cross-border identity of its own and that its resurgence serves both integration and development.

References

Abu-Lughod, J. (1989). *Before European Hegemony: The World System, 1250–1350.* New York: Oxford University Press, Chap. 8.

Bernstein. (2001). Ultimate Journey. Vintage Departures.

Braudel, F. *The Mediterranean and the Mediterranean World in the Age of Philip II* (2 vols., New York: Harper and Row, 1972–73).

Chanda, N. (2007). *Bound Together: How Trades, Preachers, Adventurers, and Warriors Shaped Globalization.* New Haven: Yale University Press.

Dalrymple, W. (2002). *White Mughals: Love and Betrayal in Eighteenth-Century India.* London: Penguin Books, p. 347.

Das Gupta, A. (2001). *The World of the Indian Ocean Merchant, 1500–1800, Collected Essays.* Oxford: Oxford University Press, pp. 37–38.

Das Gupta, A. India and the Indian Ocean, C. 1500–1800: The Story. In *World of the Indian Ocean Merchant*, A. Das Gupta (ed.), p. 49.

Derrett, J. D. M. (1975). Social and Political Thought and Institutions. In *A Cultural History of India*, A. L. Basham (ed.), Oxford: Oxford University Press, pp. 134–40.

Devare, S. (2006). *India and Southeast Asia: Towards Security Convergence.* Singapore: Institute of Southeast Asian Studies, Chap. 3.

Doniger, W. (2009). *The Hindus: An Alternative History.* New York: Penguin Press.

---

[14] For a more complete discussion of Asia's current regionalisation and the roles of the private sector and technology, see (Frost, 2008).

Frost, E. L. (2008). *Asia's New Regionalism*. Boulder, CO: Lynne Rienner Publishers; Singapore: National University of Singapore Press; and New Delhi: Viva Books, Chaps. 4 and 5.

Hamashita, T. (1997). The Intra-Regional System in East Asia in Modern Times. In *Network Power: Japan and Asia*, P. J. Katzenstein and T. Shiraishi (eds.), Ithaca, NY: Cornell University Press, p. 115.

Kulke, H., K. Kesavapany and V. Sakhuja (eds.), (2009). *Nagapattinam to Suvarnadwipa: Reflections on the Chola Naval Expeditions to Southeast Asia*. Singapore: ISEAS.

Lewis, M. W. and K. Wigen (1997). *The Myth of Continents*. Berkeley, CA: University of California Press, pp. 2–3, 151–157, 187–188, 200.

Lieberman, V. (2003). *Strange Parallels: Southeast Asia in Global Context, c. 800–1830*. Vol. I, Cambridge: Cambridge University Press, pp. 66–84.

Mahbubani, K. (2008). *The New Asian Hemisphere*. New York: Public Affairs/Perseus Group, Chap. 2.

McPherson, K. (1998). *The Indian Ocean: A History of People and the Sea*. Delhi: Oxford University Press, p. 123.

Mungello, D.E. (1999). *The Great Encounter of China and the West, 1500–1800*. Lanham, MD: Rowman & Littlefield, p. 3.

Ostler, N. (2005). *Empires of the Word: A Language History of the World*. New York, London, Toronto, and Sydney: Harper Perennial, p. 179.

Pempel, T. J. (2005). *Remapping East Asia: The Construction of a Region*. Ithaca: Cornell University Press, pp. 2–4.

Rana, P. B. (2009). The Integration and 'Re-Centering' of Asia — Historical and Contemporary Perspectives. *ISAS Working Paper No. 86*, 9 September.

Reid, A. (1988). *Southeast Asia in the Age of Commerce, 1450–1680*. Vol. I: The Lands Below the Winds. New Haven: Yale University Press, p. 128.

Reid, A. *Charting the Course of Early Modern Southeast Asia*.

Tagore, R. (1961). Talks in China. A. Chakravarty, (ed.), In *The Tagore Reader*. Boston: Beacon Press, pp. 209–210.

Wales, H. G. Q. (1967). *The Indianization of China and of Southeast Asia*. London: Bernard Quaritch, p. 127.

Wang, G. (2000). *The Chinese Overseas: From Earthbound China to the Quest for Autonomy*. Cambridge: Harvard University Press, passim.

Weatherford. (2004). *Genghis Khan and the Making of the Modern World*. New York: Crown Publishers, pp. 200–206.

Wheatley, P. (1961). *The Golden Khersonese* (reproduced) by Greenwood Press: Westport, CT: First Published in Kuala Lumpur: University of Malaya Press, p. 184, quoted in Shaffer, Maritime Southeast Asia to 1500, p. 2.

Wolters, O. W. (1999). *History, Culture and Region in Southeast Asian Perspectives*. Ithaca, NY: Southeast Asia Program Publications in cooperation with the Institute of Southeast Asian Studies, p. 46.

Horizontal Asia[1]

Anthony Bubalo and Malcolm Cook

Conventional wisdom now intones that the 21st century will be the
Asian century, with power inexorably shifting away from the West
toward that vast and, for many Westerners, rather vague entity called
Asia. If this is the case, and there are grounds for believing that it is, we
need to clarify what exactly (or even approximately) we mean by "Asia."

Geographical terms in themselves, do not change the lines on
maps, but they do shape conceptions and consequently, behaviour.
"Asia" is certainly a term whose meaning has changed with historical
circumstances and their contexts. In the heyday of Western imperialism, "Asia" typically referred to everything from Suez to Shanghai,
with a particular emphasis on those parts of Asia readily accessible to
Western navies and merchant ships. But by the third quarter of the
20th century, a series of events — the War in the Pacific, the rise of a
communist regime in China, the Korean and Vietnam Wars, the
economic ascent of Japan and the Asian Tigers (South Korea, Taiwan,
Hong Kong and Singapore) — both narrowed what we considered to

---

[1] Reprinted with permission from the *American Interest*, Summer (May/June) 2010
(Vol. V, No. 5).

be "Asia" and underlined its growing importance. For most purposes, the north–south coastal region extending from Korea to Indonesia, came to be known as Asia. The fact that the West's key strategic inter-action with the continent was via the American naval power, reinforced this vertical maritime conception of Asia, as did the late 20th century efforts at regional organisation. Often expressed in the concept of the "Asia Pacific", this particular geostrategic artifice created some odd legacies — Asia's pre-eminent economic and political body, APEC, includes Chile but not India, Mexico but not Mongolia.

The vertical idea of Asia has now outlived its usefulness and serves to obscure reality rather than illuminate or shape it. We are not the only ones to believe this. Robert D. Kaplan sees the return of an old idea of Asia as a "continent reconfigured into an organic whole" that emphasizes its east-west connections. India's leading strategic com-mentator, C. Raja Mohan, speaks of the revival of a Curzonian perspective in Indian foreign policy that also views Asia in whole-of-continent terms. However, as these ideas gain currency, there is a risk of encouraging the adoption of one half-truth at the expense of another. Perhaps the most prominent variation thus far on the theme of Asia's strategic reorientation is the one focused on the Indian Ocean. Kaplan anticipates a competition between the naval fleets of Asia's two emerging powers, China and India. James Holmes and Toshi Yoshihara argue that China's growing naval reach prefigures its eventual adoption of Mahanian precepts, emphasising the importance of maritime power. The popular "string of pearls" thesis anticipates China building a ring of bases in the Indian Ocean.[2]

---

[2] See Kaplan, "Center Stage for the 21st Century: Power Plays in the Indian Ocean", Foreign Affairs (March/April 2009); Mohan, Crossing the Rubicon: The Shaping of India's New Foreign Policy (Viking Books, 2003); and Holmes and Yoshihara, Chinese Naval Strategy in the 21st Century: The Turn to Mahan (Routledge, 2008). The "string of pearls" thesis had its origins in a classified report written by Booz Allen Hamilton for the US Department of Defense. The first public reference was Bill Gertz, "China Builds Up Strategic Sea Lanes", Washington Times, January 17, 2005. For a general discussion of the term see Christopher J. Pehrson, String of Pearls: Meeting the Challenge of China's Rising Power across the Asian Littoral, Carlisle Papers in Security Strategy, Strategic Studies Institute, US Army War College (July 2006).

But this focus on the naval power ignores the increasing signifi-cance of Asia's vast territorial expanses. If the rise of Japan and the Asian Tigers, all island or coastal nations closely bound to the United States, accentuated Asia's vertical, maritime identity, then the rise of the great Asian land powers, India and China, and the persisting position and power of Russia, are surely re-defining Asia in more horizontal and continental terms. That will matter enormously for the West. Chinese, Indian and Russian influence will grow in the Persian Gulf and Central Asia; and a less maritime Asia will be, unsurprisingly, less amenable to Western maritime power.

This suggests that we need to read a little less Mahan and a little more Mackinder as we study up for the next half-century or so. The conceptual challenge for the West is to push out its view of Asia beyond familiar coasts, islands and archipelagos to encompass the con-tinent as a whole. To do so, we must have a firm grasp of the related economic, energy and infrastructural trends emerging before our very eyes.

Trade, Energy and Infrastructure

For a good part of the 20th century, economic exchange, or rather the lack of it, helped to keep Asia divided. The Soviet Union, India and China evinced little interest in international trade. As late as 1990, official India–China trade was a paltry US$190 million. In 1978, China, with 22.4 percent of world population, accounted for only 0.8 percent of world exports (now 19.7 percent and 9 percent, respectively). Up to the early 1990s, the vast bulk of the Russian Far East's trade was within the Russian borders. By and large, all three countries had enough critical resources to satisfy their grinding, pub-lic sector-dominated economies. The consequence was to paralyse any movement toward transcontinental economic integration.

All that has changed as Asia returns to its geostrategic roots by way of new economic networks. Decisions by Beijing (in the 1970s) and New Delhi (in the 1990s) to give up Maoist and Nehruvian versions of autarky have released long-fettered market forces in Asia. According to Chinese statistics, China is now India's largest trading partner, with bilateral trade worth US$51.8 billion in 2008. That is 30 percent more than it was in 2007, and more than 40 percent larger than India's trade with its second-largest trading partner, the United States.

The scope of this change far transcends the China–India story. According to the IMF figures, between 1990 and 2006, inter-regional trade involving "emerging Asia" increased by five times; in the same period, trade within emerging Asia increased by 8.5 times.[3] However, these data understate reality, as the IMF does not include Russia, Central Asia or the Persian Gulf in this accounting of intra-Asian trade. Between 1992 and 2007, Russian exports to China increased by six times and its imports by 15 times. In the same period, China's annual imports from Central Asia have gone from a little more than US$160 million to almost US$7 billion. Between 1990 and 2007, Chinese and Indian imports from the Persian Gulf grew from less than US $500 million and US$4 billion to US$44 and US$13 billion, respectively. In the same period, exports from China and India to the Gulf grew from around US$1 billion each to US$35 and US$20 billion, respectively. China is now the single largest merchandise exporter to the Middle East.

More limited bilateral cases are also instructive. Israel is India's third largest (and most technologically important) external source of weapons. Saudi Arabia has become India's largest supplier of imported oil and largest export market for basmati rice. In 2009, some 62 Chinese construction companies were working in the Kingdom, employing over 16,000 Chinese workers, while Saudi Arabian state-owned oil company ARAMCO, Exxon Mobil and Sinopec completed a US$5 billion refinery project in Fujian. In 1990, four of Iran's top five export markets were European countries; by 2008, four of five were Asian.

Energy has been a key factor in burgeoning Asian economic ties. China and India have joined Japan, Korea, Taiwan and others in Asia in their dependence on Persian Gulf oil, which now supplies

---

[3] The IMF defines "emerging Asia" as China, India, Hong Kong SAR, Korea, Singapore, Taiwan Province of China, Indonesia, Malaysia, the Philippines, Thailand and Vietnam.

70–80 percent of Asian import demand. Central Asian and Russian Far East energy resources are also growing elements in this transcontinental energy network. In particular, Russia, is looking at underdeveloped areas in Siberia to ensure that booming state incomes from energy resources persist in the future.

Energy and resource insecurity have become a source of Asian power competition. In particular, China's active energy diplomacy has spurred other Asian powers to follow suit. Japan's 2006 national energy strategy requires 40 percent of its imported oil to be developed by Japanese firms by 2030. (Supplies of oil, what the Japanese call "Hinomaru oil", developed overseas by Japanese companies, have recently met about 15 percent of Japan's oil needs). Accordingly, Tokyo has launched new energy diplomacy initiatives such as its "Central Asia plus Japan" dialogue. Russia has the pleasure of having both China and Japan competitively seeking access to its energy supplies and their associated pipeline needs.

These new trends in energy trade have also introduced tensions into Japan's relations with the United States. Japan has long relied on US power for the security of its oil supplies, combined with its own generous aid contributions to the Middle East. Yet, Tokyo's alliance relationship with Washington proved to be a liability in Japanese efforts to develop Iran's South Azadegan oilfield, a project that could have boosted supplies of Hinomaru oil by 60 percent. Wary of US complaints, Japan dragged its feet, and Iran cancelled the project, leaving China, Russia and India to vie to develop the field. China won. The Azadegan affair is a microcosm of a larger phenomenon: In 1990, Japan was the only Asian country among Iran's top-five export markets. By 2008, Japan was joined in the top-five by China, India and South Korea.

Competition between Asian powers over energy and resources is not just being played out in the west of Asia. There is obviously a maritime dimension to the competition too. China is developing its navy and seeking access to port facilities in the Indian Ocean to lessen the vulnerability of its long maritime supply lines to the Persian Gulf. This, in turn, is generating both insecurities and new forms of security cooperation in both the Pacific and Indian Oceans.

India recently replaced China as the largest recipient of Japanese aid, while India was the second country (after Australia) to sign a joint declaration on security cooperation with Japan. Japan's new government is likely, to accelerate its path to an independent diplomacy and security policy. It is less likely that a Japanese government looking like the present one would have deferred to the United States in the Azadegan field affair.

Asia's growing economic and energy ties are being reflected in and reinforced by an expanding network of roads, railways and pipelines that are becoming the physical infrastructure of horizontal Asia. Asian oil and gas pipelines used to attract attention due to their failure to get built; which is no longer the case. The 7,000 km pipeline linking Turkmenistan's significant liquified natural gas (LNG) reserves to China via Kazakhstan and Uzbekistan opened in December 2009. South Korea's Daewoo International is leading a consortium with Indian and Burmese corporations to build a US$5.6 billion LNG project and pipeline to feed 500 million cubic feet of gas per day from western Burma to western China by 2013. In February of last year, Russia and China agreed on a US$25 billion, 20-year investment to pipe Russian oil into China.

Even pipelines from the Persian Gulf to Asian energy consumers are edging closer to becoming a reality. The long mooted Iran–Pakistan–India gas pipeline might never be built, but the Iran–Pakistan section is under construction, providing a possible starting point — albeit for an eventual Chinese, rather than Indian, terminus. China's hesitation to finance a pipeline through Pakistan's troubled Baluchistan province to the port of Gwadar in 2009 probably will not last, given the project's potential to dramatically shorten China's sea lines of communication to the Persian Gulf.

The impact of emerging road and inland-waterway networks may be even greater than that of pipelines. In 2006, fulfilling a decades-old ambition, China completed the railway to Lhasa in Tibet. As a part of the plan to make Tibet a hub for China–South Asia trade, Beijing is looking to extend this network into northern India, Nepal, Bhutan and Bangladesh. In 2002, civil engineers connected the colonial Burma Road network to a major highway complex in China, thereby directly linking Shanghai via road to Burma's Irrawaddy Delta. It is being planned to link this highway in turn to a new Indian Ocean deep-water port supported by Chinese finance at Kyaukpyu in Burma.

Meanwhile, India, is proceeding with highway projects in the restive border province of Sikkim as a way of helping the impoverished province "grow out" of its insurgencies and asserting central government control. India has recently completed a major road project in Afghanistan connecting the southern part of the country to Iran's key port facility at Chabahar. This follows on from India's enhancement of road networks with Burma as a key land transport beachhead into Southeast Asia.

The trade, energy and infrastructure connections that we have just summarised, underline how Asia's markets, and particularly its key sources of energy, are increasingly being found on the continent rather than beyond its shores. They reflect how much the vital interests of Asia's great powers, the countries at the centre of these connections, will continue to be tied to the land even as they develop at sea.

This is not to suggest that we should ignore the growing maritime power and interests of China and India, or even the declining but still significant naval power of Russia. Indian strategists are not wrong to fret about the prospect of Sino–Indian naval rivalry and China's purported "string of pearls" strategy. It is not wrong for American strategic analysts to note that China's long sea lines of communication, particularly for energy imports, have become a key vulnerability as well as a justification for its naval build-up. But as we have suggested, it is only half the story, and very likely the less important half.

For sometime, the Chinese navy will remain poorly equipped and trained for blue-water operations. China's long-promised (or feared) aircraft carrier may eventually materialise, but the balance of its naval modernisation remains skewed toward keeping US aircraft carriers away from its eastern coastline and Taiwan. And while China's role in helping Pakistan to develop the port of Gwadar is often called the largest "pearl" in its Indian Ocean plans, it can also be seen in a different light. More significant than the port and its strategic maritime implications are the rail, road and pipelines that China is planning on using to link Gwadar to western China. (China has also helped to fund a railway line from Gwadar to Dalbandin in central Pakistan, which will be integrated with existing lines linking Pakistan to Iran). These overland connectors will eventually make China less reliant on ports and chokepoints in the Pacific, even as they generate new interests, rivalries and alliances on land.

The latter are already in train: Chinese and Indian fleets may one day maneuver against each other on the Indian Ocean, but New Delhi and Beijing are already engaged in stiff competition on land, particularly among Asia's weak states. In Burma, for example, China and India are spending huge amounts to develop trade routes and extract primary resources. In Afghanistan, India has invested heavily in infrastructure, while China has become the largest single foreign investor (unsurprisingly, in a mine). Meanwhile, what some see as a Sino–Russian rapprochement, might add only greater cordiality to their inevitable competition in Siberia and Central Asia, particularly as Russian fears about asymmetrical Russian–Chinese demographic trends in Siberia continue to fester.

Indeed, it is on land that the internal stability, territorial integrity and ambitions of China, India and Russia as regional and great powers are mostly at stake. Since World War II, all three have fought major border conflicts with each other in areas that represent the soft underbellies of these massive land powers (for example, China versus India in the Himalayas, and China versus Russia along the Amur). For Beijing, economic and infrastructure development in western China, a region that accounts for more than half of China's land area, is critical to ensure that its restive continental hinterlands are not left further behind its economically dynamic coast. India faces a similar nation-building challenge in its fissiparous northeast, even as it shadowboxes with Pakistan in Afghanistan to its northwest. For Russia, access to resources in Siberia and Central Asia is critical for it to remain as an energy superpower, particularly so if it can no longer be a military one. For all these reasons, Asia's strategic centre of gravity is shifting inland, with major implications for the maritime nations of East Asia, and others too.

In maritime Southeast Asian states, there are deep concerns that China's and India's (and even Vietnam's) economic re-awakening is marginalising them economically and strategically. In response, maritime Southeast Asia is simultaneously strengthening the economic and strategic relations with the United States, India, Japan, China and even with countries of the Persian Gulf. Different as they are from one another, the basic diplomatic strategies of Indonesia, Malaysia, Singapore, Thailand and the Philippines have become quite similar.

Unlike Southeast Asian states, Japan, as maritime Asia's premier economic and military power, is hardly to be marginalised. Yet, it too is being forced to respond to shifts in Asia's strategic fundamentals. More than any other country, Japan is simultaneously seeking closer relations with China and other countries to hedge against China's rise. In particular, the rapid growth in Japan's strategic relations with India is clear evidence that concern over China is leading Japan to seek new strategic partnerships not just across the Pacific but across Asia. Over time, this could tip Japan's century-old debate over its Asian and Western identities back in favour of its Asian one.

A Challenge for the West

If the implications of a more horizontal Asia are significant for East Asia, the implications for the West are still greater. If we understand that the Asian century is more likely to be a horizontal continental one than a vertical maritime one, then Western naval power, however formidable it remains, may become a diminishing asset. Naval supremacy will provide the West with more limited leverage on the continent than many would like to think, even as it responds to new challenges at sea.

This is particularly apparent when we look at the role of energy in forging a more horizontal Asia. There is no grand scheme behind the increasingly organic connections between Asian energy producers and consumers, but it is nevertheless occurring to the potential exclusion of both Western energy needs and strategic influence. The ability of India and China to meet an increasing proportion of their energy needs via overland pipelines, especially from Russia and Central Asia and perhaps eventually from the Persian Gulf, may well compromise the ability of Western consumers to access these resources and the importance of Western maritime power in securing them. And even where Western maritime power still matters greatly (as in policing the long sea lines of communication between the Persian Gulf and Asia), the efficacy of that power is diminishing. A more horizontal Asia reflects not just enhanced physical overland connections between Asian states, but also political and economic ones. In the past, energy suppliers have welcomed the West's ability to secure their chief export militarily, but these suppliers also crave stable markets and good prices. For the first time, their fastest-growing markets are now on their own continent, which will be a lot easier to supply if the pipelines which are now in the planning stages are built.

The politics matter particularly. For Persian Gulf producers, Asian energy consumers are far less demanding politically than their Western counterparts. For Iran, switching from European to Asian markets replaces Western sanctimony with Asian expediency. Even for the seemingly stalwart pro-Western ally, Saudi Arabia, expanding economic, political and military contacts with India, China (from whom it may once again buy medium-range ballistic missiles) and Russia are sensible hedges against over-reliance on the United States, especially if the Al-Saud comes to think that the United States is either too reckless or too timid in the way that it uses its power to protect them.

This is where geopolitics and the delicate matter of geopolitical reputation come together. The permanence and proximity of Asia's great powers makes for more enduring leverage, commitments and interests such that, in Central Asia and the Caucasus, for example, great power competition mostly excludes the West. Russia is asserting what it sees as its natural and historical rights, with clear implications for everything from the security of gas supplies to Europe to the future of American bases in the region. In an effort to resist this suffocating bear hug, Central Asian states are turning not to the West but to China, something implicit in the founding of the Shanghai Cooperation Organisation (SCO). Indeed, Washington's unwillingness to supply Georgia with weapons and NATO's general fecklessness during the summer 2008 Russo–Georgian war count in the region as evidence of the West's unreliability.

Washington's inability (so far) to bend Iran to its will on its nuclear program counts similarly. Regional states see this as a direct result of growing Russian and Chinese commercial and energy interests in Iran — interests that have been facilitated by Washington's three-decade political and economic estrangement from Tehran. Indeed, most regional observers understand that Moscow and Beijing's protestations against the prospect of a nuclear-armed Iran are mere diplomatic eyewash.

In Afghanistan and Pakistan, the locals question the long-term commitment of the United States and its allies for reasons particular to their own experiences and circumstances. While the West's body language is all about leaving, India and China quietly continue to build their influence in Afghanistan and, in China's case, in Pakistan as well. They will enjoy the security benefits if Western efforts there succeed and avoid local opprobrium if they fail.

Afghanistan and Pakistan are countries where Western influence has been relatively strong; what of those where it is weak? In Burma, the junta's possible nuclear activities add to already strong Western concerns about human rights and drug trafficking. The United States has tried isolation and engagement without notable success. Meanwhile, China and India compete on the ground for influence. Between high-sounding UN resolutions and occasional diplomatic forays, on the one hand, and investment, trade delegations and huge infrastructure projects, on the other, there is not much doubt about which path yields more influence.

The Regionalism Canary

One thing that should already alert us to more constrained Western influence in Asia is the continent's emerging regional institutions. For many years, "Asian" regional institutions promoted by the United States, Japan, Indonesia, Singapore and Australia, such as ASEAN and APEC, took shape on the basis of maritime strategic assumptions. Roughly 20 years after the explosion of Asia-Pacific and then East Asian regional bodies, horizontal Asia is witnessing a similar outburst. The most prominent is the China-led Shanghai Cooperation

Organisation (SCO) established in 2001 with Russia, China, Kazakhstan, Uzbekistan, Kyrgyzstan and Tajikistan as its founding members and India, Pakistan, Iran and Mongolia as observers, with Sri Lanka and Belarus recently added as dialogue partners. The annual trilateral meeting of the Foreign Ministers of Russia, China and India inaugurated in 2002 supports this. Other less–developed groupings include the Indian-led Bay of Bengal Initiative for Multi-sectoral Technical and Economic Cooperation (encompassing India, Bangladesh, Bhutan, Nepal, Sri Lanka, Burma and Thailand) and the biennial Singapore-led Asia–Middle East Dialogue, open to 49 countries and the Palestinian Authority.

Some of these are proving to be more effective than existing Asian institutions, especially in the security realm, and some considerably less so. What really distinguishes them is that, unlike the Asia-Pacific experience, most are being organised by Asia's rising powers and all exclude the United States. Even if these institutions currently coexist happily with more established organs like APEC, because they mirror Asia's gradual economic and geostrategic reorientation, they have the potential to overshadow existing bodies unless the latter adapt to new realities.

This puts into starker relief calls like that of Australian Prime Minister Kevin Rudd to re-vitalize the institutional structures of the Asia-Pacific. Unless these efforts take account of new Asian realities, they will end up being largely irrelevant. Indeed, the risk is that we in the West are already missing the different way that Asia's emerging powers define what is Asian. One of China's leading international relations experts, Professor Jia Qingguo, commenting on the Australian government's initiative, noted that if you include India in the proposal "you may well need to include such countries as Iran, Iraq and Saudi Arabia, all of which are also Asian countries." At least, they are Asian in Chinese, Indian and Russian eyes, if not yet in Western ones.

The upshot is that, we must draw for ourselves a new mental map of Asia that avoids the error of simply extending our existing maritime conception of Asia to a second ocean. Certainly the rising naval power of China and India deserves attention, but not at the expense of encouraging a peculiar kind of sea-blindness, wherein we are not blind to the sea, but blind because of it. We must rethink mindsets that reflect some three centuries of British and American maritime supremacy. We need a whole-of-Asia concept that combines north-south maritime perspectives with east-west continental ones, and economic perspectives with geostrategic ones. Given the continent's importance, nothing less will do in the Asian 21st century.

Linkages Between East and South Asia: The Contemporary Trade Perspective

Robert Scollay

Introduction

Until recently, economic integration in East Asia and South Asia were essentially separate processes. The closing decades of the 20th century saw the economies of East Asia getting increasingly integrated through expanding trade and investment linkages that were important factors both in the region's impressive growth and in its rapid recovery from the deep economic crisis of 1997–1998. South Asia presented a contrasting picture of slow and halting progress in economic integration, impeded by political conflicts and inward-looking economic policies. Trade and investment linkages between the two regions remained at a low level.

Since the turn of the century, preferential trading arrangements between the East Asian economies have been proliferating rapidly, and a proposal to create an East Asian Free Trade Agreement encompassing

13 economies of the region has also been on the table. At the same time, economic liberalisation and the associated emergence of rapid economic growth in India has led to an upsurge of interest in the expansion of economic linkages between East Asia and South Asia. Recognition of India's potential to emulate China as a rapidly-expanding economic giant has been a key factor in this upsurge of interest. The implications for countries in both regions of increasing economic interaction between these two dynamic "growth poles", as well as between India and other East Asian countries, has accordingly commanded growing attention. Reflecting this growing interest, consideration has begun to be given to the potential for, and implications of formally linking East Asia and South Asia together as a single integrated region.

This chapter sets out to examine the trade and investment issues relevant to the potential for future economic integration between East Asia and South Asia. The chapter is organised as follows. The next section presents summary data on economic characteristics of the two regions that would be expected to have some bearing on the patterns of trade relations between them. These include the scale of economic activity in the countries of the regions as well as some crude proxy indicators of openness and potential comparative advantage. This is followed by a detailed examination of patterns of trade flows, highlighting the varying extents to which the potential for integration has been exploited both between and within the two regions. The next section then briefly discusses aspects of preferential trading arrangements that should be taken into account in any investigation of the possibility of new trading arrangements linking East and South Asia.

In this chapter, the East Asian region is basically divided into two sub regions: Northeast Asia comprising of China, Japan, Korea, Chinese Taipei and Hong Kong China and Southeast Asia, comprising of the 10 members of the Association of Southeast Asian Nations or ASEAN (Brunei Darussalam, Indonesia, Malaysia, the Philippines, Singapore, Thailand, Cambodia, Laos, Myanmar and Vietnam). In the data displayed in the following section, this subdivision is modified to separate China from other countries of the region, to bring

Hong Kong, China and Singapore together as a group of countries with common characteristics and to divide the Southeast Asian countries into two sub-groups, based on income levels. Later in the chapter, India is separated from the other South Asian economies for some purposes, since its trade structure is quite different from the other four.

Selected Economic Indicators and their Implications

The data in Table 5.1 on the size of East and South Asian economies is useful in establishing the focal points of economic activity in the two regions. When GDP is measured at official exchange rates, which are the rates used in most international trade and investment transactions, the leading economic role of Northeast Asia is very clear. The combined GDP of the Northeast Asian economies comprises 20 percent of world GDP, almost eight times the combined GDP of both the Southeast Asian and South Asian economies. Japan remains the largest economy in the combined region, accounting for 9 percent of world GDP, while the Chinese economy, also at 9 percent of world GDP, easily outranks all the other economies of the combined region in size.[1] India dominates economic activity in South Asia, with 2.3 percent of world GDP, or just over 80 percent of the combined GDP of the South Asian economies. India's GDP is just over a quarter of that of China, the other emerging giant. In contrast with South Asia, economic activity in Southeast Asia is more widely dispersed, with Singapore, Indonesia, Malaysia, the Philippines and Thailand, all accounting for a significant share.

GDP measured at purchasing power parity (PPP) exchange rates emphasises the economic weight of the two emerging giants, China and India. China is easily the largest economy among the two regions, while the Indian economy is substantially larger than all other economies in the table except China and Japan, although still less than half the size of the Chinese economy. The shares in world GDP of South Asia and Southeast Asia on a PPP basis are much larger than their shares measured at official exchange rates, but they

---

[1] In 2010 it was announced that the GDP of China, measured at official exchange rates has surpassed that of Japan.

Table 5.1. East and South Asian economies.

	Share of World GDP 2009 (in percent)	
	At Official Exchange Rates (current US$)	At Purchasing Power Parity (current international $)
Japan	8.7	5.7
Korea	1.4	1.8
Chinese Taipei*	1.3	1.1
China	8.6	12.6
Hong Kong	0.4	0.4
Singapore	0.3	0.3
Malaysia	0.3	0.5
Thailand	0.5	0.7
Indonesia	0.9	1.3
Philippines	0.3	0.4
Brunei Darussalam*	0.0	0.0
Cambodia	0.0	
Laos	0.0	0.0
Myanmar*	0.0	0.2
Vietnam	0.2	0.4
India	2.3	5.2
Pakistan	0.3	0.6
Sri Lanka	0.1	0.1
Bangladesh	0.2	0.3
Nepal	0.0	
Northeast Asia	20.1	21.8
Southeast Asia	2.5	3.8
South Asia	2.8	6.3

Sources: World Bank World Development Indicators (except Chinese Taipei)
IMF World Economic Outlook/Taiwan National Statistics (Chinese Taipei).
Note: *2006

are still far outranked in economic size by the economies of Northeast Asia, by a factor of over three in the case of South Asia and a factor of over five in the case of Southeast Asia.

A key point highlighted by this data is that the rapid development of economic linkages within East Asia has offered the countries of the region, the benefits of closer integration within one of the three major poles of economic activity in the global economy and in particular, has allowed Southeast Asia, the opportunities provided by integration into the greater East Asian economy. South Asia has lacked a centre of activity of comparable magnitude and as noted earlier, its links with the East Asian growth pole lacked dynamism until recently. Closer economic linkages with East Asia thus offers a dramatic enlargement in the size of the regional market to the South Asian economies with which they can become integrated. By contrast, closer economic integration with South Asia offers East Asia a relatively modest increase in market size, although the future potential of the rapidly growing Indian market is clearly greater than what is indicated by its current GDP levels.

Table 5.2 further highlights the greater scope for beneficial integration that has existed in East Asia. The economies of the region exhibit a wide range of levels of development and factor endowments and a corresponding diversity of comparative advantages. Per capita income levels range from US$38,268 in Japan to US$239 in Myanmar, a ratio of 160:1, and there is a wide dispersion of per capita incomes within that range. Natural resource endowments range from virtually non-existent in Hong Kong and Singapore to the resource riches of economies like Indonesia and Brunei Darussalam. Population densities are very high in the resource-poor industrialised economies of Northeast Asia and Vietnam, but significantly lower in the Southeast Asian economies that enjoy substantial endowments of natural resources, as well as in China. Thus, East Asian economies have been able to exploit the enormous potential for beneficial specialisation that exists within their region.

By contrast, South Asian economies exhibit a much narrower range of development levels and factor endowments. Without exception, they are low-income developing countries, with per capita

Table 5.2.   GDP per capita and population densities of East Asian and South Asian economies.

	2008 GDP Per Capita (current US$)	Population Density (people per sq. km)
Japan	38,268	350
Korea	19,162	502
Chinese Taipei	17,154	637
China	3,422	142
Hong Kong	30,683	6,696
Singapore	39,950	6,943
Malaysia	8,187	82
Thailand	4,043	132
Indonesia	2,246	125
Philippines	1,854	303
Brunei Darussalam*	32,501	74
Cambodia	710	82
Laos	882	27
Myanmar*	239	74
Vietnam	1,051	278
India	1,065	383
Pakistan	994	215
Sri Lanka	2,020	312
Bangladesh	497	1,229
Nepal	438	201

Sources: World Bank World Development Indicators (except Chinese Taipei)
IMF World Economic Outlook (Chinese Taipei).
* 2006

incomes ranging from US$2020 in Sri Lanka to US$438 in Nepal. Population densities are uniformly high and increasing, ranging from 1229 persons per square kilometre in Bangladesh to 201 persons per square kilometre in Nepal in 2008. Among the lower-income developing economies in East Asia, only Vietnam and the Philippines have population densities higher than Nepal and both these economies have lower population densities than Bangladesh, India and Sri Lanka. Natural resource endowments in South Asian economies range from being substantial to meagre.

A qualification that needs to be noted is that India, like China, contains a number of large regions with considerable diversity in factor endowments and therefore, in comparative advantages. Nevertheless, the range of comparative advantages on which specialisation can be based is clearly much narrower in South Asia than in East Asia. Integration with East Asia will thus potentially allow South Asian economies to engage in specialisation within a region with a much more complete range of comparative advantages, with correspondingly greater potential benefits. Within this wider region, the data suggests that South Asia would specialise in labour-intensive manufactures, supplemented by country-specific specialisations in some agricultural and other natural-resource products and possibly also by somewhat more capital-intensive manufacturing in more advanced regions of India. Among East Asian economies, the Philippines and Vietnam most closely resemble Sri Lanka and Pakistan respectively in terms of income levels and population densities. Cambodia and Laos have higher incomes but lower population densities than Bangladesh and Nepal.

The data in Table 5.3 provides some further indications as to the segment of the manufacturing spectrum likely to be occupied by South Asian economies if trade with East Asia occurs on the basis of comparative advantage. The selected indicators of educational attainment (literacy rates, secondary and tertiary school enrolment) and access to information (internet usage rate) for South Asian economies other than Sri Lanka are significantly lower than those for China and the larger Southeast Asian developing economies. This suggests that average skill levels in South Asian work forces are also likely to be lower, pointing toward specialisation in manufacturing characterised

Table 5.3. Indicators of technology levels, education levels, and access to information in East Asian and South Asian economies, 2004.

	High-Technology Exports (% of manufactured exports)	Literacy Rate, Adult Total (% of people ages 15 and above)	School Enrolment, Secondary (% gross)	School Enrolment, Tertiary (% gross)	Internet Users (per 1,000 people)
Japan	24		102	54	587
Korea	33		91	89	657
China	30	91	73	19	73
Hong Kong	32		85	32	506
Singapore	59	93			571
Malaysia	55	89			397
Thailand		93	77	41	109
Indonesia	16	90	64	17	67
Philippines	55	93	86	29	54
Cambodia		74	29	3	3
Laos		69	46	6	4
Myanmar		90	40		1
Vietnam		90	73	10	71
India	5	61	54	12	32
Pakistan	1	50	27	3	13
Sri Lanka	1	91	83		14
Bangladesh	0				2
Nepal		49		6	7

Source: World Bank, World Development Indicators.

by lower technology levels as well as labour-intensity. This seems to be borne out by the figures for the share of high-technology products in total manufacturing exports, which are much lower even for India than for China and the larger Southeast Asian developing economies and very low indeed for Bangladesh, Pakistan and Sri Lanka.

In order to realise the potential benefits of specialisation, countries must be open to international trade. Table 5.4 indicates that the South Asian economies generally lag far behind East Asia in terms of openness. In East Asia, even in economies with relatively lower values for the openness indicator such as Indonesia, the Philippines and

Table 5.4. Openness of East Asian and South Asian economies, 2005.

Merchandise Trade (% of GDP)	
Japan	25
Korea	69
China	64
Hong Kong	334
Singapore	368
Malaysia	196
Thailand	129
Indonesia	54
Philippines	89
Cambodia	126
Laos	36
Viet Nam	132
India	28
Pakistan	37
Sri Lanka	65
Bangladesh	38
Nepal	37

Source: World Bank, World Development Indicators.

Vietnam, for example, the values of the openness indicator are uniformly higher than for all South Asian economies, with the exception that the value for Sri Lanka is higher than that for Indonesia.

Another summary indication of the degree of engagement in international trade is obtained by comparing shares of world GDP with shares of world imports and exports, as is done in Table 5.5, showing the shares of world imports and exports of the East and South Asian economies over the three-year period 2002–2004, along with their shares of world GDP for 2003, the mid-year of that period. The closest correspondence between shares of world GDP and that of world exports and imports is in Northeast Asia, although within that sub-region, there is considerable diversity, between Japan, whose shares of world exports and imports are much smaller than its share of world GDP, and the other four Northeast Asian economies, whose shares in

Table 5.5. East Asian and South Asian countries percentages of world exports, world imports, and world GDP.

	World Exports (in percent) 2002–2004	Percentage of World Imports (in percent) 2002–2004	World GDP (in percent) 2003
Japan	6.3	4.9	11.78
Korea	2.6	2.4	1.66
China	6.0	5.4	3.9
Chinese Taipei*	1.9	1.7	0.8
Hong Kong	3.0	3.0	0.4
Singapore	1.9	1.7	0.3
Indonesia	0.8	0.5	0.6
Malaysia	1.4	1.1	0.3
Philippines	0.5	0.5	0.2
Thailand	1.1	1.0	0.4
Vietnam	0.3	0.3	0.1
Brunei Darussalam	0.1	0.0	0.1
Cambodia	0.0	0.0	0.0
Laos	0.0	0.0	0.0
Myanmar	0.0	0.0	0.0
Bangladesh	0.1	0.1	0.1
India	0.8	1.0	1.6
Nepal	0.0	0.0	0.0
Pakistan	0.2	0.2	0.2
Sri Lanka	0.1	0.1	0.0
Northeast Asia	19.8	17.4	18.5
Southeast Asia	6.2	5.2	1.9
South Asia	1.4	1.4	2.1

Notes: Northeast Asia: Japan, Korea, China, Chinese Taipei, Hong Kong China.
Southeast Asia: Indonesia, Malaysia, Philippines, Singapore, Thailand, Vietnam, Brunei.
Cambodia, Laos, Myanmar.
South Asia: Bangladesh, India, Nepal, Pakistan, Sri Lanka.

world exports and imports are much larger than their shares of world GDP. There is a remarkable difference between Southeast Asia and South Asia.

Southeast Asia's share of world exports and imports is a multiple of its share of world GDP and this is also true for individual Southeast

Asian countries. By contrast, South Asia's share of world exports and imports is about two-thirds of its share of world GDP, reflecting a lower degree of overall engagement in international trade. Among the South Asian countries, this pattern is especially marked for India and less marked for Sri Lanka.

Figure 5.1 shows the share of world exports for the three sub regions over the period 1999–2006. Northeast Asia's share of world exports grew steadily from 2001 onward, and reached 22 percent by 2006. The share of Southeast Asia remained relatively stable over the period, at just under 7 percent. The share of South Asia in world exports remarkably rose by over a third from 1999 to 2006, but was still less than 1.5 percent in the latter year.

The rapid rise of South Asia in world exports indicates strong growth, albeit from a very low base, and Fig. 5.2 shows that this is indeed the case. South Asia's exports grew more rapidly over the period than those of every Asia-Pacific sub region shown, except for Pacific Latin America.

One feature that clearly distinguishes South Asia from East Asia and which is undoubtedly an important factor underlying its lower degree of engagement in international trade, is its higher level of

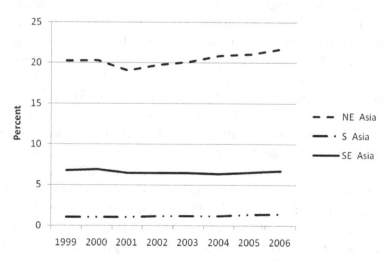

Fig. 5.1:   Share of world exports 1999–2006.

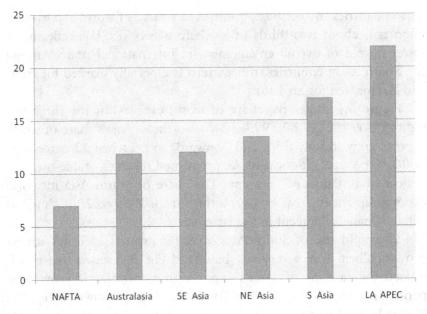

Fig. 5.2: Average export growth in Asia-Pacific sub-regions, 1999–2006.

protection. As illustrated in Table 5.6, the average applied MFN tariff of even Sri Lanka, the most open economy in South Asia, is still higher than the average registered by East and Southeast Asian countries. This difference in protection levels remains despite the progressive reduction of tariff barriers in South Asia, especially in the last decade. Bangladesh, for instance, has brought down its average applied MFN tariff from 58 percent in 1992 to 15 percent in 2006; India from 35 percent (1997) to 19 percent (2005); and Pakistan from 39 percent (1991) to 14 percent (2006).

Southeast Asia mirrors the asymmetries in protection, generally observed in the whole Asian region, as it brings together the most open economies of Singapore and Brunei and the still relatively protected markets of Vietnam, Cambodia, Thailand and Laos. Northeast Asian countries, in turn, display higher levels of agricultural protection than most of Southeast Asia. In fact, as Table 5.7 shows, South Korea's average MFN tariff for agriculture, pegged at 48 percent in 2006 is even higher than that of India (38 percent in 2005).

Table 5.6. Applied MFN tariffs 2006.

South Asia	MFN	SE Asia	MFN	Northeast Asia	MFN
India	19.2	Vietnam	16.8	Korea	12.1
Pakistan	14.3	Cambodia	14.3	China	9.9
Nepal	14.0	Thailand	10.0	Japan	5.6
Sri Lanka	11.2	Laos	9.7	Northeast Asia	9.2
Bangladesh	15.2	Malaysia	8.5		
South Asia	14.8	Indonesia	6.9		
		Philippines	6.3		
		Myanmar	5.6		
		Brunei	3.3		
		Singapore	0.0		
		SE Asia	8.14		

Source: WTO Trade Profiles, 2006.

Table 5.7. Agriculture vs non-agriculture MFN tariffs, 2006.

	Agri	Non-agri
South Korea	47.8	6.6
India	37.6	16.4
Japan	24.3	2.8
Vietnam	24.2	15.7
Sri lanka	23.8	9.2
Thailand	22.1	8.2
Laos	19.5	8.5
Cambodia	18.1	13.7
Bangladesh	17.3	14.9
Pakistan	16.3	14
China	15.7	9
Nepal	14.9	13.7
Malaysia	12.3	7.9
Philippines	9.6	5.8
Myanmar	8.7	5.1
Indonesia	8.2	6.8
Brunei	5.2	3

Source: WTO Trade Profiles, 2006.

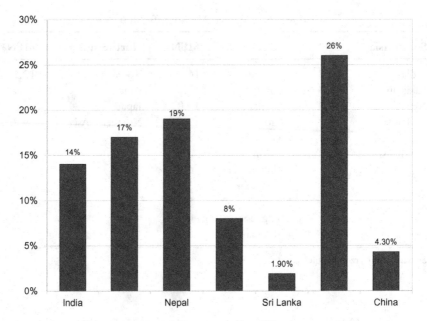

Fig. 5 3: Importance of tariff revenues.

Source: ADB Country Studies (various), 2007.

The fact that tariffs still constitute important revenue sources, particularly for South Asian countries, could lead to some reluctance to further liberalise trade. Although the trend is toward reduced influence, trade taxes continue to take up more than a quarter of total government revenues for Bangladesh, 19 percent for Nepal, 17 percent for Pakistan and 14 percent for India (see Fig. 5.3). In 1992, import tariffs contributed 19 percent to total Thai government earnings, but that has fallen to less than 10 percent at present.

The lesser degree of engagement in international trade of South Asian economies is likely to have a significant bearing on their trade performance relative to the East Asian economies, including on the trade between the two regions. Continued progress in opening their economies will clearly be essential if the South Asian economies are to realise the potential benefits of closer integration with East Asia.

Table 5.8.   Growth of East Asia–South Asia trade. East Asian economies' trade with South Asia. South Asia economies' trade with East Asia (percentage increases from 1999/2000–2004/5 unless otherwise indicated).

	Percentage	Increase
	Export	Imports
(1) East Asia trade with South Asia		
China	305	509
Japan	11	12
Korea	109	98
Hong Kong	68	60
Singapore	65	237
Indonesia	130	113
Malaysia	78	84
Philippines	70	87
Thailand	129	89
Cambodia (2000–2004)	36	157
(2) South Asia trade with East Asia		
India (1999/2000–2004)	145	132
Bangladesh (1999/2000–2004)	–17	13
Sri Lanka (2000–2004)	4	25

Source: Calculated from Comtrade data.

East Asia–South Asia trade and its Future Potential and Implications

Recent growth in East Asia–South Asia trade

It has been correctly observed that recent years have seen a surge in trade between East Asia and South Asia, albeit from a very low base (Rana, 2005). When this trade is disaggregated by economy, as is done in Table 5.8, it is clear that the aggregate trade flow masks very considerable variation across the inter-regional trade flows of individual economies.

Table 5.8 summarises the recent growth in trade of East Asian economies with South Asia and of South Asian economies with East Asia over the period 1999/2000–2004/2005 (or the nearest period for which comparable data was available). The trade of East Asian economies with South Asia has grown rapidly, albeit from a relatively low base, with Japan being the conspicuous exception to this statement. The most dramatic growth is obviously observed in China's trade with South Asia but several other East Asian economies have had growth of around 100 percent or more in their export and or import trade with South Asia — Korea and Indonesia for both exports and imports, Thailand for exports and Singapore and Cambodia for imports. Hong Kong, Malaysia and the Philippines all recorded export and import increases over the period in the range of 60–90 percent.

India is the only one of the South Asian economies listed to have shown comparable growth in trade with East Asia over the same period. This implies that a very large share of the increased trade of East Asian economies with South Asia over the period consisted of increased trade with India. The exports of Bangladesh to East Asia actually fell over the period, and export growth of Sri Lanka to East Asia was minimal. The imports of the latter two economies from East Asia continued to grow modestly, despite the weak performance of exports in the opposite direction.

It seems clear that generalisations about trade between East Asia and South Asia are likely to be misleading or likely to provide only a partial view. The following sections of the chapter provide analysis of the trade of the two regions from a variety of angles, including analyses disaggregated by economy and by commodity. A range of approaches are used including trade shares, trade intensity and complementarity indexes and revealed comparative advantage, as well as a more detailed analysis of recent trade trends.

Trade shares

Figures 5.4–5.6 indicate the shares of the three regions, Northeast, Southeast and South Asia in each other's and their own trade.

Northeast Asia and Southeast Asia respectively conduct just over 50 percent and 60 percent of their trade within East Asia. For Northeast Asia, intra-Northeast Asia trade accounts for over 40 percent of its trade, while the share of Southeast Asia in its trade is just over 10 percent. The share of intra-Northeast Asian trade rose

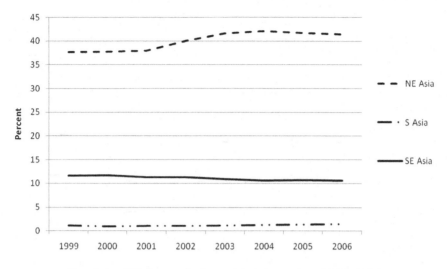

Fig. 5.4:   NE Asia trade share with Asian regions 1999–2006.

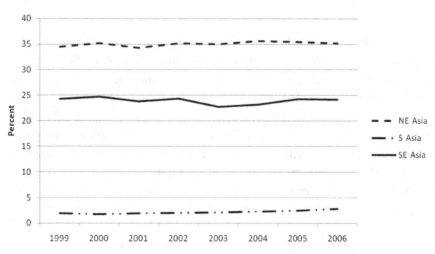

Fig. 5.5:   SE Asia trade share with Asian regions 1999–2006.

sharply from 2002–2004, while that of Southeast Asia in Northeast Asia's trade has been very gradually declining. Southeast Asia conducts 35 percent of its trade with Northeast Asia, while the share of intra-Southeast Asia in its trade is just under 25 percent. These shares have remained more or less constant.

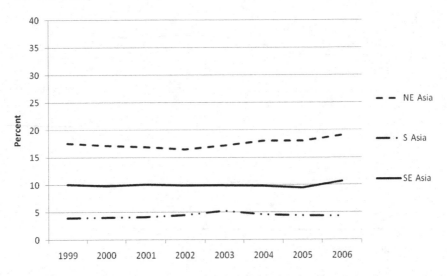

Fig. 5.6: S Asia trade share with Asian regions.

Northeast Asia and Southeast Asia conduct only about 1.5 percent and 2.75 percent, respectively, of their trade with South Asia. The share of South Asia in their trade has risen gradually over the period but still remains very low.

South Asia conducts about 30 percent of its trade with East Asia, made up of about 20 percent with Northeast Asia and 10 percent with Southeast Asia. Intra-South Asian trade accounts for less than 5 percent of South Asian trade. There is little overall upward trend in these shares over the period as a whole, although the share of Northeast Asia in South Asia's trade rose steadily from 2002.

For purposes of this study key points to note from the analysis of trade shares are:

- While intra-regional trade is highly developed within East Asia and within the East Asian sub-regions of Northeast and Southeast Asia, intra-regional trade has not developed within South Asia to the same extent;
- East Asia's share of South Asia's trade is very much higher than South Asia's share of East Asia's trade;

- Northeast Asia and Southeast Asia conduct a much higher proportion of their trade than South Asia with the three Asian sub-regions. Clearly, much of South Asia's trade is focused elsewhere.

Trade intensities

The observation that the share of countries in each other's trade may be greater than, or less than, their corresponding shares of world trade, highlights that other factors may influence these trade shares besides their overall level of engagement in global trade. Countries or regions accounting for a low share of their partners' trade, for example, may nevertheless be trading intensely with those same partners, in the sense that the low trade share might still be higher than that which might be expected on the basis of their share in world trade. Import and export trade with the same partners need not be of equal intensity; the intensity of one flow can be considerably greater or less than the other.

Measures of trade intensity are used to capture the propensity of countries to trade more or less with partners than would be expected on the basis of the corresponding shares of world trade. The **bilateral trade intensity index** reflected in Figs. 5.7–5.9 measures the intensity of a country or region's trade, both imports and exports, with a partner country or region, in a sense whether the partner's share in its overall trade is greater or less than that would be expected on the basis of the partner's share in world trade. An index value of greater than one indicates the extent to which the partner's weight in the trade of the country or region concerned exceeds its weight in world trade, while an index value of less than one indicates a less-than-expected intensity of trade, interpreted in the same way. In the discussion that follows, for the sake of brevity, index values of greater than or less than one are respectively described as "above average" or "below average".[2]

---

[2] This convention is also followed in describing the values of other indexes that are above or below their threshold value.

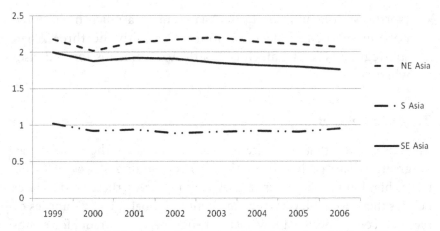

Fig. 5.7:   NE Asia's trade intensity with Asian regions 1999–2006.

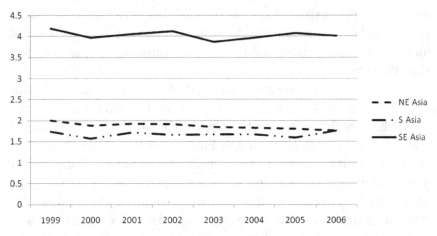

Fig. 5.8:   SE Asia's trade intensity with Asian regions 1999–2006.

Both intra-Northeast Asia trade and Northeast Asia's trade with Southeast Asia are approximately double the level that would be expected on the basis of the two region's shares of world trade. The intensity of Northeast Asia's trade with Southeast Asia showed a tendency to decline over the period. On the other hand Northeast Asia trades with South Asia approximately at the level that would be expected based on South Asia's share of world trade and the relevant intensity index remained more or less stable over the period.

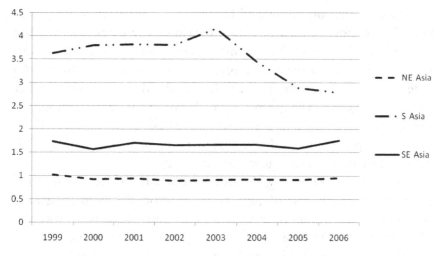

Fig. 5.9:   S Asia's trade intensity with Asian regions 1999–2006.

The trade intensity data for Southeast Asia shows that, remarkably, the level of intra-Southeast Asian trade is approximately four times the expected level based on Southeast Asia's share of world trade. The intensity indexes for Southeast Asia's trade with Northeast Asia and South Asia both lie between 1.5 and 2, with a somewhat declining trend over the period in the former and a stable trend in the latter.

The intensity of intra-South Asian trade appears to have been high and rising until 2002 but thereafter fell quite rapidly. South Asia trades approximately one-and-half times more with Southeast Asia than would be expected based on the former's share of world trade, while its trade with Northeast Asia is more or less in line with expectations based on Northeast Asia's share of world trade.

Thus, the intra-regional trade of all three sub-regions displays a high level of intensity, especially in Southeast Asia and South Asia, although the intensity of intra-South Asian trade fell rapidly over the latter part of the period. Southeast Asia's trade with Northeast Asia and South Asia is intense in both directions, while the trade between Northeast Asia and South Asia in both directions corresponds broadly to what would be expected based on the shares in world trade of the two sub-regions.

Separate import and export intensity indexes focus respectively on the export and import sides of the bilateral trade flow, allowing the influence of each on the overall bilateral trade intensity to be identified. The **export intensity index** measures the extent to which a partner accounts for a larger or smaller share of the exports of a country or region, compared to the partner's share of world imports. An index value of one again provides the threshold, with a value greater than one indicating the extent to which exports are more focused on the partner than would be expected on the basis of the partner's share in world imports, and a value of less than one indicating a lower than expected share of exports going to the partner.

In exactly the same way, the **import intensity index** measures the extent to which the share of imports sourced from the partner is greater or less than what would be expected on the basis of the partner's share of world exports. An index value of one again provides the threshold.

The export and import intensity indexes for the trade of Southeast Asia and South Asia with each other are interesting. Figures 5.10 and 5.11 illustrate these indexes for South Asia's trade with East Asia. Figure 5.10 shows the export intensity of South Asia's exports to Southeast Asia increasing strongly, while Fig. 5.11 shows a steady decline in the intensity index for South Asia's imports from Southeast Asia. The same indexes for Southeast Asia show an apparently corresponding rise in the intensity of Southeast Asia's imports from South Asia and fall in the intensity of its exports to South Asia.

Commodity composition of trade

The commodity composition of trade also has an important bearing on actual and potential trade levels. Here again, different measures are used to capture different dimensions of the influence of the commodity composition of trade.

The index of **revealed comparative advantage (RCA)** measures the extent to which the share of a product in a country's exports exceeds or falls short of the share of the same product in world exports. The threshold value of the RCA index is one, which indicates that the product concerned accounts for an identical share of both the exports of the country in question and of world exports. RCA is generally taken as a measure of a country's competitiveness in exporting the product in

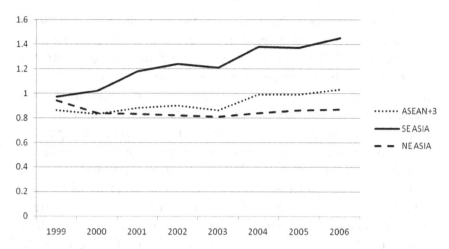

Fig. 5.10:   Export intensity indexes for South Asias exports to East Asia 1999–2006.

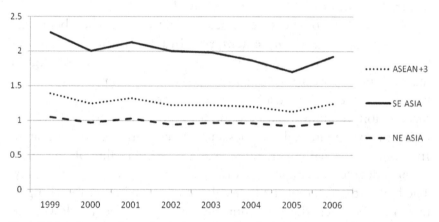

Fig. 5.11:   Import intensity indexes for South Asia's imports from East Asia 1999–2006.

question. The higher/lower the value of the index, the more/less competitive the country as an exporter of the product in question.[3] Changes in the range of the products with an RCA above the threshold level,

---

[3] Here the original version of the RCA index is used. This has a threshold value of one, a lower limit of zero, and no upper limit. An alternative is the symmetric RCA index, which takes a value between −1 and 1, and has a threshold value of zero.

together with changes in the average RCA of those products can also be taken as an indication of whether a country is extending the range of products in which it is an internationally competitive exporter. RCA is not a measure of true comparative advantage, since while the trade flows on which it is based reflect the underlying comparative advantage albeit to an unknown degree, they also reflect the distortions of the underlying comparative advantage created by whatever trade barriers are in place.

Comparisons of RCAs between countries can indicate the extent to which they are likely to be competitors in world markets. Countries with a high RCA value for the same product are likely to be leading competitors in the export markets for that product. In trade flows, the potential for bilateral trade based on specialisation will be higher, and the greater is the difference in RCA profiles between the two countries. However, similar RCA profiles do not rule out bilateral trade if intra-industry trade is involved.

Another type of measure indicating the potential for beneficial specialisation is the **Complementarity Index**. This index measures the degree to which the export profile of one country or region matches the import profile of another, or the "matching" in the commodity profile of the trade of two countries or region. In one formulation, the index takes a value between 0 and 100, with 0 indicating no overlap in trade profiles and 100 indicating a perfect match. In another formulation, the index has a threshold value of one, indicating a degree of matching that is "average" for the global economy. The higher the value of the index above one, the higher the complementarity between the two countries or regions and the lower the index value, the lower the complementarity.

Revealed comparative advantage

Table 5.9 summarises the RCAs for the three sub regions for the 21 HS Sectors, for the year 2006. As a first approximation, these sectors can be subdivided into "uncontested sectors", where only one of the sub-regions has an RCA greater than one and "contested sectors", where two or three of the sub-regions have an RCA greater than one. This is shown in Table 5.10.

Table 5.9. Revealed comparative advantages of Asian regions in 21 HS sectors 2006.

	HS Sections	NE Asia	SE Asia	S Asia
S01	Animal Products, Animals	0.28	0.75	1.29
S02	Vegetable Products	0.22	0.85	2.36
S03	Oils and Fats	0.06	4.83	0.95
S04	Foodstuffs	0.27	0.85	0.83
S05	Mineral Products and Fuels	0.16	1.09	0.99
S06	Chemical Products	0.55	0.61	0.97
S07	Plastic and Rubber Products	1	1.31	0.69
S08	Hides Skins and Leathers	1.8	0.44	3.37
S09	Wood and Wood Products	0.46	1.65	0.15
S10	Pulp and Paper Products	0.42	0.58	0.22
S11	Textiles	1.75	1.05	6.5
S12	Footwear and Headgear	2.15	1.51	1.7
S13	Stone and Glass Products	1.08	0.58	0.96
S14	Gemstones	0.61	0.69	5.5
S15	Metals and Metal Products	0.97	0.48	1.08
S16	Machinery and Electronics	1.65	1.59	0.23
S17	Transport Equipment	0.92	0.26	0.26
S18	Instruments	1.51	0.6	0.21
S19	Arms and Ammunition	0.24	0.1	0.3
S20	Miscellaneous	1.93	0.76	0.51
S21	Art and Antiques	0.22	0.16	1.3

Source: WITS.

Analysis at the sub-regional level indicates only four sectors where more than one sub-region has an RCA greater than one (Table 5.10). However, the sub-regional level is probably too high a level of aggregation to produce a meaningful analysis of the degree of head to head competition between the sub-regions. An earlier analysis (Scollay and Pelkmans-Balaoing, 2007) based on 2004 data employed a breakdown within the sub-regions into groups of countries with similar trade profiles. This analysis showed that South Asian countries generally face formidable competition from East Asian countries in all of the products in which they have above-average revealed comparative advantage. For the most part, these are labour-intensive manufacturing

Table 5.10. "Uncontested" and "contested" sectors (based on RCAs of regions for each sector).

Uncontested Sectors	Region with RCA > 1
Stone and Glass Products	NE Asia
Instruments	NE Asia
Miscellaneous	NE Asia
Oils and Fats	SE Asia
Mineral Products and Fuels	SE Asia
Plastic and Rubber Products	SE Asia
Wood and Wood Products	SE Asia
Animal Products, Animals	S Asia
Vegetable Products	S Asia
Gemstones	S Asia
Metals and Metal Products	S Asia
Art and Antiques	S Asia
"Contested Sectors"	**Regions with RCA > 1**
Hides, Skins and Leathers	NE Asia, S Asia
Textiles	NE Asia, SE Asia, S Asia
Footwear and Headgear	NE Asia, SE Asia, S Asia
Machinery and Electronics	NE Asia, SE Asia
Sectors where no region has RCA>1	
Foodstuffs	
Chemical Products	
Pulp and Paper Products	
Transport Equipment	
Arms and Ammunition	

Source: Table 5.9.

sectors and natural-resource based sectors, although India also has above-average RCAs in sectors such as chemicals and metals and metal products. Above-average revealed comparative advantages are conspicuously lacking in South Asia in sectors characterised by more advanced technology, where East Asian economies have considerable strength (Scollay and Pelkmans-Balaoing, 2007).

Complementarity index

Figures 5.12–5.14 illustrate the commodity complementarity indexes for each sub-region with the other two sub-regions. In this case, the index takes a value of 0 to 100, with zero indicating no matching of trade profiles and 100 indicating a perfect match.

Figure 5.12, for Northeast Asia indicates high and increasing complementarity over time with Southeast Asia and much lower

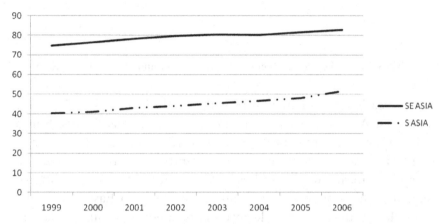

Fig. 5.12: NE Asia complementarity with SE Asia and S Asia.

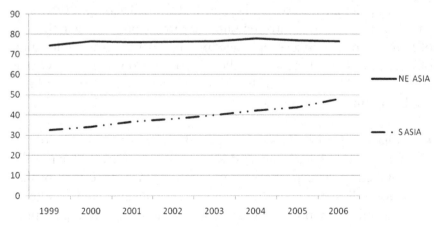

Table 5.13: SE Asia complementarity with NE Asia and S Asia 1999–2006.

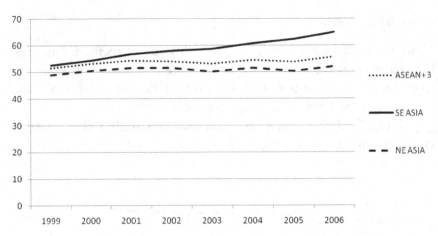

Table 5.14: S Asia complementarity with NE Asia and SE Asia 1999–2006.

but increasing complementarity with South Asia. Figure 5.13, for Southeast Asia, shows high but stable complementarity with South Asia. Figure 5.14, for South Asia, indicates low and stable complementarity with Northeast Asia and low but increasing complementarity with Southeast Asia. These results are symptomatic of a high degree of trade integration within East Asia, and a much lower degree of trade integration between South Asia and East Asia, which is nevertheless on the increase between South Asia and Southeast Asia in particular.

The earlier analysis of Scollay and Pelkmans-Balaoing (2007) was based on a breakdown into the same country groups as their analysis of RCAs, and utilised a complementarity index with a threshold value of one, as described earlier, to allow a comparison with the average level of complementarity in the world economy. Their main findings can be summarised as follows:

• India's export profile is well-matched to the import profiles of the rest of South Asia, Japan, and Korea and its import profile is well-matched to the export profile of Southeast Asia. Its export profile is not well-matched to the import profiles of China and Southeast Asia and its import profile is not well-matched to the export profile of the rest of South Asia, Japan, Korea and China.

- The rest of South Asia has an export profile well-matched to the import profiles of Japan and Korea and of Hong Kong and Singapore and its import profile is well-matched to the export profile of Southeast Asia. The export profile is not well-matched with the import profiles of India, China and Southeast Asia, and its import profile is not well-matched to the export profiles of Japan, and Hong Kong and Singapore.

- Southeast Asia's export profile is well-matched to the import profiles of all other groups except Japan and Korea, for which it is neutral and its import profile is well-matched to the export profiles of Japan and Korea and of Hong Kong and Singapore. Its import profile is not well-matched to the export profiles of India and the rest of South Asia.

- China's export profile is well-matched to the import profiles of Hong Kong and Singapore, and its import profile is well-matched to the export profiles of Japan and Korea and of Hong Kong and Singapore. Its export profile is not well-matched to the import profile of India and its import profile is not well-matched to the export profiles of India and the rest of South Asia.

- Japan and Korea have export profiles that are well-matched to the import profiles of all East Asian groups, and import profiles that are well-matched to the export profiles of India and the rest of South Asia.

- Hong Kong and Singapore have export profiles that are well-matched to the import profiles of Southeast Asia and China, and import profiles that are well-matched to the export profiles of China, Japan and Korea, and the rest of South Asia. Their import profiles are not well-matched to the export profiles of the rest of South Asia. (Scollay and Pelkmans-Balaoing, 2007).

Summarising in a different way, commodity complementarity has either a favourable or neutral influence on intra-East Asian flows, while its influence on South Asia–East Asia trade is mixed, but with a predominance of unfavourable influences. The influence on intra-South Asian trade is mixed, with the influence on exports of other South Asian countries to India being particularly unfavourable.

Increasing trade integration between East and South Asia, and the role of preferential trade agreements (PTAs)

Preferential trading arrangements (PATs) are playing an increasingly prominent role in trade within East Asia and South Asia, and appear likely to also play a growing role in trade between the two regions. Existing PTAs range from partial preference agreements, generally following a positive list approach, to more comprehensive agreements designed to satisfy GATT Article XXIV, usually following a negative list approach. Partial preference agreements have tended to be more popular with the South Asian countries, while East Asian economies have shown a greater willingness to engage in more comprehensive agreements, although not all East Asian PTAs are comprehensive. Defensive motivations for the establishment of PTAs are becoming increasingly important as countries seek to avoid being disadvantaged relative to their competitors in the markets of their trading partners.

India's pursuit of PTAs with East Asian partners seems likely to accelerate the tendency for India to move away from its South Asian neighbours in its trade relations. India has concluded an FTA with the ASEAN group as a whole and also a separate bilateral FTA with Singapore. FTAs have also been announced between India and Korea and between India and Japan, the latter very recently. India is also part of the 'ASEAN Plus Six' group (comprising of the 10 ASEAN members, China, Japan, Korea, Australia, New Zealand and India) that is considering a possible FTA within the framework of a Comprehensive Economic Partnership for East Asia (CEPEA).

Apart from an FTA between Pakistan and China, which appears to be at least as much politically as economically motivated, there are no comparable arrangements involving other South Asian countries. Three South Asian countries are members of the Asia Pacific Trade Agreement (APTA), formerly known as the Bangkok Agreement, a "positive list", partial preference agreement between Bangladesh, China, India, Korea and Sri Lanka. BIMSTEC (the Bay of Bengal Initiative for Multisectoral Technical and Economic Cooperation) links Bangladesh, India, Sri Lanka, Bhutan, Myanmar and Nepal with Thailand. Neither APTA nor BIMSTEC, however, have the same potential as vehicles for economic integration between South Asia and East Asia as the various initiatives involving India outlined in the preceding paragraph, even though the latter also have their limitations.

One of the challenges for South Asian countries, if they seek to intensify trade linkages with East Asia, is to move beyond the "partial preference", "positive list" approach that has characterised most of their PTAs hitherto, and to accept deeper commitments on trade in goods than they have previously considered comfortable. After considerable early struggles, India has moved much further along this path than the other South Asian countries.

Therefore, on the basis of current trends the other South Asian countries are likely to fall further behind India in the push for integration with East Asia and to face increasing erosion of their preferential position in the Indian market.

References

Rana, P. D. (2005). Economic Relations Between South and East Asia: The Evolution of Pan-Asian Integration (paper prepared for the High Level Conference on Asian Economic Integration, New Delhi, 18–19 November).

Scollay, R. and A. Pelkmans-Balaoing (2009). Current Patterns of Trade and Investment. In *Pan-Asian Integration: Linking East and South Asia*, J., Francois, Rana, P.B. and Wignaraja, G. (eds.), Asian Development Bank and Palgrave Macmillan, London, pp. 63–162.

Transport and Trade Facilitation for South Asia–East Asia Trade

Douglas H. Brooks and Barbara Dizon*

Introduction

After the financial crisis in 1997–1998, Asia recovered and reached greater heights of economic growth and development, partly through the expansion and focus on international trade both within Asia and with other regions. Contributing to this success in international trade are a strong support for trade facilitation and investments in domestic or international infrastructure. Infrastructure development supports a reduction in trade costs and stimulates total trade through greater economies of scale and increased potential for manufacturers to produce better quality products for sale to international or domestic markets. There are three forms of infrastructure development that facilitate trade and increase its overall performance. The first is

---

* The views expressed in this chapter are the authors' own and do not necessarily reflect those of ADB or its Board of Governors.

physical or hard infrastructure improvements, such as expanding capacities of roads or improvements and development in ports. Hard or physical infrastructure is mostly tangible and costly.

The second is soft infrastructure, which refers to streamlining trade operations such as improvements in port rules, reducing tariff and non-tariff barriers, neutral administration and governance of systems and decreased red tape associated with trade. Complementing soft infrastructure development are improvements in the conditions for investment, shifts in production methods that lead to more trading activities and new technologies for procurement and marketing beyond the national borders. A supporting environment of legal and judicial rights and procedures, equitable and enforceable competition policy and a sound regulatory framework are other examples of soft infrastructure that are crucial for physical infrastructure efficiency.

A third form of trade infrastructure development is improvement of logistics and supporting financial intermediation services in which risk management opportunities and payment and clearing services are crucial. Infrastructure finance, through the presence of a long-term, local currency bond market is important. Externalities that arise with the development of infrastructure services clearly indicate an important role for regional coordination to increase efficiency and trade facilitation. Regional coordination in trade facilitation, promotes regional growth and allows greater regional investment opportunities in cross-border infrastructure, creating a virtuous cycle in trade operations.

Asia's trade infrastructure is currently inadequate. Existing infrastructure lacunae, combined with inefficiencies in transporting goods and people and shortages such as the lack of power supply to operate machineries and facilities, create macroeconomic and microeconomic imbalances. While East Asia as a whole does relatively better than other developing regions in its infrastructure performance, comparison with high income countries still shows significant room for improvement in its trade operations.

Reductions in trade costs explain more than half of the (1870–1913) pre-World War I surge in trade and roughly a third of post-World War trade growth while a steep rise in trade costs explains the entire trade collapse in the inter-war period (Jacks *et al.*, 2008).

Globally, tariffs and quotas have been reduced through multilateral negotiations under the General Agreement on Tariffs and Trade, its successor the World Trade Organisation, and a raft of bilateral and regional trade agreements. Tariff barriers constitute an average cost increase of 10–20 percent of a traded product's factory-gate price in developed countries, as suggested by Anderson and van Wincoop (2001).

This chapter presents an overview on the importance of trade facilitation between East Asia and South Asia. With the nature of trade in Asia as well as its investments in infrastructure that reduce transport costs, intra-regional and inter-regional trade is expanding, creating a global chain of economic links that make it possible for regions to integrate and cooperate, as production networks are formed in response to an ever-changing environment of globalisation.

Trade in Developing Asia

Description of trade in developing Asia

Table 6.1 shows the various growth rates of Asian countries in their export and import performance for 20 years prior to the 2008–2010 global economic crisis. The table reveals growth in exports and imports in East Asia over 20 years, particularly in China with a huge increase in its value of exports from US$33.3 billion in 1987 to US$1.5 trillion in 2007, overtaking the exports of Japan; Hong Kong; Taipei, China; Korea; and Singapore. India, the only South Asian country which entered the top ten in Asia's leading exporters, had an export value of US$175.4 billion in 2007. Seven of the eight emerging Asian economies in the list had double-digit import growth rates of more than 10 percent while Japan, which used to be an aggressive performer in Asian trade, had an average export growth of 8.6 percent. India's exports expanded 17 times while that of China increased by 30 times. China, also the largest importing country, recorded an import value at US$1.1 trillion, registering 18.5 percent average annual import growth from 1987–2007.

Table 6.2 shows the increase in share of intra-regional exports in trade in East Asia (15) at 15.2 percent annually from 1990–2007. Its

Table 6.1.   Trade growth in Asia's 10 leading exporters (1987–2007)[a].

	Exports			Imports		
	US$[b] Billion 2000 Constant Prices		Average Growth Rate	US$[b] Billion 2000 Constant Prices		Average Growth Rate
Countries	1987	2007	1987–2007	1987	2007	1987–2007
1. China	33.3	1464.0	20.8	37.2	1109.7	18.5
2. Japan	297.4	739.9	4.7	172.8	898.6	8.6
3. Hong Kong, China	40.9	420.0	12.3	14.7	429.6	12.4
4. Taipei, China[c]	83.3	361.1	10.3	79.9	262.3	8.3
5. Republic of Korea[d]	51.6	289.5	10.1	27.9	421.6	16.3
6. Singapore	35.2	272.8	10.8	30.4	283.9	11.8
7. Malaysia	15.1	211.8	14.1	10.9	170.5	14.7
8. Thailand	9.8	184.6	15.8	11.2	166.9	14.5
9. India	10.2	175.4	15.3	14.8	253.8	15.3
10. Indonesia	14.5	137.2	11.9	10.6	86.4	11.0

[a] Ranking based on 2007 Exports.
[b] United States dollar.
[c] First year of data for Taipei, China is 1992.
[d] First year of data for Republic of Korea is 1989.
Source: United Nations COMTRADE database: http://comtrade.un.org/db/.

intra-regional export share in world trade also increased by roughly 7 percent points over the same period. In South Asia, the trade share of intra-regional exports also showed a strong increase for the same time period, but from a lower base. East and South Asia had annual average export growth rates of over 10 percent for the 17 year period. The remarkable performance of East and South Asia in exports surpassed the performance of other trade blocs such as the European Union, MERCOSUR and NAFTA.

With export growth rates soaring in East Asia and South Asia, the shares of components in exports and imports within the regions increased much faster than in trade with the rest of the world. Exports within the region were 60 percent of total component exports. For component imports, the share was even higher in 2005–2006. An increase in component intensity has been noticeable

Table 6.2. Exports 1990–2007.

	Total Exports ($ billion)					Share of World Trade (in percent)					Share of Intraregional Exports in Total (in percent)					Annual Growth (in percent)
	1990	1995	2000	2005	2007	1990	1995	2000	2005	2007	1990	1995	2000	2005	2007	1990–2007
East Asia (15)	417.8	870.4	1193.9	2136.6	3075.3	13.0	17.9	19.2	21.7	22.2	100.0	100.0	100.0	100.0	100.0	12.5
Intra-regional	136.1	344.7	456.4	901.7	151.7	4.2	7.1	7.3	9.1	11.0	32.6	39.6	38.2	42.2	49.4	15.2
Extra-regional	281.7	525.7	737.5	1234.9	1557.6	8.7	10.8	11.8	12.5	11.3	67.4	60.4	61.8	57.8	50.6	10.6
East Asia (16)	704.7	1313.3	1673.1	2731.5	3789.5	21.9	27.1	26.8	27.7	27.4	100.0	100.0	100.0	100.0	100.0	10.4
Intra-regional	284.0	646.2	797.8	1389.5	1853.4	8.8	13.3	12.8	14.1	13.4	40.3	49.2	47.7	50.9	48.9	11.7
Extra-regional	420.7	667.1	875.3	1342.0	1936.1	13.0	13.7	14.0	13.6	14.0	59.7	50.8	52.3	49.1	51.1	9.4
Central and West Asia (8)	—	5.6	14.9	34.7	62.2	—	0.2	0.3	0.6	0.4	—	100.0	100.0	100.0	100.0	22.2
Intra-regional	—	1.9	1.2	2.9	3.9	—	0.1	0.0	0.0	0.0	—	33.4	8.1	8.4	6.3	6.4
Extra-regional	—	3.7	13.7	31.8	58.3	—	0.1	0.3	0.5	0.4	—	66.6	91.9	91.6	93.7	25.7
South Asia (7)	27.2	43.7	60.7	125.8	194.4	0.8	0.9	1.0	1.3	1.4	100.0	100.0	100.0	100.0	100.0	12.3
Intra-regional	0.9	2.1	2.9	8.4	12.1	0.0	0.0	0.0	0.1	0.1	3.5	4.7	4.8	6.7	6.2	16.2
Extra-regional	26.3	41.6	57.8	117.4	182.3	0.8	0.9	0.9	1.2	1.3	96.5	95.3	95.2	93.3	93.8	12.1
EU (27)	1521.6	2010.8	2424.3	4054.3	5316.8	47.2	41.4	38.9	41.1	38.4	100.0	100.0	100.0	100.0	100.0	7.6
Intra-regional	1018.6	1401.3	1641.5	2732.1	3601.1	31.6	28.9	26.3	27.7	26.0	65.9	62.1	61.1	59.7	67.7	7.7
Extra-regional	503.0	609.5	782.8	1322.2	1715.7	15.6	12.6	12.6	13.4	12.4	34.1	37.9	38.9	40.3	32.3	7.5
NAFTA (3)	546.1	853.6	1223.6	1478.7	1834.6	16.9	17.6	19.6	15.0	13.3	100.0	100.0	100.0	100.0	100.0	7.4
Intra-regional	225.8	392.9	681.6	824.4	930.8	7.0	8.1	10.9	8.4	6.7	41.3	46.0	55.7	55.8	50.7	8.7
Extra-regional	320.4	460.7	542.1	654.3	903.8	9.9	9.5	8.7	6.6	6.5	58.7	54.0	44.3	44.2	49.3	6.3
MERCOSUR (5)	64.6	89.1	122.5	219.4	324.3	2.0	1.8	2.0	2.2	2.3	100.0	100.0	100.0	100.0	100.0	10.0
Intra-regional	4.9	16.8	20.0	24.2	38.5	0.2	0.3	0.3	0.2	0.3	8.9	20.5	20.9	13.1	11.9	12.9
Extra-regional	59.7	72.3	102.5	195.2	285.8	1.9	1.5	1.6	2.0	2.1	91.1	79.5	79.1	86.9	88.1	9.6

(Continued)

Table 6.2.   (*Continued*)

	Total Exports ($ billion)					Share of World Trade (in percent)					Share of Intraregional Exports in Total (in percent)					Annual Growth (in percent)
	1990	1995	2000	2005	2007	1990	1995	2000	2005	2007	1990	1995	2000	2005	2007	1990–2007
WORLD EXPORTS	3224.8	4853.9	6233.1	9859.0	13830.0	100.0	100.0	100.0	100.0	100.0	—	—	—	—	—	8.9
MEMO ITEM																
Japan	286.9	442.9	479.2	594.9	714.2	8.9	9.1	7.7	9.0	5.2	12.2	14.4	11.7	10.4	8.8	5.0
China	62.1	148.8	249.2	762.0	1218.1	1.9	3.1	4.0	7.7	8.8	5.8	6.2	6.9	11.0	12.2	18.2
United States	392.9	583.0	780.3	904.3	1162.2	12.2	12.0	12.5	9.2	8.4	14.8	13.1	11.4	7.7	7.1	5.7

Source: Calculated from UN Comtrade data (S2, items-total) and Direction of Trade and Statistics 2008.

Notes:

1. East Asia (15): Brunei; Cambodia; China; Hong Kong, China; Indonesia; Korea; Lao PDR; Malaysia; Mongolia; Myanmar; Philippines; Singapore; Taipei; China; Thailand; Vietnam.

2. East Asia (16): East Asia (15) plus Japan.

3. Central and West Asia (8): Armenia, Azerbaijan, Georgia, Kazakhstan, Kyrgyz Republic, Tajikistan, Turkmenistan, Uzbekistan.

4. South Asia (7): Afghanistan, Bangladesh, India, Maldives, Nepal, Pakistan, Sri Lanka.

5. EU (27): Austria, Belgium, Bulgaria, Cyprus, Czech Republic, Denmark, Estonia, Finland, France, Germany, Greece, Hungary, Ireland, Italy, Latvia, Lithuania, Luxembourg, Malta, Netherlands, Poland, Portugal, Romania, Slovakia, Slovenia, Spain, Sweden, and the United Kingdom.

6. MERCOSUR: Argentina, Brazil, Paraguay, Uruguay, and Venezuela.

7. NAFTA: Canada, Mexico, and the US.

8. Japan, China and United States share of regional export to world is only intra-regional export (share of individual country's export to the region to total regional export).

9. Annual Growth of Central and West Asia is for 1995–2005.

in Southeast Asia's trade with other developing countries, most notably China. Korea and Taipei also show substantial component trade with other countries in the region (ADB/ADBI, 2009).

To compete with other markets, South Asia may feel the need to invest for improvements in its trading environment and infrastructure. Intra-regional and extra-regional trade in East Asia provides opportunities and avenues as markets are still open. However, stiff competition arises as manufacturers now produce quality goods for trade. Establishing international network links, opening communication for a smooth flow of information and promoting interaction with other Asian countries would contribute toward creating more unified Asian cooperation and regionalisation.

Changing nature of trade in Asia

As the nature of Asia's trade changes, so does the region's infrastructure needs and its efficiency in international transactions. Hummels (2009) notes that these are influenced by (1) changes in the weight-value ratio of traded goods; (2) demand for timeliness and the shift toward increased air shipping; (3) new trade flows of both products and geographical routes and variations in the size of shipments; and (4) product fragmentation. Complex relationships arise since the developments are inter-linked. For example, declining weight-value ratios and vertical specialisation in the fragmentation of new production supply chains generate new trade flows and patterns that stimulate the rapid growth in the air cargo shipments, since ocean shipment tends to be more expensive and late in delivery.

Asia's goods for trade have become lighter and are now often higher-valued goods and weightless services. An example is the onset of the information and communication technology (ICT) revolution, which has generated increased trade in ICT products and outsourced services, as well as greater migration of highly-skilled professionals. This has implications for the choice of transport mode, the distance and destination of trade flows, the location and break-down of production processes, harmonisation and standardisation of customs clearing and inspections, and the demand for supporting infrastructure to facilitate trade. Improvements in infrastructure for air freight and containerisation are examples of changes in transport technology in response to increased demand for time sensitive goods. Multimodal shipping and improvements in logistics have made it possible to trade with more destinations in less time and at lower average costs. The use of containerisation facilitates cost savings by allowing goods to be packed once and moved over long distances via a combination of several transport modes such as rail, truck, and ocean liner, without being unpacked, re-inspected and repacked. Air cargo shipment has grown faster with an increasing number of international flights as Asia experiences rapid growth. Demand for air freight increases, as consumers get richer and prefer more expensive imports and therefore, transport costs now are a smaller fraction of the delivered price. One such case is the huge imports of meat that requires trade facilitation in terms of infrastructure in cold storage facilities and air cargo so that timely delivery to the final consumer preserves the quality of the meat.

The combination of increased trade in parts and components within Asia and greater long-distance air shipments is generating many more but smaller new shipments, which benefit SME's, while the biggest shipments get bigger. Such is the case of exports from China where the mean shipment is getting bigger and the median is falling. This pattern is similar for other Asian countries.

Transport Costs as Associated with Trade Facilitation

Transport costs, which account for a large share in the prices of delivered goods, influence demand. Both the quantity of investment and infrastructure services and efficient coordination of logistics services that lower transport costs influence trade performance. Nordas and Piermartini (2004) characterise four dimensions of the relationship between infrastructure and trade transaction costs: (a) direct monetary outlays, such as cost of communications, business travel, freight, insurance and logistics services; (b) timeliness, even more than freight rates, as this is influenced by geography and the nature of infrastructure; (c) risk, such as damaged cargos resulting in increased losses and high insurance costs resulting from poor and inadequate infrastructure; and (d) lack of access to basic services such as transport and telecommunications services leading to high opportunity costs as this limits access and information to markets and trading opportunities. Recent changes in the composition of trade also affect the demand for transportation services.

Infrastructure development lowers the marginal cost of trade, increasing exports at both the intensive and extensive margins. At the extensive margin, this comes in the form of small shipments from small firms, which influence the infrastructure services demanded, especially transportation infrastructure, differently than the deepening of existing trade flows at the intensive margin.

In East Asia, as infrastructure expands trade facilitation, a corresponding reduction in trade costs occurs and alters the comparative advantages of countries relative to other regions, making greater fragmentation of production supply chains possible and spurring the region's intra-regional trade in intermediate products. When inputs are sourced from wherever costs are lowest, the production processes are dispersed geographically; timeliness and reliability of delivery become very important factors and the influence of both physical and institutional infrastructure services become more apparent.

Among different indicators of infrastructure services' contribution to trade, port efficiency appears to have the largest influence, reflecting that the vast bulk of developing countries' trade uses seaports. The dominance of sea freight over land transport and associated cost savings emphasise the need to address the challenges faced by land-locked regions attempting to compete in global markets as well as the importance of improving efficiency at the ports.

A study by Jon Haveman *et al.* (2009) confirms that specific types of infrastructure investments are highly-correlated with reductions in port costs. Mumbai, India in South Asia experienced the greatest improvement in relative costs between 1997 and 2005 while Penang, Malaysia in East Asia has the lowest costs of nine ports studied. Operating with new harbors, wharfs or terminals, and procurements of new cranes are found to reduce port costs by 2 percent and 1 percent, respectively. Increasing the number of berths and deepening channels at ports have smaller effects.

Investing in port infrastructure not only lowers costs and raises port efficiencies for current trade flows but can also increase port capacity to handle new flows and influence the composition of business. Port costs vary across products and even at a single port, new infrastructure can influence the relative costs for loading or unloading containers vs bulk commodities. With advantages derived from the use of containerisation for certain products, relevant port infrastructure developments can contribute to reducing unit costs further as the share of such trade rises.

Interactions between changes in the composition of trade, mode of packing and capacity expansion effects of new port infrastructure, all influence the profitability and bankability of investing in it. In planning port expansions or developing improvement projects, both the efficiency and capacity effects need to be considered for projecting or maximising potential benefits.

The relative weights of different aspects of trade costs are surprising. As De (2007a) notes, the ocean freight for importing a container to India was two thirds more than that for exporting, while the rate for importing a container to China from six Asian countries was lower than that for exporting. Auxiliary shipping charges, such as documentation fees, container handling charges, government taxes and levies among others, may sometimes be more expensive than ocean freight charges, particularly in cases where shipments experience the greatest congestion at ports or borders. Improvements in soft infrastructure such as better country liaison and coordination actions could lower average and variable costs.

The composition of freight charges is variable across countries and commodity categories. As Prabir De notes, the share of total inland freight charges is often greater than that for ocean freight. The actual balance depends on the country, suggesting an inland focus for trade-related infrastructure priorities where the inland share is greater.

Looking at various commodity groups, the weight-to-value ratio often influences transport costs. So the preferred mode of transport for heavy goods by order of preference is sea transport, followed by rail and then land. Hummels and Skiba (2004) found that a 10 percent increase in the ratio of product weight to value results in a 4 percent increase in ad-valorem shipping costs. Landlocked countries and inland regions that export heavy goods should therefore develop streamlined rail connections to efficient ports. Rail has the additional advantage of being a less-carbon intensive transport mode and is therefore more environmental-friendly than road transport.

Infrastructure and logistics need to adjust to the impact of long-term changes in oil prices on trade. High rise in oil prices in the first half of 2008 to US$142.99 per barrel increased shipping and import costs, shifting the balance in favour of domestically produced goods. Such changes have double impact on products from international supply chains since the prices of both imported and exported goods are increased. Steel from China produced with Brazilian iron ore for export to the US would be hit twice by higher fuel charges. The effect of a rise in oil prices is greater where the goods (or their imported components) are shipped by air or have a high weight-to-value ratio. However, improvements in transport technology and reductions in oil prices would have the opposite effect.

Time is an important factor for perishable or time-sensitive goods. As Hummels (2001) has emphasised, the time cost of one day in transit for US imports is equivalent to the ad-valorem tariff rate of 0.8 percent or to an imposed 16 percent tariff on an average trans-Pacific shipment of 20 days. Improvements in infrastructure that reduce delays at the border, in transit, or in ports will increase a country's propensity to trade and reduce accompanying costs.

As land and labour costs continue to rise in the coastal regions of Asia, investors search for areas to locate production facilities further inland. But poor and inadequate infrastructure connections raise transport costs to and from these areas. In the case of China, this realisation has led to shifts in infrastructure policy to prioritise hinterland access. Again, there is a clamor for the use and construction of railways to be prioritised since railways are more suitable for transporting bulky and heavy goods.

Infrastructure development is vital for connecting remote areas and land-locked countries with regional and global trade. The median land-locked country has 55 percent higher transport costs than the median coastal one and transporting goods over land is around seven times costlier for a similar distance by sea. Estimates of the elasticity of trade flows with respect to transport costs range from –2 to 3.5, which means that lowering a land-locked country's trade costs by 10 percent through regional infrastructure increases its exports by over 20 percent. Most land-locked countries in Asia, struggle with poor physical infrastructure and small domestic markets that are remote from world markets and are highly-vulnerable to external shocks. To avoid transporting by the expensive use of air shipment, traded goods must pass through at least one nearby state, often resulting in a high transaction cost.

Customs and transport inefficiencies hamper access to global markets, deter foreign direct investment (FDI) and raise import costs, calling for a multidimensional approach to fix the problem. Developing adequate national transport networks and efficient transit systems, promoting regional or sub-regional economic integration and encouraging FDI in economic activities are recommended. The Global Framework for Transit Transport Cooperation between Land-locked and Transit Developing Countries and the Donor Community as endorsed by the United Nations General Assembly sought to enhance transit systems by preventing land-locked and developing countries from being marginalised from world markets.

Most small and developing Asian countries have remote areas with poor connections to other domestic market areas as well as to international sea and air gateways due to inadequate transport infrastructure, combined with low population density and remoteness in location. Poor infrastructure requires the use of small, inefficient vehicles or vessels that have high operating costs resulting in high transport costs. Transport systems are poorly developed and lack streamlined procedures to guide movement of containers between coastal and inland areas. Border procedures are cumbersome and time consuming. South Asia displays some of these characteristics of a poor trade structure. Hence, inland transport is slow and expensive and intra-regional trade is relatively low. Land border crossings are overcrowded. Complex border-crossing requirements expand possibilities for corruption and informal trade. With greater policy attention to efficiency concerns, delays and monetary costs can be reduced.

As infrastructure improves, exports reach new destinations, often through small shipments from small firms. When new markets are developed inland, air shipment can become a viable mode of transportation rather than sea or land freight, avoiding port congestion and saving time. Similarly as individual incomes rise, air shipment may be preferred to transport goods, particularly as the ratio of weight-to-value declines. More goods are now manufactured according to product specifications demanding a quick and timely delivery. Air shipment has the huge advantage of speed, and advances in technology have lowered transportation costs over time. As noted by Hummels (2009), air freight cost fell by 90 percent between 1955 and 2004. Long-distance trade has become more attractive and markets for traded goods expand along with air shipment routes. The fall in weight-to-value ratio of traded goods and the declining share of trade costs in delivered goods prices in effect leads to a shrinkage of economic distance. Trading with far-off markets is then no longer much more costly than trading with neighbouring ones. The marginal cost of sending an additional mile by air shipment falls rapidly. Hence, average air shipments are travelling longer distances while the average ocean shipment is going a shorter distance (Hummels, 2007). Furthermore, the rapid decline in air shipping costs increased the demand for air cargo.

Intra-regional trade in Asia causes rapid trade growth but congestion occurs at the port when increase in traffic outpaces transport infrastructure service. Ports may become overcrowded due to neglect by port authorities to open access routes or improve logistics. Improving trade facilitation and rationalisation of the customs transit system in order to reduce inspection times and simplify declarations and documentation procedures are crucial elements in improving the reliability of soft infrastructure.

Infrastructure to Support Trade Facilitation in Asia

Efficient infrastructure lowers transaction costs and increases potential profits for producers while increasing and expanding linkages to global supply chains and distribution networks. A study by Francois and Manchin (2006) incorporated threshold effects and found that infrastructure is an important determinant not only of export levels, but also of the likelihood of exporting. Investments that expand and upgrade transport and telecommunications infrastructure are vital in trade but FDI is unlikely to finance and develop significant amounts of infrastructure by itself, without significant changes in trade facilitation. The study by Francois and Manchin highlights the complementarity between greater government involvement, domestic transport and communications infrastructure and export performance.

Financing infrastructure projects depends on the capacity of the government as such investment is complicated by size, bulkiness, long time horizons and public good characteristics of projects. The overall fiscal and monetary conditions of a country depend on its dynamics of trade balances, debt and reserve accumulation, and these factors serve as feedback loops between trade and infrastructure. Also, the choice of mode for financing investments in infrastructure can have macroeconomic implications that can vary depending upon the country's initial conditions (Brooks and Zhai, 2008). Demographics, government debt levels and intergenerational equity are all relevant concerns in decision-making processes for infrastructure financing. If too little is spent on maintenance of existing facilities relative to new investments, allocation of infrastructure expenditures across sub-sectors may suffer from the political economy of such decisions. Allocation of spending in infrastructure sub-sectors for differing modes of transportation also requires careful analysis of potential risks, externalities and scale effects in order to avoid inequities and problems that these can cause in the operations of different production sectors.

Bottlenecks arise along Asia's borders causing inefficiencies in its logistics systems and impeding trade. Table 6.3 illustrates the border trade costs for imports and exports in various regions. South Asia takes 33.3 days to process exports while East Asia accomplishes the task in 10 days less. Roughly the same observation for the two regions may be made for processing of imports, though it takes a longer time to process imports compared to exports.

Table 6.3. Border trade costs 2009.

Sub-region	Sub-Saharan Africa	East Asia and Pacific	South Asia	Central and West Asia	Latin America and Caribbean	OECD
Exports						
Documents needed (average number)	8	7	9	7	7	5
Time required (days)	34.7	23.3	33.3	29.7	19.7	10.7
Cost to (US$ per container)	1,878.8	902.3	1,339.1	1,649.1	1,229.8	1,069.1
Imports						
Documents needed (average number)	9	7	9	8	7	5
Time required (days)	41.1	24.5	32.5	31.7	22.3	11.4
Cost to (US$ per container)	2,278.7	948.5	1,487.3	1,822.2	1,384.3	1,132.7

Source: World Bank (2009a).
Note: OECD = Organisation for Economic Co-operation and Development.

Besides physical infrastructure, other priorities for boosting trade in Asia are streamlining processes, reducing bureaucracy and improving port efficiency in logistics and services. With the bulk of Asia's trade transported by sea, nearby coastal areas, inland areas and landlocked countries will benefit from trade as this is channelled through road and rail links to ports. Clark *et al.* (2004) found that infrastructure improvements that raise port efficiency from the 25th to the 75th percentile can reduce shipping costs by more than 10 percent. Both the quantity of infrastructure investment and quality of infrastructure services influence trade performance. Table 6.4 shows the intraregional comparisons of infrastructure for trade between East Asia and South Asia, with comparator regions. Investment in infrastructure in East Asia corresponds to greater merchandise trade as a percentage of GDP, larger nominal values in FDI flows, higher investments in fixed capital formation and larger gross domestic savings.

Table 6.4.   Intra-regional comparisons.

	Period	Africa	East Asia	South Asia	Latin America and Caribbean
Merchandise trade (percent of GDP)	2005	57.8	74.6	31.2	44.2
Gross fixed capital formation (percent of GDP)	2004	18.4	33.8	22.9	19.5
Gross domestic savings (percent of GDP)	2004	17.9	37.9	20.1	23.8
Cumulative inward FDI flows (Bn US$)	1990–2005	125.0	1340.0	65.0	725.0
Intra-regional shares (percent)	2003	12.2	55.0	6.0	15.0
Infrastructure					
Electricity consumption (kWh per capita)	2003	513.0	1184.3	393.9	1614.5
Fixed line and mobile subscribers (per 1000)	2004	90.6	431.7	75.3	496.0
Intranet users (per 1000)	2005	29.0	88.6	49.0	156.1
Electric power transmission and distribution losses (percent of output)	2003	12.0	7.3	26.4	16.1
Paved Roads (percent of total)	1999–2003	12.5	32.3	53.9	26.8

Source: World Bank, World Development Indicators 2007.

Congestion at the ports in China has been a perennial problem for trading partners since the bulk of its goods are transported by sea. Lack of collaboration among stakeholders contributes to inefficiencies from overloading the physical infrastructure at the ports. Trade facilitation is difficult to achieve as administrative procedures at customs areas are unclear and unreliable. Irrelevant information and repetitive procedures in the process can be eliminated (Ma and Zhang, 2009). The customs transit system needs to be rationalised to minimise inspection times and to simplify declarations and customs

Table 6.5. Road transport by region, 1996 and 2004.

Road Transport Region	Paved Roads (Percent of Total Roads)		Transport Network (Thousand Kilometres)	
	1996	2004	1996	2004
Developing Asia and the Pacific	49.1	65.3	5,407.9	7,385.1
East Asia	58.7	83.9	1,319.1	2,022.1
Central and West Asia	75.0	68.6	579.0	598.4
The Pacific	23.7	...	27.9	...
South Asia	41.1	46.0	2,673.7	3,745.3
Southeast Asia	47.2	62.5	808.2	1,019.4
Other developing	40.6	46.4	7,531.9	...
OECD	81.4	79.9	11,300.0	14,000.0
World	47.6	55.5	24,300.0	...

Source: World Bank 2007.
Notes:
1. Czech Republic, Hungary, Mexico Poland, Slovak Republic, Turkey, and Republic of Korea are not included in OECD average as they are grouped into developing countries. Other 23 OECD economies are included.
2. The world aggregates were estimated based on available data from 179 countries.

processes to maintain the status of Chinese ports as regional hubs and gateways to international markets and suppliers.

Exploring complementarities with other modes of transport infrastructure is urgent. Ports can move more goods in containers when served by efficient rail, road and inland waterway networks, ICT infrastructure, storage yards and trained human resources. Table 6.5 presents indicators of road infrastructure and total transport network in various regions. While East Asia has a considerably shorter transport network than South Asia, the percentage of paved roads completed is larger in East Asia.

Similarly, Table 6.6 shows the effect on goods transported and passengers carried as rail line infrastructure for Asia has increased. The average growth rate in goods transported by railway in East Asia in

Table 6.6. Railway, transport, by region 1996 and 2005.

Region	Rail Lines, Total (Route Km)		Good Transported (Million Ton-Km)		Passengers Carried (Million Passenger-Km)	
	1996	2005	1996	2005	1996	2005
Developing Asia and the Pacific						
East Asia	170,965.8	181,713.0	1,730,980.0	2,593,743.0	784,091.0	1,259,855.0
Central and West Asia	60,910.0	67,402.0	1,307,730.0	1,953,577.0	367,347.0	594,556.0
The Pacific	28,496.0	33,768.0	133,430.0	218,801.0	21,593.0	40,061.0
South Asia	...	597.0	...	...	...	...
Southeast Asia	66,922.1	66,379.0	278,457.4	408,432.0	363,869.6	584,724.0
Other developing	14,637.7	13,567.0	11,363.5	12,933.0	31,281.4	40,514.0
OECD[1]	237,473.5	373,127.0	1,593,484.0	2,627,406.0	395,613.4	352,108.0
World[2]	396,453.5	472,102.0	3,196,582.0	3,389,390.0	322,348.1	492,256.1

Source: World Bank 2007[b].
Notes:
1. Czech Republic, Hungary, Mexico Poland, Slovak Republic, Turkey, and Republic of Korea are not included in OECD average as they are grouped into developing countries. Other 23 OECD economies are included.
2. The world aggregates were estimated based on available data from 179 countries.

the span of nine years from 1996 to 2005 is 4.6 percent while the average growth in rail lines for the same time span is just 1.13 percent. Trade growth along a particular shipping route also encourages entry of new competition to lower marginal costs, especially when it is complemented with efficient and effective competition policies that constrain monopoly power and remove barriers to entry (Brooks, 2008). A study by Hummels *et al.* (2007) reveals that ocean liners charge a higher freight rate for goods whose import demand is relatively inelastic, indicating that shipping firms are possibly exercising monopoly market power for that good. In 2006, one in six importer-exporter pairs were served by a single liner service and over half were served by three or less.

Increasing port efficiency enables countries to reap large economies of scale. Larger and faster ships that are accommodated in ports built for huge volumes of containerisation reduce the average time shipments spend at sea and in ports. Service becomes more frequent, facilitating timely delivery. A densely-traded route also allows an effective use of hub and spoke arrangements such that small container vessels transport shipments into a hub where containers are aggregated into much larger and faster container ships for longer hauls. Using standardised containers yields savings by allowing goods to be packed only once and moved over long distances by a combination of multiple transport modes.

ICT complements physical transport infrastructure as it helps reduce costs of finding information on suppliers, agreeing on contract terms, monitoring trade implementation and tracking location and status of shipments. Fink *et al.* (2002) found that higher telecommunications costs dampen bilateral trade flows, especially for differentiated products. The demand for ICT services is increasing as small shipments of a wide variety of value-added products proliferate. The same may be said for growth in trade in general as it outpaces manufacturing. Trade in banking and communication services depends on well-developed ICT infrastructure in both exporting and importing countries.

Table 6.7 shows telephone lines used and subscribed by regions as an indication of ICT. East Asia's average growth rate in telephone

Table 6.7.   Telephone lines by region.

Region	Telephone Mainlines (per 1000 people)		Telephone Subscriber (per 1000 people)	
	1996	2005	1996	2005
Developing Asia and the Pacific				
East Asia	78,100	378,000	89,500	819,000
Central and West Asia	8,573	13,000	8,680	23,700
The Pacific	158	208	165	382
South Asia	15,200	52,600	15,700	155,000
Southeast Asia	16,900	45,800	22,300	190,000
Other developing countries	150,000	268,000	158,000	924,000
OECD	455,000	482,000	569,000	1,200,000
World	723,931	1,239,608	863,345	3,312,082

Source: World Bank 2007b.
Notes:
1. Czech Republic, Hungary, Mexico Poland, Slovak Republic, Turkey, and Republic of Korea and not included in OECD average as they are grouped into developing countries. Other 23 OECD economies are included.
2. The world aggregates were estimated based on available data from 179 countries.

lines is 19.1 percent as compared to South Asia's at 14.8 percent. However, South Asia's average growth rate in telephone line subscribers is 25.7 percent compared to East Asia's at 24.8 percent. With few telephone lines available, traders are blocked from retrieving vital information about ready markets, revisions to changes and procedures, pricing systems and availability of transport modes.

Improving logistics services is a vital component of Asia's global competitiveness as they are relied on by supply chains that span the region and shape the location of FDI. Improvements in infrastructure service efficiency can lead to cost savings equivalent to moving production to locations which are thousands of kilometres closer to trading partners. Countries in East Asia such as China; Hong Kong, China; Republic of Korea; Malaysia; Singapore; and Thailand have well-built logistics systems to facilitate trade but more investments are required if economic activities are to expand inland from the coastal areas where they are currently concentrated.

The World Bank's logistics performance index (LPI) indicates that East Asian economies perform relatively well compared to South Asian countries but most still lag far behind the high-income economies of Singapore and Hong Kong, China. As countries progress toward more complex and higher value manufacturing and as production processes become fragmented, challenges of providing efficient logistics support rise. Premiums are now imposed for timeliness and reliability of delivery, care and security in handling and transporting, and certification and standardisation of product quality. Freight forwarding, warehousing, storage, packaging, shipping services and ICT infrastructure services are becoming increasingly important. Goods, which are easily perishable such as cut flowers and food products deteriorate rapidly and tend to face relatively high costs when delays are incurred. Fashion and high technology items are also vulnerable. The importance of logistics services is directly proportional to the increasing importance of a product's value and demand for its timely delivery. Both quantity and quality of logistics services in cross border trade create competitiveness. Fortunately, the private sector responds well to the profit incentive to stimulate efficiency improvements in trade and logistics services.

Infrastructure service quality differs across countries in Asia as this is largely shaped by the nature of the country's trade, investment and production patterns. The interaction of forces of agglomeration and dispersion varies widely across product categories in accordance with production technologies. Kimura *et al.* (2007) found that geographical distance reduced trade in machinery parts and components much less in East Asia than in Europe, implying much lower costs of production fragmentation in the former, contributing to large differences in the development of international production and distribution networks. Kuroiwa (2008) on the other hand, found that the automotive industry in Southeast Asia is geographically concentrated as parts and components are heavy and bulky and transporting them is costly. Hence, the share of local content rose and that of imported components declined during the 1990s.

Increases in FDI, often for international production networks, further boost regional trade, adding to the direct effect of improvements in trade facilitation across borders. If the advantages of splitting production processes across economies in a region have greater impacts than those from concentrating it together, reductions in transport costs make FDI complementary to trade. There is an indirect impact of trade facilitation on reduced transport costs and FDI inflows as it reduces the cost of spreading production across countries in order to exploit their comparative advantages. Southeast Asia's electronics industry components are generally small and light with relatively low transport costs. Cross-border production networks proliferated there in the 1990s which created a cycle of cross-border infrastructure development, trade and investment that fosters economic growth.

Countries have striven to improve trade and infrastructure services to compete for larger shares of regional supply chains. The Malaysian government has actively promoted infrastructure development in order to strengthen its competitive and comparative advantages. It pursued an FDI-led export oriented development strategy, which contributed much to the economy's integration into global production networks through the development of its high-quality infrastructure services.

In a related study, Tham *et al.* (2009) explained the role of infrastructure in attracting export-oriented FDI by analysing the sector and location patterns in Malaysia through interviews with local managers of foreign firms with subsidiaries involved in international trade. FDI was drawn to areas with good infrastructure and amenities, as improving infrastructure helps attract FDI which in Asia has been directed toward the export sectors and thus influences production patterns and quantities of imported raw material and intermediate inputs.

Similarly, Amiti and Javorcik (2008) find that access to markets and suppliers are the most important factors affecting FDI entry. Their findings revealed that the influence of facilitating infrastructure on FDI was four times greater than that of production costs. A one standard deviation increase in the number of sea berths increases foreign entry by some 11 percent while an equivalent increase in railway length increases FDI by 7 percent.

Regional Cooperation and Trade Facilitation (East and South Asia)

At the international level, countries gather to cooperate, contribute further to trade and formulate investment agreements, which will strengthen structural reforms and increase the attractiveness of foreign direct investment in a particular country or location. Policies are formulated to leverage domestic policy actions and negate adverse impacts on growth, equity, and efficiency, and help reduce corruption. Synergies exist among trading partners and cross-border cooperation in building and maintaining soft infrastructure as measures for trade facilitation can lead to reductions in trade costs, stimulating investments in infrastructure and expansion in trade. The increased production and trading serves as a stimulus to corresponding increases in employment and inclusive growth.

Regional integration can help less-developed countries and regions open access to new markets, suppliers, technologies and opportunities and help internalise negative spillover effects and capitalise on economies of scale. The effects of progress have not been even and equal across sub-regions. East and Southeast Asia are generally ahead of other Asian sub-regions in terms of trade and regional integration because trade-related infrastructure projects are more commonly available and are of higher quality. In South Asia, infrastructure performance and logistic services are lower and so are intra-regional and inter-regional trade. Cooperation in trade in East and Southeast Asia *vis-à-vis* South Asia is seen to improve the performance of trade in South Asia. Providing efficiencies that generate investment and improvements in the structure of trade of South Asia enables it to attract FDI that can help improve the overall trading outlook.

International trade brings benefits not only across an economy but to the region as a whole. Economic growth is one of the benefits spurred by international trade, as this strengthens regional trade in Asia, enabling it to capitalise on global patterns of production fragmentation and to diversify opportunities. Half of world trade takes place between countries less than 3,000 km apart. Trade within East Asia grew faster between 1990 and 2005 than the region's trade with the rest of the world. In contrast, trade among and within other Asian sub-regions is still small.

South Asia has a total population of more than 1.5 billion, with an estimated 400 million people living with less than US$1 a day, and has been growing at an average annual growth of 6 percent per annum since 2001. Similar to East Asia, South Asia looked forward to deeper integration of the region. The South Asia Free Trade Agreement (SAFTA) was signed on 1 July 2006 and it will be fully operational by 2016. India is the largest trading partner for the rest of South Asian countries with 73 percent of intra-South Asia exports. South Asia trade is characterised by a high incidence of tariffs and transport costs. Most of South Asia's trade is by land and with high trade transaction costs. These costs range from as low as 10 percent to as high as 81 percent (De, 2007b).

Trade in South Asia is congested at the borders where externalities such as the formation of unplanned and informal markets and long queues of trucks arise. High trade transaction costs escalate as a result of border crossing delays, the number of documents to process and copies of documents required at the borders. Regulations, poor institutions and poor infrastructure penalise South Asia trade. Technology asymmetry and high barriers of all sorts at the port borders and disincentives to regional transport and production networks result in low overland traffic and high costs of movement of factors of production.

The bottlenecks that transpire at Asia's borders causing inefficiencies in its logistics systems, clearly indicate that tariffs and freight rate charges are still high in Asia's ports, especially where bulk goods transported by sea are traded. Facilitating trade and streamlining movements of goods and services across borders through improvements in port efficiency infrastructure is therefore important, enabling countries to reap large economies of scale. As an example, accommodating larger and faster ships and container facilities reduces the average time that shipments spend at sea and in ports. At the same time, congestion at the ports from smaller ships is reduced. Service can become more frequent, facilitating the timely delivery of goods.

While East and South Asia belong to the lower middle-income countries, LPI assessment and trade facilitation indicators in East and South Asia show a remarkable contrast in the trade performance and implementation of these regions at the international and domestic levels. The international LPI results show that China has an LPI score of 3.49 as compared to India with a score of 3.12. China's performance in several trade performance indicators such as custom services, infrastructures, international shipments, logistics quality and competence in tracking and tracing of shipments and timeliness also shows better scores relative to India. The indicators measured were based on the level of fees and charges, quality of infrastructure, competence and quality of service, efficiency of processes and sources of major delays and changes in the logistics environment since 2005. Increased propensity to trade by South Asia with East Asia is increased if inefficiencies are improved on those LPI indicators showing poor performance results. The robust performance of trade in East Asia on the other hand signifies that more trade can be performed with South Asia if its products are accommodated.

In a study of bilateral trade costs between China and India, Brooks and Ferrarini (2010) found that there has been a substantial reduction in trade costs between the two countries from 117 percent tariff equivalent in 1990 to 44 percent in 2008, accompanied by a substantial increase in trade volume (Fig. 6.1). The bulk of the trade cost reduction was found to be on the part of China. A simple decomposition of the sources of trade growth between growth in GDP and reduction in trade costs attributed to about three fourths of the trade expansion to reduced trade costs.

The high port, airport and land supply chains costs for exports and imports in South Asia mean a high cost to trade in South Asia. More goods can be traded and can open areas to increase production functions that lead to bigger trading opportunities and at lower costs. The case of Suzhou Park in China demonstrates how a free-trade zone with streamlined customs procedures and distinct transport routes to ports can reduce both costs and waiting times (Hausman *et al.*, 2005).

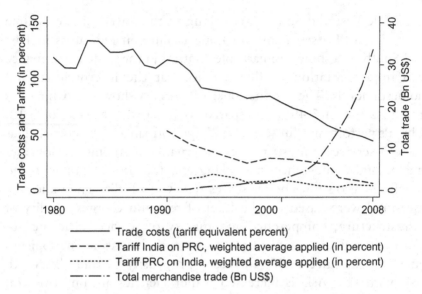

Fig. 6.1:   China and India — Bilateral trade, tariffs and costs.

Source: IMF DOTS, WB WDI, UN TRAINS. Brooks and Ferrarini (2010).

Conclusion

Improving trade facilitation and services through investments in infrastructure that reduce transport costs and coordinating border arrangements and improvements in logistics services make regional trade integration between East and South Asia possible. Where lapses occur, efforts should be focused on fixing and removing the inefficiencies. Investing in physical and soft infrastructure to attract more FDI, requires joint efforts from both public and private sectors as capital infusion is provided by the private sector while administration and public goods are handled by the government. In trade facilitation, the quality of service rendered is commensurate with its current logistics networks.

Trade in Asia is promising as the region is expected to be among the fastest growing markets in the world as a result of business expansion, regional integration and deepening of capital flows. The continuous development of regional production networks and supply chain improvements and investments in trade facilitation in

Asia will support and sustain the region's economic growth, regional integration and status as a hub for trade. With trade facilitation that reduces transport costs, cooperation and regional integration between East and South Asia will broaden and enhance inclusive economic growth.

References

Amiti, B. and B. S. Javorcik (2008). Trade costs and location of foreign firms in China. *Journal of Development Economics*, 85, pp. 129–149.

Anderson, J. E. and E. Van Wincoop (2000). Borders, Trade and Welfare. *NBER Working Paper Series 8515*.

Asian Development Bank (2009). Supporting Regional Trade and Investment, *Infrastructure for Seamless Asia*, Tokyo: Asian Development Bank Institute.

Brooks, D. H. and F. Zhai (2008). The macroeconomic effects of infrastructure financing: A tale of two countries. *Integration and Trade*, 28, pp. 297–323.

Brooks, D. H. and B. Ferrarini (2010). Trade Costs between People's Republic of China and India. *ADB Economics Working Paper No. 203*.

Brooks, D. H. (2008). Linking Asia's Trade, Logistics, and Infrastructure. *ADB Institute Working Paper No. 128*.

De, P. (2007a). Presentation on the Role of Infrastructure in Reducing Trade Costs: India Country Study. *ADBI*, Tokyo, 25–26 June 2007.

De, P. (2007b). Impact of Trade Costs on Trade: Empirical Evidence from Asian Countries. Asia-Pacific Research and Training Network on Trade. *Working Paper Series, No. 27*.

Fink, C., A. Matoo and H. C. Neagu (2002). Assessing the Impact of Telecommunication Costs on International Trade. *World Bank Policy Research 2552*.

Francois, J. F. and M. Manchin (2007). Institutions, Infrastructure and Trade. Available on the Social Science Research Network: http://ssrn.com/abstract= 964209 (accessed 21 September 2008).

Hausman, W. H., H. L. Lee and U. Subramanian (2005). Global Logistics Indicators, Supply Chain Metrics, and Bilateral Trade Patterns. *World Bank Policy Research Working Paper 3773*. Washington, DC: World Bank.

Haveman, J., A. Ardelean and C. Thomberg (2009). Trade Infrastructure and Trade Costs: A Study of Select Asian Ports. In *Infrastructure's Role in Lowering Asia's Trade Costs: Building for Trade*, edited by D. H. Brooks and D. Hummels. Cheltenham, UK, and Northampton, MA: Edward Elgar Publishing.

Hummels, D. (2009). Trends in Asian Trade: Implications for Transport Infrastructure and Trade Costs. In *Infrastructure's Role in Lowering Asia's Trade Costs: Building for Trade*, edited by D. H. Brooks and D. Hummels. Cheltenham, UK: Edward Elgar Publishing.

Hummels, D., V. Lugovsky and A. Skiba (2007). The Trade Reducing Effects of Market Power in International Shipping. *NBER Working Paper 12914.* Cambridge, MA: National Bureau of Economic Research.

Hummels, D. (2007). Transportation costs and international trade in the second era of globalization. *Journal of Economic Perspectives,* 21, pp. 131–154.

Hummels, D. (2001). Time as a Trade Barrier. *GTAP Working Papers 1152.* Center for Global Trade Analysis, Purdue University.

Jacks, D. S., C. M. Meissner and D. Novy (2008). Trade costs, 1870–2000. *American Economic Review,* 29(2), pp. 529–534.

Kimura, P., Y. Takahashi and K. Hayakawa (2007). Fragmentation and parts and components trade: Comparison between East Asia and Europe. *North American Journal of Economic and Finance,* 18(1), pp. 23–40.

Ma, L. and J. Zhang (2009). Infrastructure Development in a Fast Growing Economy — the People's Republic of China. In *Infrastructure's Role in Lowering Asia's Trade Costs: Building for Trade,* edited by D. H. Brooks and D. Hummels. Cheltenham, UK: Edward Elgar Publishing.

Nordas, H. K. and R. Piermartini (2004). Infrastructure and Trade. World Trade Organisation Staff Working Paper ERSD-2004-04.

World Bank (2010). Connecting to Compete: Trade Logistics in the Global Economy.

Connecting South and East Asia for Pan-Asian Integration: Prospects and Challenges

Biswa Nath Bhattacharyay

Introduction

Economic integration within and between economies promotes intra-regional trade and economic growth; it can narrow development gap and income disparities. Over the past 25 years, East Asian economies have prospered through an outward-oriented strategy. The major drivers of East Asia's[1] strategy have been market-driven trade, foreign direct investment and finance; and the formation of regional production clusters and supply chains linked to international production network through the development of infrastructure connectivity. Despite rapid and remarkable growth, Asian economies face

---

[1] In this chapter, East Asia refers to countries belonging to Southeast Asia that are members of the Association of South East Asian Nations (ASEAN) and China.

considerable challenges in improving the quality of life and standard of living as well as in addressing several socio-economic and environmental issues. In the 1970s–1980s, South Asia stagnated due to its inward-oriented growth strategy and lack of infrastructure connectivity — resulting in low trade integration and regional connectivity within the region and with East Asia. However, in recent years, South Asia, particularly India has adopted a "look East" policy and opened its market, raising huge potential for economic integration between South and East Asia.

However, the increase in international linkages and growing interdependence among the world's economies has accentuated the global financial and economic crisis through a strong contagion impact. What began as a financial crisis in a handful of industrialised economies continues to spill over into the real economy, engendering massive contractions in consumer demand, rising unemployment and mounting protectionist pressures worldwide. Traditionally, Asian countries have prioritised exports especially to the US and Europe. Developing and emerging countries in South[2] and East Asia have not been spared from the fallout. Many are now facing slumping demand for their export products, significant reductions in foreign investment and remittances and a more general liquidity shortage (WEF-GCR, 2009). Furthermore, the global crisis has also reduced Asia's industrial production, employment, and adversely affected consumer spending. In addition, the recent unprecedented triple disasters (earthquake, tsunami and nuclear plant accident) in Japan would adversely impact Asian economies, particularly the East Asian production network.

At this juncture, it is of utmost importance to address the impact of the global and Japanese crisis and the prospect of a prolonged downturn in major markets by speeding up economic recovery and to help sustain growth by reorienting Asia's export-dependent economies toward increasing demand within the region to become more resilient against external shocks and thus, reducing global

---

[2] South Asia refers to countries that are members of the regional grouping, South-Asian Association for Regional Cooperation (SAARC).

imbalances. It is in Asia's interests — and the world's — that the region directs more of its energies toward satisfying local needs.

Asia, factory of the world as it is today, has a good potential to be a leading consumer of the world. To realise this potential, it is imperative to strengthen regional connectivity through a better regional infrastructure network among other policy measures. Among the high-priority areas is infrastructure connectivity within and between East and South Asia. These two regions are not well interlinked and thus, remedying this can create huge potential for trade and economic integration. Increased infrastructure can lead to better connectivity; it can enhance intra-regional trade, investment, demand and consumption within the region through the facilitation of smoother movement of goods and services and the reduction of trade and logistics cost. This will create large benefits for the region, particularly for South Asian economies, which are the least integrated sub-regions.

This chapter examines the role of connectivity in South and East Asia for increased Pan-Asian integration and for catalysing the socioeconomic transformation of the region as well as associated prospects and challenges. It highlights the benefits of seamless infrastructure connectivity within Asia. It also provides policy recommendations for building East and South Asia connectivity for Pan-Asian Integration.

The Concept and Benefits of Regional Connectivity

This section presents the concept of seamless infrastructure connectivity and its associated benefits.

Concept of connectivity

Regional connectivity is defined as the establishment of linkages across the region through "hard" and "soft" infrastructure to facilitate smooth and cost-effective movement of goods, people, services and ideas across the region. "Hard" infrastructure refers to physical construction such as energy (oil and gas pipelines and electricity grids), transport (roads, rail lines, waterways, airports, and seaports), and telecommunications (cross-border fiber optic cables and satellite connections). On the other hand, "soft" infrastructure involves facilitating infrastructure or logistics such as effective policies, rules and regulations, systems and procedures and institutions to make hard infrastructure work properly.

Connecting regional projects

Connecting regional projects are defined as hard infrastructure development projects, concerning physical construction works and/or soft infrastructure such as coordinated policies and procedures spanning two or more countries; as well as national infrastructure projects that have a significant cross-border impact (Bhattacharyay, 2010) that satisfy one or more of the following criteria:

(i) their planning and implementation involve cooperation or coordination with one or more countries;

(ii) they aim to stimulate significant amounts of regional trade and income; and

(iii) they are designed to connect to the network of a neighbouring or third country.

The concept and benefits of seamless Asian connectivity can be explained as follows:

(i) A seamlessly integrated South Asia and East Asia — a physically, economically and financially integrated region connected by world-class, efficient and environment-friendly infrastructure networks in transport, energy, and telecommunications that facilitate trade of goods and services; movement of people, ideas and investments within the region and with global markets, wider access to markets and public services thereby facilitating inclusive and sustainable economic growth; narrowing development gap and reducing poverty;

(ii) Expanding, deepening and integrating regional production network and supply chains by streamlining policies, systems, mechanisms and procedures such as customs procedures and other bureaucratic impediments and thus increasing their efficiency;

(iii) Integrating and deepening regional financial markets as well as enhancing their efficiency that channel Asia's large savings and that of the rest of the world to productive investments, particularly infrastructure development across the region; and

(iv) Efficient, cost-effective and seamless connections within South Asia and East Asia and with the rest of the world for a more competitive, prosperous, and integrated region, and to utilise the diversity and huge untapped economic potential of the two sub-regions (adapted from Bhattacharyay, 2010a).

There is a considerable development gap between developed and emerging Asian economies and less-developed economies. Regional physical integration through cross-border infrastructure development is an important tool for narrowing the development gap between poor and rich economies in Asia by bringing poorer countries into the regional and international supply chain and production network and providing access to large markets.

Furthermore, proper connectivity between people, institutions and businesses can facilitate smooth and speedy movements of ideas and knowledge. Throughout history, ideas and knowledge flowed in Asia, particularly between East and South Asia at different speeds and for different reasons. Efforts need to be made to facilitate free movements of ideas, technology, best practices and other knowledges across the region for addressing common challenges.

Trade and Economic Gains from Better Connectivity

Development of international production networks through better connectivity and dramatic economic growth in Asia began in Japan in the 1960s. It then spread to the newly industrialised Asian economies of Hong Kong, China, Republic of Korea (henceforth, Korea), Singapore, and Taipei, China during the 1970s–1980s. This was followed successfully by some of the larger ASEAN countries — Malaysia,

Thailand and Indonesia — in the 1980s–1990s. Subsequently, China, India and Vietnam have witnessed rapid economic growth from the 1990s up to the present.

A special characteristic of East Asian growth and trade integration is the internationalisation of production network and supply chains through exchange of intermediate goods within East Asia. Expansion of intra-regional trade has been remarkable, with East Asia's trade rising from 37 percent in 1980 to 55 percent in 2006. East Asia's share is higher than the peak figure of 49 percent for NAFTA area, achieved in 2001, though still lower than the peak figure of 66 percent for EU-15, achieved in 1990 (Table 7.1). ASEAN's trade share has been stagnant since 2005 whereas South Asia is least integrated with a share of 3.51 percent in 2008. This indicates a large potential for further trade enhancement within and beyond East Asia, particularly between South and East Asia (ADB, 2009).

According to Goldman Sachs (2007), in 2050, the combined GDPs of China and India will become US$70 trillion, exceeding that of the US while India will catch up with the US economy at US$38.2 trillion. In terms of demographics, the two regions have complementarities which could be utilised in the years to come. India

Table 7.1.   Intra-regional trade share, 1990–2008 (in percent).

	1990	1995	2000	2005	2006	2007	2008
ASEAN	18.84	23.95	24.69	27.19	27.07	26.92	26.71
ASEAN+3	29.41	37.52	37.33	38.9	37.93	37.66	37.53
East Asia*	43.07	51.88	52.24	55.44	54.46	53.76	52.06
South Asia	2.12	3.8	3.77	4.8	3.79	3.75	3.51
East Asia + South Asia	45.19	55.68	56.01	60.24	58.25	57.51	55.57
EU 27	65.4	65.4	65.1	65	65.5	65.8	67.18
NAFTA	37.2	42	46.8	42.9	42	41	49.47

Sources: IMF Direction of Trade Statistics CD-ROM (June 2008). Data for Taipei, China sourced from the Bureaus of Foreign Trade website and Statistical Yearbook published by the Directorate-General of Budget, Accounting, and Statistics.

Note: ASEAN+3 = ASEAN economies and Japan, Korea and China.

will strongly benefit from its demographic dividend as 70 percent of India's 1.5 billion population is under 35 years of age, while China is expected to soon face an ageing population. Asia as a whole has around 980 million middle class citizens, a large portion of which live in China and India, providing an attractive market opportunity for Asian economies. With a combined population of more than 3.2 billion, integrating East Asia and South Asia can have profound implications for not only Asia, but also for the rest of the world.

Developing infrastructure networks and connectivity is essential for integrating the core, wider economic activities and basic services in the South and East Asia region. The latest WEF-GCR (2010) and the Infrastructure Quality assessment included herein, illustrates the importance of infrastructure quality in global competitiveness. It is worth noting that countries that have a higher ranking in infrastructure have a corresponding higher ranking in the global competitiveness index as well (Table 7.2). This correlation highlights the importance of building a reliable and efficient transport infrastructure network — especially in developing and emerging Asian economies. Moreover, various research studies have also shown that the quality, effectiveness and extensiveness of infrastructure networks greatly impact economic growth and reduce income inequalities and poverty (ADB/ADBI, 2009).

The World Economic Forum (WEF) also considers infrastructure as one of the key pillars of competitiveness. Improvements in connectivity through effective modes of transport for goods, people, and services — such as quality roads, rail roads, ports and air transport — enable entrepreneurs to get their goods and services to market in a secure and timely manner and facilitate the movement of workers to the most suitable jobs. Economies also depend on electricity supplies that are free of interruptions and shortages so that the work of businesses and factories is unimpeded. Finally, a solid and extensive telecommunications network allows for a rapid and free flow of information, which increases overall economic efficiency by helping to ensure that businesses can communicate, and that decisions made by economic actors take into account all available relevant information (WEF-GCR, 2009).

Table 7.2. Socio-economic development, competitiveness, infrastructure quality and business environment of selected South, and East Asian countries.

	Population (2008 millions)	GDP Per Capita (current US$)	Human Development Index		WGI[1] Composite		GCI[2]		Infrastructure Quality		Doing Business Ranking
			Rank	Score	Rank	Score	Rank	Score	Rank	Score	
South Asia											
Bangladesh	160	494	146	0.543	179	−0.923	106	3.6	126	2.93	119
India	1,139.96	1,068	134	0.612	106	−0.171	49	4.3	76	3.47	133
Nepal	28.58	441	144	0.553	176	−0.888	125	3.34	131	2.03	123
Pakistan	166.04	1,013	141	0.572	190	−1.086	101	3.58	89	3.06	85
Sri Lanka	20.16	2,020	102	0.759	150	−0.535	79	4.01	64	3.88	105
Southeast Asia											
Cambodia	14.7	651	137	0.593	168	−0.785	110	3.51	95	2.94	145
Indonesia	228.25	2,254	111	0.734	143	−0.501	54	4.26	84	3.2	122
Laos	6.21	837	133	0.619	184	−0.99	NA	NA	NA	NA	167
Malaysia	26.99	7,221	66	0.829	79	0.263	24	4.87	26	5.05	23
Philippines	90.35	1,847	105	0.751	139	−0.484	87	3.9	98	2.91	144
Singapore	4.84	37,597	23	0.944	14	1.574	3	5.55	4	6.35	1
Thailand	67.39	3,869	87	0.783	124	−0.298	36	4.56	40	4.57	12
Vietnam	86.21	1,052	116	0.725	153	−0.555	75	4.03	94	3	93

(*Continued*)

Table 7.2. (*Continued*)

	Population (2008 millions)	GDP Per Capita (current US$)	Human Development Index		WGI[1] Composite		GCI[2]		Infrastructure Quality		Doing Business Ranking
			Rank	Score	Rank	Score	Rank	Score	Rank	Score	
North East Asia											
Japan	127.7	38,443	10	0.96	25	1.203	8	5.37	13	5.83	89
S. Korea	48.61	19,115	26	0.937	56	0.703	19	5	17	5.6	15
Mongolia	2.63	1,998	115	0.727	116	-0.257	117	3.43	132	1.98	60
China	1,325.64	3,263	92	0.77	138	-0.465	29	4.74	46	4.31	19

[1] WGI = World Governance Index;
[2] GCI = Global Competiveness Index.
Source: World Economic Forum (2001) (2008) (2009).

Notes: On Score-1=underdeveloped, 7=extensive and efficient by international standards.

Trade integration through enhanced connectivity can reduce poverty, particularly in small, low income land-locked countries like Laos. The aforementioned WEF report also shows that trade between ASEAN and China grew from US$156 million in 1990 to US$3.4 billion in 2008, with these countries' share of Laos trade increasing from 75–82 percent over the same period, averaging 7.5 percent growth of GDP between 2003–2008. The region has also seen a decline in poverty incidence to 28 percent in 2008 from 33.5 percent in 2002.

Increased connectivity is essential for East Asia–South Asia trade and economic cooperation and integration. Connecting South Asia and East Asia through intra-regional infrastructure connectivity projects is quite important but this is not an easy task. There are several regional cooperation programs involved in regional connectivity. ASEAN has been driving the ASEAN+3 (Japan, Korea and China) trade and economic cooperation processes and also ASEAN+6 (ASEAN+3 and Australia, New Zealand and India) processes, toward a free trade agreement (FTA) covering the whole of East Asia. Connectivity can facilitate trade integration between East and South Asia using India as a gateway to South Asia. There are wider cooperation agendas among ASEAN+6 countries for a so-called "comprehensive economic partnership" in East Asia, which is equivalent to an ASEAN+6 FTA. This is a trade and industrial cooperation framework among ASEAN+6 countries that involves India. ASEAN+6, the East Asian Summit group, have identified five priority areas of cooperation including: energy, education, finance, avian influenza and natural disaster management with more areas being added. Furthermore, the performance of the Bay of Bengal Initiative for Multi-sectoral Technical and Economic Cooperation (BIMSTEC) initiative, which involves Bangladesh, India, Myanmar, Nepal, Bhutan, Sri Lanka and Thailand is crucial to the integration between these two sub-regions, especially through East Asia's integration with India.

India needs to play a critical and leading role to integrate South Asia within and with East Asia. To achieve larger and sustainable gain, India has to carry other South Asian countries into this process rather than simply joining East Asia.

Challenges for Connectivity

Having large geographic areas and populations, the economies of South and East Asia are facing a huge infrastructure gap, which imposes large costs on society, from lower productivity to reduced competitiveness and hence, loss of potential growth to lack of basic needs, like electricity, roads, waters, etc.

South and East Asian economies face many challenges in infrastructure connectivity. The major challenges include: (i) socio-economic, geographic and demographic diversity within and between countries; (ii) huge and rising infrastructure needs in transport, energy, water and sanitation and communications; (iii) adverse impact of infrastructure development on environmental and climate change; (iv) lack of deep and integrated financial markets to meet large financing needs across the region; (v) lack of adequate knowledge, capacity and technology. This section discusses the above challenges except for the challenge concerning financial markets which will be discussed later.

Socio-economic, geographic and demographic diversity

South and East Asia encompass a large area with quite diverse economies (geographical and market size, income level, natural resources, technical capacity, financial resources, access to regional and global markets, language and culture). Their level of infrastructure development, financial and technological capacities, business environment, public private partnership experiences, tradition or culture and their practices for managing infrastructure are also widely different. Table 7.2 shows the region's diversity in terms of population size, stages of development, quality of life, competitiveness and quality of hard and soft infrastructure (including business environment).

Due to rapid growth and urbanisation of Asian emerging economies, their infrastructure needs continue to rise. Sustaining rapid growth and competitiveness of these economies will be difficult unless serious infrastructure deficiencies are addressed. The problem is particularly acute in the energy sector for most economies.

The two regions include the most populous countries in the world — 3.7 billion inhabitants with large economies like China and India in addition to many small economies. These include island countries or far inland and remote areas that remain isolated from economic centres. For instance, Indonesia, Japan, Malaysia and the Philippines are archipelagic in nature with numerous islands. Bhutan, Laos and Nepal are small and land-locked countries with mountainous borders. South and East Asia also have four land-locked countries namely — Afghanistan, Bhutan, Nepal and Laos. Lack of access to ports combined with a dependence on neighbouring countries is an economic disadvantage that could be addressed with improved intra-regional connectivity.

As seen from Table 7.2, the Global Competitiveness Index (GCI) score of countries are significantly higher when their ranking in infrastructure is correspondingly high. This high correlation highlights the importance of building a reliable and efficient transport infrastructure network — especially in developing and emerging Asian economies. Moreover, various research studies have also shown that the quality, effectiveness and extensiveness of infrastructure networks greatly impact economic growth and reduce income inequalities and poverty (ADB/ADBI, 2009).

Most countries in South and East Asia need to enhance their infrastructure connectivity to improve their global competitiveness to attain the level of advanced economies in Asia. The quality of an infrastructure network depends on its weakest link and therefore, convergence of infrastructure quality of all participating economies is essential.

Rapid economic growth and basic infrastructure needs

Countries in both South Asia and East Asia have been experiencing a steady increase in GDP growth over the last decade (2000–2010) as can be seen from Table 7.3. There has been a corresponding increase between GDP growth and exports of goods as a percentage of GDP, especially in China, India and Korea as well as increase in savings rate. This rapid expansion has created significant pressure on infrastructure. Even though connectivity has improved across large parts of the

Table 7.3.   Growth trends in South & East Asian countries (2000–2010).

Countries	Growth Rate[1] (annual percentage of GDP)							Exports of Goods and (as percentage of GDP)					Gross Domestic Savings (percentage of GDP)				
	2000	2005	2006	2007	2008	2009	2010	2000	2005	2006	2007	2008	2000	2005	2006	2007	2008
Cambodia	8.8	13.3	10.8	10.2	5.2	-1.5	3.5	49.8	64.1	68.6	65.3		5.6	9.8	13.1	13.2	
Indonesia	4.9	5.7	5.5	6.3	6.1	4.3	5.4	41	34.1	31	29.4	29.8	32.8	29.2	30.8	29	28.9
Malaysia	8.9	5.3	5.8	6.3	4.6	-3.1	4.2	120	118	117	110		46.1	42.8	43.2	42.2	
Philippines	6	5	5.3	7.1	3.8	1.6	3.3	55.4	47.6	47.3	42.5	36.9	23.1	10.4	13.8	15.6	13.4
Singapore	10.1	7.3	8.4	7.8	1.1	-5	3.5		236	243	230	234	46.9	48.8	50.3	52.4	50
Thailand	4.8	4.6	5.2	4.9	2.6	-3.2	3	66.8	77.2	76.4	76		31.5	31.7	33.3	35.8	
Viet Nam	6.8	8.4	8.2	8.5	6.1	4.7	6.5	55	69.4	73.6	76.8		27.1	31.4	31.7	28.2	
PRC	8.4	10.4	11.6	13	9	8.2	8.9	23.3	37.4	39.9	42.5	35	37.5	49.6	52.4	53	49.2
India	4	9.4	9.7	9.1	7.1	6	7	13.2	19.9	22.2	21.2	24	23.2	32	33.3	35.2	32.9
Japan	2.9	1.9	2.4	2.1	-0.7	0.7	0.5	11	14.3	16.1			26.9	25	25.2		
Korea	4	4	5.2	5.1	2.2	-2	4	38.6	39.3	39.7	41.9	52.9	33.4	32.4	31	30.9	30.2

[1] Projected GDP Growth rate 2009 and 2010 from Asian Development Outlook (2009) and ASEAN (2008).
Source: World Development Indicators (2009), Asian Development Outlook (2009), and ASEAN (2008).

South and East Asia region, much more needs to be done to improve the quality of existing infrastructure and develop new ones.

The challenges of connectivity are highlighted by the huge gap in supply and demand for basic necessities of life — roads, electricity, water, and communication networks. About one billion people (224 million in East Asia and 706 million in South Asia) are without access to any electricity service; 638 million with no access to improved drinking water; only 53.4 percent of a total road network of 5.66 million km is paved, and only one in three persons have access to telephone connections (IMF, 2006; and ADB, 2007).

As shown in Table 7.4, enhancing transportation and energy infrastructure in developing countries remains an important issue. Asian economies exhibit a wide variation in road and rail densities as well as in the rate of electrification. Even though marked improvements in road and electrification have been seen over the last two decades, there is still a long way to go for Asia in order to fulfill basic infrastructure needs.

Telephone and internet connectivity is yet another indicator of the disparities that exist within the region. On one hand, there are countries like Singapore and Korea whose communications infrastructure matches that of advanced countries, on the other hand, countries like Myanmar, Afghanistan, Bangladesh, Nepal and India lag far behind with their relatively low levels of subscription to telephone per 100 people (both mobiles and fixed lines) as well as internet users (see Table 7.5).

One important input that is necessary for building and maintaining basic infrastructure and business activities of an economy is energy. Asian energy demands are huge, particularly large Asian economies such as China, India, Japan, Korea and Indonesia and therefore its energy security is a major concern. According to International Energy Agency (IEA's) World Energy Outlook for 2008[3], world primary energy demand was expected to increase by 45 percent between 2006 and 2030 at an annual growth rate of 1.6 percent. A large proportion of this rise in demand comes from the South and East Asian region. During 2000–2030, the primary energy demands for China and India are expected to increase

---

[3] www.iea.org.

Table 7.4. Basic infrastructure quantity in the South Asia and East Asia region.

	Road Density (km/1000 sq km land)			Rail Network Density (km/1000 sq km land)			Household Electrification Rates (percentage of households)			
	1990	Latest Year		1990	Latest Year		Earliest Year		Latest Year	
East and Southeast Asia										
Cambodia	203	217	2004	3	4	2005	17	2000	21	2005
China	127	371	2006	6	7	2007	...	...	...	...
Indonesia	159	216	2005	...	3	1998	49	1991	91	2007
Laos	61	129	2006	...	...	...	...	...	46	2002
Malaysia	262	283	2005	5	5	2007	...	...	...	...
Myanmar	38	41	2005	5	...	...	...	...	47	2002
Philippines	539	671	2003	2	2	2006	65	1993	77	2003
Thailand	141	352	2006	8	8	2006	...	...	99	2005
Vietnam	295	717	2004	9	10	2007	78	1997	96	2005
South Asia										
Bangladesh	1444	1838	2003	21	22	2007	18	2000	47	2007
Bhutan	50	171	2003	...	...	...	...	...	41	2003
India	673	1116	2006	21	21	2007	51	1991	68	2005
Nepal	48	121	2004	...	...	...	18	1996	61	2006
Pakistan	220	338	2006	11	10	2007	60	1990	89	2006
Sri Lanka	1439	1505	2003	23	19	2005	...	...	81	2002

Source: ADB (2009b).

Table 7.5.   Telephone and internet connectivity in South Asia and East Asia region (2008).

Country/Region	Mobile and Fixed Line Telephone (subscriptions per 100 people)	Internet Users (per 100 people)
East and Southeast Asia		
Cambodia	29.4	0.5
China	74.1	22.5
Indonesia	75.2	7.9
Korea, Republic of	137.7	75.8
Laos	34.6	8.5
Malaysia	118.5	55.8
Myanmar	2.4	0.2
Philippines	79.9	6.2
Singapore	170.1	69.6
Thailand	102.4	23.9
Vietnam	115.5	24.2
South Asia		
Afghanistan	27.6	1.7
Bangladesh	28.7	0.3
Bhutan	40.5	6.6
India	33.8	4.5
Nepal	17.1	1.7
Pakistan	55.6	11.1
Sri Lanka	72.1	5.8

Source: World Development Indicators, World Bank. http://data.worldbank.org/indicator.

sharply from 1122 Mtoe[4] and 460 Mtoe to 3885 Mtoe and 1280 Mtoe, respectively. Even though maximum increase in demand comes from the power-generation sector through the rising demand for coal, oil remains the dominant fuel in the primary energy mix. Similarly, the demand for gas was expected to increase at 1.8 percent per annum (IEA-WEO, 2009).

Energy consumption too is expected to see a sharp increase over the next 10 years (Table 7.6). In the major economies of South and

---

[4] Mtoe = Million tons of oil equivalent.

Table 7.6. Primary energy consumption in Asia and other regions (Mtoe).[a]

Economy/Region	Actual		Forecast		Annual Ave. Growth Rate (in percent)		
	1990	2000	2010	2020	1990–2000	2000–2010	2010–2020
People's Rep. of China	673(40.5)	932(35.5)	1406(42.2)	2063(45.1)	3.3	4.2	3.9
Japan	439 (25. 4)	525 (21.7)	543(15.3)	561 (12.3)	1.8	0.3	0.3
Rep. of Korea	93(5.6)	191(7.9)	262(7.9)	303(6.6)	7.5	3.2	1.5
India	187(11.3)	322(13.3)	452(13.6)	684(15.0)	5.6	3.4	4.2
Indonesia	52(3.1)	98(4.1)	144(4.3)	209(4.6)	6.5	3.9	3.8
Taipei, China	48(2.9)	83(3.4)	110(3.3)	132(2.9)	5.6	2.9	1.9
Singapore	13(0.8)	25(1.0)	36(1.1)	48(1.1)	6.3	4	2.9
Malaysia	20(1.2)	47(1.9)	74(2.2)	110(2.4)	8.7	4.6	4
Philippines	18(1.1)	33(1.4)	57(1.7)	96(2.1)	5.9	5.6	5.5
Thailand	29(1.7)	58(2.4)	89(2.7)	145(3.2)	7.3	4.4	5
Viet Nam	5.8(0.3)	14(0.6)	33(1.0)	54(1.2)	9.5	8.7	5.2
Hong Kong, China	11(0.6)	15(0.6)	18(0.5)	20(0.4)	3.8	1.7	1.1
Other Asian countries	71(4.3)	80(3.3)	111(3.3)	144(3.2)	1.2	3.4	2.6
Asian total	60 (21.2)	2423 (25.8)	3335(30.2)	4570(33.6)	3,9	3.2	3.2

(Continued)

Table 7.6.   (Continued)

Economy/Region	Actual		Forecast		Annual Ave. Growth Rate (in percent)			
	1990	2000	2010	2020	1990–2000	2000–2010	2010–2020	
North America	2137(27.4)	2555(28.2)	2863 (25.9)	3196(23.5)	1.8	1.1	1.1	
Central and South America	382(4.9)	526(5.8)	710(6.4)	980(7.2)	3.2	3	3.3	
OECD Europe	1624(20.8)	1764(19.5)	1953(177)	2116(15.5)	0.8	1	0.8	
Non-OECD Europe	1468(18.8)	100(11.1)	1197(10.8)	1385(10.2)	-3.8	1.8	1.5	
World total	7811	9057	11053	13593	1.5	2	2.1	
	(100.0)	(100.0)	(100.0)	(100.0)				

[a] Number in parentheses indicates the percentage in relation of the world total; TOE stands for ton of oil equivalent. For measurement, 1 TOE = 0.93 tons.

Source: Infrastructure for a Seamless Asia, ADB-ADBI (2009).

Note: Based on data from "Energy Balances of OECD Countries" and "Energy Balances of Non-OECD Countries", International Energy Agency; forecast figures prepared by the Institute of Electrical Engineering,

East Asia, the average growth in energy consumption exceeds 3.2 percent with countries like Vietnam and the Philippines seeing higher than average growth rates of 8.7 percent and 5.6 percent respectively. In comparison, the energy consumption growth in developed economies is either stagnant or declining (ADB-ADBI, 2009).

It is necessary to note that these infrastructure links are useful only if they are well maintained throughout the year for ensuring necessary quality. An assessment of the quality of transport infrastructure (Table 7.7) shows that in many countries of South and East Asia, the quality of road, rail, port and air-transport infrastructure falls below the world

Table 7.7. Transport infrastructure quality assessment (2008).

Region/Country	Overall Infrastructure	Road	Railroad	Port	Air Transport
World Average	3.8	3.8	3	4	4.7
G7 Average	5.7	5.7	5.4	5.4	5.8
Asia Average	3.8	3.7	3.6	3.9	4.6
East Asia Average	4.6	4.7	4.8	4.8	5.1
PRC	3.9	4.1	4.1	4.3	4.4
Hong Kong, China	6.3	6.4	6.2	6.6	6.7
Korea, Rep	5.6	5.8	5.8	5.2	5.9
Taipei, China	5.5	5.6	5.7	5.5	5.7
South Asia Average	2.9	3.1	2.8	3.4	4.2
Bangladesh	2.2	2.8	2.3	2.6	3.4
India	2.9	2.9	4.4	3.3	4.7
Nepal	1.9	1.9	1.3	2.9	3.5
Pakistan	3.1	3.1	1.6	3.4	4.2
Southeast Asia Av.	4.2	4.2	3.2	4.3	5.1
Brunei Darussalam	4.7	5.1	n.a	5	5.6
Cambodia	3.1	3.1	1.6	3.4	4.2
Indonesia	2.8	2.5	2.8	3	4.4
Malaysia	5.6	5.7	5	5.7	6
Philippines	2.9	2.8	1.8	3.2	4.1
Singapore	6.7	6.6	5.6	6.8	6.9
Thailand	4.8	5	3.1	4.4	5.8
Viet Nam	2.7	2.6	2.4	2.8	3.9

Source: World Economic Forum (2008).

Note: Ranking – 1 = poorly developed and inefficient; 7 = among the best in the world.

average. The problem of quality infrastructure seems particularly acute in South Asian countries — India, Nepal, Pakistan and Bangladesh.

Impact on environment

Perhaps the most important regional challenge to connectivity in general, and for Asian transport infrastructure in particular is the issue of energy security — ensuring the access of reliable, adequate and affordable energy supplies. However, energy production and consumption are also the leading sources of pollution and greenhouse-gas emissions. According to International Energy Agency (IEA), in its report on the World Energy Outlook (WEO) for 2009, fossil fuels remain the dominant sources of primary energy worldwide, accounting for more than three-quarters of the overall increase in energy use between 2007 and 2030. Oil demand (excluding bio-fuels) is projected to grow by 1 percent per year on average over the projection period, from 85 million barrels per day in 2008 to 105 million barrels per day in 2030. In this scenario, the transportation sector accounts for 97 percent of the increase in oil use (IEA-WEO, 2009).

Transportation is thus becoming the fastest growing major contributor to global pollution and climate change, accounting for 23 percent of energy-related CO_2 emissions. If there are no changes in investment strategies and policies, experts foresee a three to five fold increase in CO_2 emissions from transportation in Asian countries by 2030, compared to that in 2000 (ADB, 2010). The total per-capita carbon dioxide emissions from the consumption of energy for Asian countries have increased significantly during the period of 1998–2008. This gives us an indication, not only of increasing volume of energy being consumed for road, rail and air transportation, but it also points to the broader issues of energy security, particularly environment-friendly or green energy supply and managing energy demand through energy efficiency.

While it is important to have quality transport infrastructure, it should be noted that energy production and consumption by this sector, also has negative externalities, most significant of which is increased carbon dioxide emissions causing adverse environmental impact and climate change. Emissions from fuel consumption by the transport sector has been a major contributor to the increase in emission of Green House Gases (GHGs) that are harmful not only to the local population but also causes long-term effects such as global warming and climate change.

Furthermore, pollution has indirect costs on health and productivity. In addition, the construction of a large number of power-plants and hydro dams, and coal mining operations may cause displacement of local populations and their resettlement, and loss of livelihood.

Table 7.8 shows that the contribution of the transportation sector to CO_2 per-capita emissions is significant in most East and South Asian

Table 7.8. Per-capita carbon dioxide emission from the consumption of energy and transport sector.

Country/Sub-region	Emissions from Transport (2007, million metric tons)		
	Total Emission from Fuel Consumption	Transport CO_2 Contribution	Percentage of Transport Contribution
East and Southeast Asia			
Cambodia	307	81	26
China	4,575	310	7
Indonesia	1,179	106	9
Malaysia	2,620	50	2
Myanmar	6,681	1,507	23
Philippines	254	80	31
Singapore	817	295	36
Thailand	3,537	844	24
Vietnam	1,099	274	25
South Asia			
Bangladesh	252	31	12
India	12,082	1,571	13
Nepal	114	31	27
Sri Lanka	643	322	50

Source: IEA, (2009).

countries. Moreover, transportation consumes a large chunk of fuel consumption, particularly in Southeast Asia and some South Asian Economies (e.g. 50 percent for Sri Lanka) (IEA, 2009).

It would also be in the long-term interests of the South and East Asian region to include environmental sustainability as one of its key considerations in improving competitiveness and productivity. This could be achieved through energy-efficient green infrastructure connectivity e.g., hydro-power and renewable energy electricity grids, and a green railway network.

Capacity, knowledge and technology

The quality of regional transport networks depends on its weakest link. Therefore, it is of utmost importance to enhance institutional capacity of participating countries for development and maintenance of quality hard and soft infrastructure. In order to attain and maintain an acceptable level of global competitiveness, it is necessary to nurture institutional specialisation, building capacities and knowledge and developing and adopting appropriate technology, particularly for developing green infrastructure. Lack of transparency and accountability and poor governance in general, leading to unmanageable political risk can discourage private sector participation and funding. Regional institutions including multilateral development banks such as the Asian Development Bank (ADB) and the World Bank (WB) can play an important role in these areas by providing guarantees against major risks and technical assistance and training for capacity building. Aspects of good governance including autonomy, transparency, accountability, and effective decision-making processes using proper decision tools are essential for building and maintaining quality, sustainable and cost-effective infrastructure (ADB, 1995; 2006 and ADB/ADBI, 2009).

ADB has highlighted four aspects of sound governance that are relevant for all Asian countries:

• Accountability: Officials must be answerable to the entity from which they derive their authority; work must be conducted according to agreed rules;

- Participation: Public employees must be allowed a role in decision-making; citizens, especially the poor, must be empowered by promoting their rights to access and secure control over basic entitlements that allow them to earn a living;
- Predictability: Laws, regulations and policies must be applied fairly and consistently;
- Transparency: Low cost, understandable and relevant information must be made available to citizens to promote effective accountability, and clarity about laws, regulations and policies (ADB, 1995, 2006; and Wescott, 2005).

Financing and coordinating cross-border connectivity projects involving multiple countries are highly challenging. It is essential to maximise the benefits of regional infrastructure projects among participating countries as well as to minimise adverse socio-economic and environmental impacts. In order to encourage Asian countries to participate in regional projects, the development and implementation of projects should produce a win-win situation for all parties, particularly small- and low-income participating countries. This requires among others strong coordination, development and harmonisation of good policies, rules and regulations, standards, systems procedures especially in custom and border procedures; capacity and governance of institutions. This calls for building a strong capacity, skill and knowledge base as well as adoption of appropriate technology.

Efforts need to be made to enhance the capacity of national and sub-regional institutions involved in connecting South and East Asia, such as, ASEAN, Greater Mekong Sub-region (GMS), Brunei Darussalam Indonesia Malaysia Philippines — East Asian Growth Area (BIMP-EGA), South Asian Association for Regional Cooperation (SAARC) and BIMSTEC. As intra-regional connectivity is very low in South Asia, special efforts are needed to strengthen South Asian institutions. The next section will discuss these initiatives in details.

Pan-Asian and Inter-Sub-regional Connectivity Initiatives

East and South Asia have a long history of economic and cultural exchanges spanning several centuries and these have shaped the distinct identity of the Asian region. Since ancient times, the legendary Silk Road, the Pan-Asian road connectivity had been a conduit for vibrant flows of goods and services, labour and capital across Asia. The 19th century colonial powers in Asia provided the framework for wide and liberal trade. This is now called the First Wave of Globalisation (1870–1914) under which an Anglo-French agreement resulted in a combination of falling transport-costs and reduction in tariff barriers. As a result, British and French colonies in South Asia and East Asia were integrated with each other, and with the markets in Western Europe. The Second Wave of globalisation (1950–1980) was triggered by multilateral trade liberalisation under the auspices of GATT, while the ongoing Third Wave (1980 onwards) is being spurred by technological advances in transport and communication technologies, involving developing countries for the first time (World Bank, 2002).

Even during the first half of the 20th century, especially during the rise of Japan, the intra-regional trade ratio was estimated to be over 50 percent. While trade and investment flows were disrupted due to political and military factors during the colonial period and in the post-war Asia, the exchange of ideas continued.

Regional and sub-regional infrastructure cooperation

Infrastructure links in East and South Asia so far are being realised through 8 major sub-regional initiatives including GMS, ASEAN, SAARC, BIMP-EGA, BIMSTEC, South Asia Sub-regional Economic Cooperation (SASEC), Mekong–Ganga Cooperation Initiative (MGCI) and Indonesia–Malaysia–Thailand Growth Triangle (IMT-GT). In addition, Pan-Asian initiatives such as the Asian Highway (AH) and the Trans-Asian Railway (TAR) have been implemented as part of sub-regional and national programs. Of the sub-regional initiatives, GMS has made the most significant progress in strengthening connectivity, mainly through cross-border transport corridors (Bhattacharyay, 2010).

Major initiatives undertaken to enhance connectivity between South and East Asia are presented below:

Pan Asian connectivity for East-South Asia connectivity

In 1992, the concept of Pan-Asian transport connectivity was revived by the United Nations Economic and Social Commission for Asia and the Pacific (UNESCAP). The Asian Land Transport Infrastructure Development (ALTID) initiative is comprised of three pillars, the Asian AH, the TAR and the facilitation of land transport projects through inter-modal transport terminals (UNESCAP, 2010a).

AH (Fig. 7.1) seeks to improve economic links between Asia, Europe and the Middle East through road connectivity. It is planned as a network of 141,271 km of standardised highways — including 155 cross-border roads — that criss crosses 32 Asian countries.

Similarly, the TAR network aims to link Pan-Asian and Pan-European rail networks at various locations, connecting major ports of Asia and Europe and providing land-locked countries with better access to seaports either directly or in conjunction with highways.

These regional networks would enhance connectivity between East and South Asia. One additional and important benefit of a rail-way network is that, in the long run, it is a much more efficient and environmentally-sustainable mode of passenger and freight transport compared to roadways. Rail transport of goods is substantially less energy intensive than shipment via trucking. In terms of energy use per ton-kilometre, freight movement by rail is at least two times as energy efficient as by truck in virtually all International Energy Agency (IEA) member countries[5], and many times greater in some cases — especially in US, Denmark and Japan (IEA, 1991). More recently, it has also been demonstrated that rail transportation releases less than a fifth of the emissions per passenger-mile of those of automobiles and less than a fourth of those of airplanes. Air travel

---

[5] IEA has 28 member countries, mostly from Western Europe and North America. The only two Asian members are Japan and South Korea. Website — http://iea.org/about/membercountries.asp

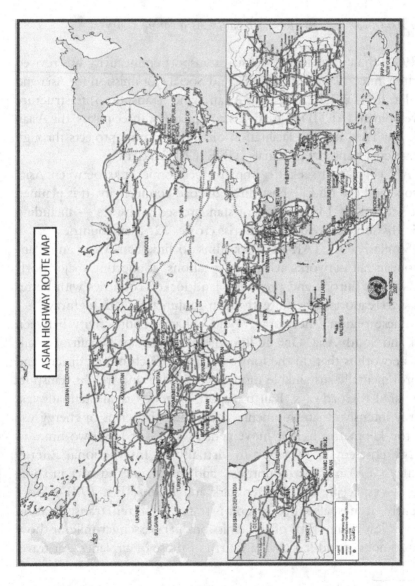

Fig. 7.1:   Proposed Asian highway network.

Source: UNESCAP (2010).

emissions are particularly damaging to the environment because the nitrogen oxides and water vapour they release magnify the global warming effect (Glaeser, 2009).

Sub-regional connectivity

BIMSTEC

Among the existing sub-regional institutions, BIMSTEC could have a special role to play in bringing together the economies of South and East Asia, by virtue of the fact that its member countries straddle across both these regions. Established in 1997, this organisation aims for economic integration through free trade agreement and improving transport infrastructure and logistics among its member countries — Bangladesh, India, Myanmar, Sri Lanka, Thailand, Bhutan and Nepal (Bhattacharyay, 2010a).

This institution has 12 priority sectors, including transport and communications, and energy, led by India and Myanmar respectively. Expert groups for each of these sectors coordinate, monitor and review progress in projects being implemented and will report on the same to the Sectoral Committee.[6]

Greater Mekong Sub-region (GMS)

Greater connectivity has been particularly significant for the GMS. Total exports of GMS countries grew by more than 300 percent from 1992 to 2005 and intra-regional trade increased even more dramatically; in 2004, it was 12 times of the 1992 level. Annual tourist arrivals doubled from 10 million in 1995 to an estimated 20 million in 2005. Net FDI inflows to the GMS increased from about US$3 billion in 1992 to about US $5.5 billion in 2005 (excluding inflows to China and Myanmar). Competitiveness of GMS economies improved due to greater connectivity, simplified

---

[6] BISTEC — for further details, please see URL — http://www.bimstec.org/sector.html.

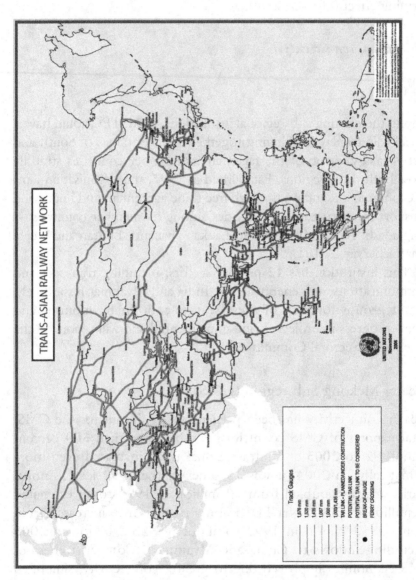

Fig. 7.2:   Trans-Asian railway network.

Source: UNESCAP (2010).

rules/processes governing the cross-border movement of goods and people, development of trade logistics systems, establishment of a regional power market to rationalise energy supply, and the harnessing of information and communication technology (ADB, 2006).

Since 1992, the countries of the GMS — Cambodia, China, Laos, Myanmar, Thailand, and Vietnam — have participated in a comprehensive program of economic cooperation covering transport (see Fig. 7.3), energy, telecommunications, human resource development, environment and natural resources management, trade. ADB (and its other development partners) is assisting GMS countries to achieve the MDGs through increased connectivity, improved competitiveness, and a greater sense of community. ADB has been acting as the de facto secretariat, and coordinator of the GMS Program; providing technical, advisory, administrative, financial and logistical support to the GMS program institutional mechanisms (ADB, 2006).

The success and effectiveness of the GMS network could serve as a good model for building similar connectivity between East and South Asia as well as within the South Asian region.

Mekong–Ganga Cooperation Initiative (MGCI[7])

Mekong–Ganga Cooperation Initiative focuses on four sectors of cooperation: tourism, culture, education, and transport and communications. In terms of regional connectivity, MGCI's intentions concerning transport and communications consisted of two aspects: (i) road networks, which implied collaboration in the Trans-Asian Highways, and (ii) rail connectivity. The India–Myanmar Tamu–Kalewa road was inaugurated in February 2001, followed by the East-West Corridor linking the Bay of Bengal to the South China Sea, a project finalised in December 2006. The South Corridor linking Thailand, Cambodia and Vietnam, and the North-South Corridor, linking Kunming in Yunnan to Bangkok are expected to be completed around 2010–2011. As for rail connectivity, the feasibility

---

[7] Mekong–Ganga Cooperation Initiative (MGCI) is a sub-regional organisation founded in Vientiane on 10 November 2000.

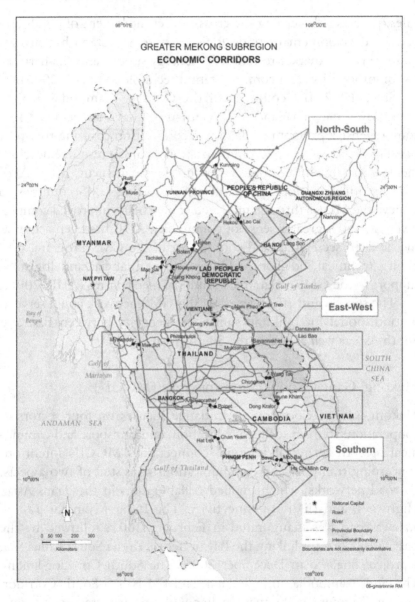

Fig. 7.3: Greater Mekong sub-region — Economic corridors.

Source: ADB (2006).

study to link New Delhi with Hanoi has been completed but construction has not yet begun (RIS; 2005, Levesque, 2007).

Other infrastructure cooperation initiatives include ASEAN, BIMP-EGA, IMT-GT, SAARC and SASEC.

Priority projects for connectivity

Myanmar plays a strategic role in the ASEAN context as it possesses considerable natural resources and it functions as a node connecting Southeast Asia with the People's Republic of China as well as with India and other South Asian countries. The involvement of Myanmar is very important for connecting East Asia and South Asia, particularly ASEAN economies and South Asia. Northeast India's role is also very important in connecting neighbouring land-locked small countries — Bhutan, Nepal, and Bangladesh. East Asia–South Asia connectivity cooperation is contingent on the challenging task of connectivity between India's northeastern region, which is an under-developed region in India and Myanmar.

In this context, the BIMSTEC initiative comprising East Asia and South Asian countries can lead the connection between these two regions especially with India. Some examples of sub-regional projects for connectivity involving East Asia and South Asia are AH, TAR, energy connectivity projects (*Myanmar–Bangladesh–India Gas Pipeline, and Myanmar–India Hydro Power Project*) and Transport connectivity Projects (*China–Nepal 2nd Friendship Bridge and India–Myanmar–Thailand Vietnam Railway Cooperation*).

Inter-regional integration also gives land-locked countries the opportunity to prosper by facilitating inter-linkages. Laos in particular, has already benefited greatly from integration with its neighbours and the region in general, becoming a primary thoroughfare for trade between China, Vietnam, and Thailand. It now acts as the land-link among GMS countries, including Vietnam, Thailand and China. Nepal shares full borders with India and China, two of the region's largest economies. Increased connectivity within the South and East Asian region can further improve the prospects for land-locked economies.

Some countries in the region also face the problem of entering territories across constricted corridors, which could be more easily accessed through neighbouring countries. A typical example is the "chicken's neck" corridor separating mainland India from its seven north-eastern states. National connectivity or integration of North-East India with the rest of the country depends on a minor connectivity between India and Bangladesh. The shipment of Assam tea to Europe is required to travel 1,400 km to reach Kolkata port along the "chicken neck," since no agreement exists for India to use the traditional route through Chittagong port, which would be shorter by 60 percent. The Southern border of Tripura State is only 75 km from Chittagong port but goods from Agartala are required to travel 1,645 km to reach Kolkata port through the "chicken neck." If transport cooperation were there, goods would have travelled only around 400 km across Bangladesh to reach Kolkata (World Bank, 2010).

Due to the lack of adequate transport cooperation between India and Bangladesh, India and Myanmar are jointly implementing "Kaladan project" to link Sittwe port of Myanmar with Mizoram State of India, partly through Kaladan River and partly by road. This alternative would be quite expensive compared to the existing route through the "chicken neck." Transport cooperation with Bangladesh could have given India a much shorter route across Bangladesh. India allows a transit between Nepal and Bangladesh across the "chicken neck" for bilateral trade only and not for the third country trade of Nepal, which now has to pass through already congested Kolkata port. If transport cooperation existed, Nepal could have used Mongla port in Bangladesh, which has spare capacity (World Bank, 2010).

Financing South and East Asia Connectivity

Another significant challenge for connectivity is meeting financing needs. In this regard, it is very important to assess the magnitude of national infrastructure financing needs and financing gaps of Asian economies by key sectors such as transport, energy, telecommunications, water and sanitation, as well as the regional infrastructure financing needs for identified regional projects. Estimates of needed national and regional infrastructure financing can facilitate planning and development of solutions for identifying appropriate investment strategies and financial resources, as well as prioritising projects for utilisation of limited resources.

National connectivity needs

This section presents the estimation of national transport infrastructure financing needs for 32 Asian developing economies during 2010–2020 using a "top-down" econometric approach based on the projected growth of key economic parameters such as GDP and population as well as regional transport infrastructure financing needs using a "bottom-up approach". The selected 32 countries of South and East Asia include: Bangladesh, Bhutan, Cambodia, Indonesia, India, Laos, Philippines, China, Malaysia, Nepal, Pakistan, Sri Lanka and Vietnam. The projections covered airports, ports, railways and roads under transport (for details, see Bhattacharyay, 2010).

During the 10-year period of 2010–2020, 32 ADB developing member countries are expected to require almost US$8.22 trillion (2008 US$) for its overall infrastructure investment needs for electricity, transportation, telecommunications, water and sanitation. Of this amount, it was estimated that the transportation sector alone — constituting airports, ports, rails and roads — would require US$2.9 trillion or 35 percent of the total infrastructure investment needs. This translates to an annual investment of US$508 billion over 2010–2020 for new capacity investments in infrastructure (Table 7.9).

Table 7.9 also provides a detailed breakdown of transport estimates by country per year and as a percentage of GDP. South Asian countries are expected to see half of their total infrastructure investment needs being diverted to the transportation sector, amounting to about US$1.1 trillion. In absolute terms, the top five countries with the largest transport needs are: China, India, Indonesia, Bangladesh and Pakistan. It is worth noting that land-locked countries in East Asia (e.g., Laos) are also projected to invest a large portion of their

Table 7.9. Estimated transport infrastructure investment needs for national connectivity in energy, transport and telecommunications: 2010–2020

Country	Investment as Percentage of Projected GDP		Total Investment Needs	Transport Needs	Total Investment Per Year	Transport Investment Per Year
	Transport	Total	(US$ millions)	(US$ millions)	(US$ millions)	(US$ millions)
East & SE Asia	**1.61**	**5.54**	**5,472,327**	**15,90333**	**497,484**	**144,576**
Cambodia	4.43	8.71	13,364	6,797	1,215	618
China	1.39	5.39	4,367,642	1,126,349	397,058	102,395
Indonesia	3.88	6.18	450,304	282,715	40,937	25,701
Laos	10.62	13.61	11,375	8,876	1,034	807
Malaysia	1.94	6.68	188,084	54,623	17,099	4,966
Mongolia	12.04	13.45	10,069	9,013	915	819
Myanmar	2.70	6.04	21,698	9,699	1,973	882
Philippines	2.30	6.04	127,122	48,407	11,557	4,401
Thailand	0.58	4.91	172,907	20,425	15,719	1,857
Vietnam	2.07	8.12	109,761	27,981	9,978	2,544
South Asia	**5.55**	**11.00**	**2,370,497**	**1,196,023**	**497,484**	**108,729**
Bangladesh	4.92	11.56	144,903	61,672	13,173	5,607
Bhutan	2.84	4.07	886	618	81	56
India	5.67	11.12	2,172,469	1,107,725	197,497	100,702
Nepal	1.65	8.48	14,330	2,788	1,303	253
Sri Lanka	4.23	6.85	37,908	23,409	3,446	2,128
Total East and South Asia	**2.30**	**6.52**	**8,222,503**	**2,900,576**	**747,500**	**263,689**

Source: Author, ADB/ADBI (2009), ADBI (2009) and Centennial Group Holdings (2009).
Note: Estimates obtained using the low case scenario.

infrastructure investments to improve their transport connectivity. The total annual transportation financing needs as a percentage of GDP are higher in several small economies such as Laos, Cambodia, Mongolia, Bangladesh and Sri Lanka.

It has been estimated that the total cost for building transport infrastructure for South and East Asia would cost about US$290 billion (Table 7.9). The above data also points to another common challenge for countries in the South Asia–East Asia region regarding reliable funding to meet the huge requirement for connectivity. Benefits for transport infrastructure investment for the construction of airports and ports itself could be quite substantial. Countries of developing Asia — especially those that have the potential of being linked through road and rail connections to China and India stand to gain the most from improvements in regional transport infrastructure.

Airports and seaports are considered regional infrastructure projects as defined above. As seen from Table 7.10, cumulative investments for airports and ports over the period 2010–2020 are quite substantial

Table 7.10. Projection of annual investment needs for transportation–airports and sea-ports for selected countries in East & South Asia (2010–2010, US$ million).

Country	Airports	Ports	Total
Bangladesh	1,998	8,718	10,716
Cambodia	45	0	45
China	23,867,244	80,802,819	104,670,063
India	503,073	2,163,041	2,666,114
Indonesia	75,287	337,870	413,157
Laos	20	0	20
Malaysia	45,317	520,054	565,371
Nepal	75	0	75
Pakistan	9,864	52,970	62,834
Philippines	4,931	63,459	68,390
Sri Lanka	658	28,437	29,095
Thailand	44,408	182,592	227,000
Vietnam	2,735	64,181	66,916
Total	24,555,655	84,224,141	108,779,796

Estimates obtained using the low case scenario.
Source: Author, ADBI (2009) and Centennial Group Holdings. (2009).

for China and India. For the 13 countries listed, total investments for airports and ports stand at US$24 trillion and US$84 trillion respectively.

Regional connectivity needs

This section presents regional connectivity financing needs using a bottom-up approach by reviewing infrastructure investment demand at the project level specifically for regional or cross-border projects. Table 7.11 exhibits investment estimations for regional infrastructure for planned projects and breaks down demand into the following groups and programs at Pan-Asian and sub-regional levels: (i) Pan-Asian, such as the ALTID project; and (ii) Sub-regional, including the GMS, SASEC, and the Pacific Countries; Greater Mekong Regional Program (GMRP) and cross-sub-regional programs, such as

Table 7.11. Asia's total regional indicative investment needs for identified infrastructure projects connecting South and East Asia by regional/sub-regional program: 2010–2020 (US$ million).

Regional/ Sub-regional Program	Energy	Transport				Total	Grand Total
		Airport/ Port	Rail	Road	TF/ Logistics		
AH	—	—	—	17,425	—	17,425	17,425
TAR	—	—	107,469	—	—	107,469	107,469
ACP*	—	51,446	—	—	—	51,446	51,446
GMS	2,604	200	1,523	3,972	163	5,858	8,462
ASEAN	11,583	—	16,800	—	—	16,800	28,383
BIMP-EAGA	100	—	—	—	—	—	100
SASEC	133	—	—	—	203	203	336
Other**	61,929	—	—	—	90	90	62,018
Total	**76,348**	**51,646**	**125,792**	**21,397**	**456**	**199,291**	**275,639**

* ACP = Asian Container Ports.

** Includes projects connecting East/Southeast–Central–South Asia that do not explicitly fall under a sub-regional program.

Source: Bhattacharyay (2010c) and Author.

within and between South Asia, East Asia–Southeast Asia, and ASEAN.

One under-utilised option for overcoming the financing gap in infrastructure development is to tap into the huge savings and surpluses that exist in some South and Southeast Asian economies as well as other Asian economies. At present, Asian savings are heavily invested in developed countries in more secured, but low yielding, securities, such as US treasury bills. At the same time, due to under-developed local capital markets and lack of appropriate long-term financing instruments, much Asian savings are invested in non-productive sectors such as real estate or stock market speculation. This has created a global imbalance through financing advanced economies' consumption with cheap money supplied from huge Asian savings.

To attract these savings into investments in productive sectors, there is a need to develop indigenous financial markets, particularly a strong bond market, as well as appropriate and innovative financial instruments. Furthermore, innovative instruments and incentives will be needed to create bankable projects and attract private sector participation.

In order to utilise Asian savings for regional infrastructure needs, Asian financial markets need to be integrated. Various sources of fund such as Sovereign Wealth Fund and Islamic finance should be explored. Initially, a special joint financing facility by ADB and other Multilateral Development Banks (MDBs)[8] and bilateral contributors, such as the Japan International Cooperation Agency (JICA), needs to be created to help identify, prioritise, design, prepare and promote bankable cross-border projects. The quality of this process is critical because the goal is to produce a list of well-designed, bankable projects that accurately describe the benefit, costs and risks of projects in ways that make clear how they are good bets for large public and private investments. This facility needs to provide grants and concessional financing to Asian countries that have low-incomes and poor technical capacities to reduce asymmetric costs and distribute benefits among participating countries (for details refer to Bhattacharyay (2010b)).

---

[8] Multilateral Development Banks, such as ADB and World Bank.

Conclusions and Recommendations

Regional connectivity can be achieved at three inter-linked levels: (i) improving national (domestic) connectivity, particularly in large economies; (ii) connectivity between countries within sub-regions; and (iii) connecting sub-regions. Connecting the sub-regions will be the building blocks for Pan-Asian connections.

Infrastructure investment and development is a key instrument for enhancing competitiveness, productivity, sustaining economic growth, improving social conditions, and promoting peace and prosperity. East Asia's and South Asia's economic integration through a seamless physical connectivity is essential and a solid building block for the creation of a seamless Asia — an integrated region connected by world-class environment-friendly infrastructure networks.

East and South Asia are key engines of global economic growth. Economic links between the two regions are growing fast due to the rapid economic growth of China and India. Asia can benefit more from greater trade and economic integration through regional connectivity. Meanwhile, green regional transport and energy connections can mitigate negative impacts of transport and energy investments on environmental degradation and climate change.

Financial market integration at the regional-level is needed to enhance investment within the sub-region and to utilise Asia's robust savings for its productive investments, including infrastructure investment. As a response to the ongoing financial crisis, existing and planned investments under fiscal stimulus packages and the long-range development plans can be coordinated to commit countries to undertake large infrastructure investment as part of the stimulus package and bring forward projects that connect sub-regions.

In view of enormous untapped economic potential, both regions will benefit immensely in terms of a more competitive, prosperous, inclusive and integrated region through efficient and seamless connections across East and South Asia. This will require a top-down approach with a strong partnership and commitment from regional leaders who share a common vision for these two regions together with the bottom-up market-driven approach.

There is a need to develop strong institutional capacities, governance, regulations and coherent development plans at the national-, sub-regional- and regional-levels for effective planning, coordination and implementation of projects to ensure "win-win" outcomes among participating countries and managing negative socio-economic impacts.

Appropriate infrastructure strategies need to be developed to prioritise projects and required investments and formulate policies conducive for effective project implementation. For meeting huge financing needs, an effective financing framework needs to be developed to help mobilise the region's vast savings and encourage public-private partnerships. It is not realistic for MDBs such as ADB, World Bank (WB) or bilateral donors such as JICA to fill in the entire financing gap. Instead, they should work together to facilitate private participation in various ways, for example, by assisting well-structured projects through PPP preparation and operation. At the same time, it is important to promote good governance and capacity building, where MDBs such as ADB can play a larger role in helping member countries.

Asian economies together with international and regional development partners (e.g., ADB, WB, and UNESCAP) and bilateral organisations (e.g., JICA) can work together to achieve a seamless connectivity between East and South Asia, which is a key building block for Pan-Asian connectivity. Asian connectivity will pave the way for an integrated community utilising the most of its diversity and maintaining its openness with the rest of the world and Asia in the seamless environment can mobilise its enormous potential, which remains untapped.

Asia's major emerging economies, namely China, India and ASEAN need to play a critical role for developing infrastructure connectivity between these two regions which is essential in reducing trade and logistic costs. India's leadership is critical in carrying other South Asian countries and bridging South Asia with East Asia. This infrastructure connectivity cooperation between East Asia and South Asia would lead to wider cooperation going beyond trade and infrastructure to other major issues like environment, climate change, energy and food security, and potentially, money and finance, because of the need to mobilise private savings for infrastructure financing. Less-developed economies of South and East Asia need further economic reforms to lower tariff and non-tariff barriers, and to improve the business climate, to achieve full potential of regional connectivity.

To achieve and sustain a seamless Asia through developing a well-connected South and East Asia, an integrated knowledge society needs to be developed through developing and deepening cross-border networks of scholars, scientists, researchers, policy-makers and people as well as various educational, legal, political or governmental, research, non-governmental and private institutions.

References

ADB (1995). Governance: Sound Development Management. ADB, Manila.

ADB (2006). Greater Mekong Subregion: Regional Cooperation Strategy and Program. Manila: ADB.

ADB (2007). ADB's Infrastructure Operations-Responding to Client Needs. Manila: ADB.

ADB (2009). *Pan Asian Integration — Linking East and South Asia*. Palgrave-Macmillan.

———. (2009b). Key Indicators 2009. Manila: ADB.

ADB/ADBI (2009). Infrastructure for a Seamless Asia. Tokyo: ADBI.

ADB Evaluation Study (2010). Reducing Carbon Emissions from Transport Projects. Independent Evaluation Department, ADB.

ADBI (2009). Demand for Infrastructure Financing in Asia 2010–2020. ADBI Internal Report (prepared by Centennial Group Holdings, LLC, Washington DC. Tokyo: ADBI.

Bhattacharyay, B. N. (2010a). Institutions for Asian Connectivity, *ADBI Working Paper, No. 220*, June 2010.

_____. (2010b). Financing Asia's Infrastructure: Modes of Development and Integration of Asian Financial Markets, *ADBI Working Paper Series, No. 229*, July 2010.

Centennial Group Holdings (2009). Estimating Infrastructure Demand for Asia and the Pacific 2010–2020. ADBI commissioned report. Tokyo: ADBI.

Commission on Growth and Development (2008). The Growth Report: Strategies for Sustained Growth and Inclusive Development, 10 September 2008.

Fan, Z. (2009). Gauging the Economy — Wide Gains of Regional Infrastructure. *ADBI Working Paper No. 223*, 30 June 2010.

Goldman Sachs Global Economics Group. *Brics and Beyond* (Goldman Sachs Group Incorporated, 2007), p. 138. http://www2.goldmansachs.com/ideas/brics/book/BRIC-Full.pdf.

Glaeser, E. L. (2009). Is High-Speed Rail a Good Public Investment? New York Times Economix Series, July–October 2009.

International Energy Agency (1991). Saving Oil and Reducing CO_2 Emissions in Transport: Options and Strategies. OECD-IEA-AIE.

IEA — WEO (2009). URL Accessed on 16 August 2010 — http://www.iea.org/weo/2009.asp.

IMF (2006). World Economic Outlook. Washington D.C.: The Fund. September 2006.

Levesque, J. (2007). SAEA — Mekong–Ganga Cooperation Initiative: India's Underused Soft Power Tool, 2007. URL accessed at — http://saeagroup.com/articles/2007/december/Mekong-Ganga%20Cooperation%20Initiative%20-%20India's%20Underused%20Soft%20Power%20Tool.pdf

Research and Information System (RIS) (2005). South-South Economic Cooperation: Exploring Mekong–Ganga Relationship.

UNESCAP (2010). UNESCAP Transport Division Website. URL accessed on 23 August 2010: http://www.unescap.org/ttdw/common/TIS/ALTID/Altid.asp

Wescott, C. (2005). Improving Road Administration in the Asia-Pacific Region: Some Lessons from Experience. In *Infrastructure and Productivity in Asia: Political, Financial, Physical and Intellectual Underpinnings*, J. B. Kidd and F. J. Richter (ed.). New York, NY: Palgrave MacMillan.

WEF (2010). The Global Competitiveness Report 2009–2010. Geneva: WEF.

World Bank (2002). Globalization, Growth and Poverty — Building an Inclusive World Economy. World Bank and Oxford University Press.

_____. (2009). News & Broadcast 23 April 2009. URL accessed on 24 September, 2010 — http://web.worldbank.org/WBSITE/EXTERNAL/NEWS/0,,content MDK:22154463~pagePK:34370~piPK:34424~theSitePK:4607,00.html?cid=IS G_E_WBWeeklyUpdate_NL

_____. (2010). Promoting Economic Cooperation in South Asia — Beyond SAFTA. Chapter 7 — Transport Issues and Integration in South Asia by M. Rahmatullah, pp. 174–194, Sage Publications, New Delhi.

WEF (2001), (2008), (2009). Global Competitiveness Reports. URL — http://www.weforum.org/en/initiatives/gcp/Global%20Competitiveness%20 Report/PastReports/index.htm

Pan-Asian Economic Integration Country Perspectives from the Japanese Manufacturing Industries

Masaaki Amma

Challenges of Japanese Economy After Global Financial Crisis

The high growth of the Japanese economy in the 1960s was economically sound and inclusive, mainly supported by the strong growth of domestic household consumption and not necessarily driven by exports. During the economic recovery period of 1965–1970, the Japanese economy grew annually on average by around 12 percent, almost half of which came from household consumption. This character was also seen in the 1970s. During 1986–1991, household consumption still created as much as 2.4 percent of nearly 6 percent GDP growth.

However, this trend ended in the 1990s and 2000s. The annual rate of growth during 2002–2006, five years before the global financial crisis (GFC), declined to around 2 percent. It should be noted that the major contribution to this growth came only from two sources, net exports and domestic corporate investments. The critical underlying weakness of the Japanese economy during this period was also characterised by the fact that the two major growth drivers concentrated only on two sectors, Electrical & Electronics (E&E) and Automobile & its Component (A&C) industries. Moreover, export demand and investments ultimately depended on the high-level of US household consumption of durable goods, while the contribution of Japanese household consumption growth became very small (0.7 percent).

US household consumption increased for 17 consecutive years until the beginning of GFC. In the later years of growth, the nature of such consumption was oriented towards high-end products and high-value added items like electric appliances and automobiles. This is the very area where the Japanese manufacturing industries have still maintained their competitive edge. While they lost their international competitiveness on low-end products due to the high cost structures in Japan, they could still manage to produce high-value added products for exports at their domestic production bases. They invested to expand the production capacity for high-end products and increased exports of those items to the US, Europe and the wealthy consumers in emerging markets who benefited from sustained US economic growth. This was called "Manufacturing Comes Back Home" in Japan. It made 2 percent annual growth possible during the post–IT bubble period (2002–2007), which was a fairly good performance at that time. After GFC happened, it was clear that the continued US domestic consumption growth had been made possible by the extremely high-level of debt financing available to households, which were supported by the increased market mortgage value of real estate owned by them. US real estate prices had already peaked out after August 2006, but it was only after the Lehman Shock in September 2008 that the growth of consumption of durable goods by US households became unsustainable. Japanese exports to the US in value term in the first quarter of 2009 plunged to 43 percent of its peak during the fourth quarter in 2007 (Fig. 8.1). At the end of 2009, the recovery ratio of exports to the US represents only 59 percent of its peak.

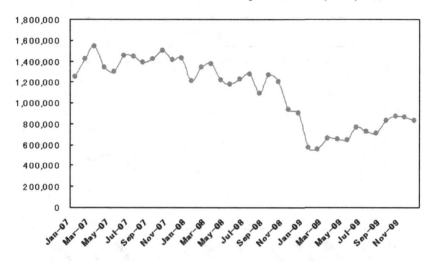

Fig. 8.1: Decline of Japanese exports to the US value (JPY million).

The Japanese economy was influenced not only by the decreased exports to the US and Europe, where banking sectors were badly affected by GFC and could not finance local household consumption growth any more. It was additionally impacted by the decline of domestic corporate investments and decreased exports to Japanese production bases in China and Asia, where they imported key intermediate components or functional chemical materials from Japan and manufactured final products for exports to the US and Europe. While the domestic consumption in China and Asia was not much affected by GFC, the Japanese exports to Asia and China decreased by 46 percent and 40 percent respectively over a year ago (Fig. 8.2) (not so different from 58 percent decline to the US and 55 percent to the EU). This indicates that Japanese exports of intermediate components and materials to China and Asia were not necessarily destined for the domestic markets in these regions but mainly for the US and European markets.

Except for the E&E and A&C industries, the Japanese economy has lost major engines for growth due to various factors. (1) The population is ageing rapidly. The productive population aged 15–64 peaked out in 1995 (87.17 million) and decreased annually by

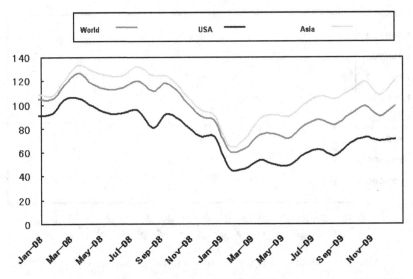

Fig. 8.2: Japanese export volume trend 2008–2010 (Volume index 2005 = 100).

0.6 million on an average. Average monthly formal wages peaked out in 2001 and have gradually decreased since then; (2) Because of the rigid permanent employment system for formal positions, the number of people employed would increase without any change in wage level during an expansionary period, while the wage would be adjusted downwards and the number employed is maintained during a recessionary period. If such process is repeated, wages would tend to continuously decline;[1] (3) Household consumption is stagnant due to the lack of certainty about the future of individual income and pessimism about the growth prospects of the Japanese economy.

The 2009 JBIC survey for the Japanese manufacturing industry[2] indicates that the momentum and commitment for business in the country's domestic market is declining. Only 27.2 percent of the respondent Japanese companies would strengthen or expand their

---

[1] The author benefited from discussions with Mr. Atsushi Nakajima, Chief Economist of Mizuho Research Institute.
[2] Report on Japanese manufacturers' Overseas Business Operations FY 2009 (http://www.jbic.go.jp/en/about/press/2009/1106-01/index.html).

business in the domestic market. Until 2007 survey, this ratio had been consistent by around 50 percent but it remarkably plunged to this level during and after the GFC. On the other hand, 65.8 percent of businesses are still committed to strengthening or expanding overseas business.

In conclusion, Japanese economic growth has been too dependent on the specific segments of Japanese industries characterised by (1) exports and domestic corporate investments; (2) the E&E and A&C industries; (3) manufacturing of high-value added products; and (4) consumption by households in the US and Europe. The Global Financial Crisis made it clear that the US economy before GFC was not sustainable. Neither was Japanese economic growth. It also made clear that the Japanese manufacturing investments in Asia and China had not yet penetrated deep into the local demand market and that the majority of production bases were still export-oriented for the US and European markets.

The 2009 JBIC survey reflects that Japanese manufacturing industries are renewing their attention to middle-income consumers in the emerging markets. However, the efforts by the Japanese manufacturing companies to target that segment are not yet strong.[3] Only a little more than 20 percent of respondent companies have already addressed the business in this segment. Their efforts and activities have so far focused on expanding the sales network, building up servicing systems or cost-cutting activities. Reviewing products specifications and quality are still limited. They are also struggling in the areas of (1) intense competition with tough local and foreign competitors; (2) challenges of further reducing the production costs; and (3) how to effectively develop sales network.

The Japanese economy has been too dependent on the manufacturing industry which has been the most globally competitive, whilst the non-manufacturing industries like financial industry, hotel & tourism, transportation & logistics, real estate development, private infrastructure operating business and business process outsourcing

---

[3] See p. 29 at http://www.jbic.go.jp/en/about/press/2009/1106-01/091106 eibun.pdf.

among others have been less viable. Even in manufacturing, the competitiveness lies entirely on technology and production process but not much on business strategy, branding, marketing and corporate services.

The following is a list of major agenda for the Japanese manufacturing industry, shared by some strategists of major globally-competitive companies in Japan: (1) shift emphasis from the US and European markets to emerging markets, particularly the growing Asian markets; (2) shift emphasis from high-end to volume zones products; (3) more strategic product development suitable for local emerging markets; (4) building more manufacturing bases overseas not only for assembly but also for production of key components; (5) locating more R&D bases close to and inside the markets; and (6) more collaboration with the local people in formulating strategies and R&D activities in markets.

Short Historical Thought: Makie (Japan)

In the author's view, the history of "Makie" (quality lacquerware products made in Japan) as an industry has potential implications in thinking about the future of the current Japanese manufacturing industry.

Lacquer[4] is produced from the refined sap of the Varnish Tree, which can be found throughout Asia. It is applied to wooden objects to give it a fine finish and lustre. The practice of lacquering objects dates back to 4000 years ago and is used to coat furniture, earrings and combs to give sturdiness and smoothness to the object. Lacquerware, in general, used to be widely produced in Asia, including China, India, Korea, Vietnam, Thailand and Japan. Initially, Chinese developed artistic techniques and added colour to make them more aesthetically pleasing. These techniques were introduced to Japan during the 5th or 6th century. The Japanese improved and

---

[4] English expressions about the lacquerware, basic facts and the history of "Makie" in this paragraph are quoted or reproduced from the home page of Toronto (Canada)-based Asian art specialists "Design by Asia" (http://www.designbyasia.com/).

matured the technology into an artistic form of art called "Makie", a high-calibre artistic form with "gold and silver lacquer finishes" and more sturdiness. Utensils and furniture items with Makie finishes were especially sought after by the upper class in Asia and Europe. They evolved into highly-sophisticated status symbols for European aristocrats. Japanese lacquerware was exported by Dutch East India Company in large numbers to various parts of Asia and Europe, including Habsburg Family like Maria Theresia and her daughter Marie Antoinette.

What happened to the Makie industry afterwards?[5] The global political and economic change forced a dramatic influence in the industry. The "Makie" lacquerware, being loved by European and Asia nobility, flourished in 16th–19th century as an industry in Japan. However, it peaked out during the mid-19th century when both European kingdoms and Japanese Shogun government collapsed and the traditional demand for Makie from the rich diminished. The Makie industry was neither able to match new demands from the emerging middle-income classes in Europe and Japan nor was it able to adjust product lines to new products demanded. There did not seem to be any major efforts in restructuring the business model by developing new products and formulating effective marketing and branding strategies worldwide. We can still have old valuable Makie items, traded and auctioned even now. However, it is no longer something of an industry but only a classic art. Maybe, they could have restructured its business model into a sustainable one.

There seems to be a similarity between Makie in the 19th century and current Japanese manufacturing. The following is a list of similarities in the author's view: (1) the technologies involved for production are sophisticated but meticulous and delicate (difficult to

---

[5] In analysing the implications of Makie in the following paragraphs in this chapter, the author especially thanks Ms. Akiko Nagashima, Curator of Lacquer, Kyoto National Museum and Ms. Monika Bincsik, Research Assistant, Art Research Center, Ritsumeikan University, for their in-depth knowledge and kind briefing about the Makie industry and its history.

transfer the technology to many artisans); (2) manufacturing is possible only with highly-developed supporting industries (refined sap, paper, powder, brush); (3) they are high-end products and very expensive; (4) international trade network between Europe, India, China and Japan existed; (5) they are exported to the wealthy people in Europe and Asia; and (6) co-existence of cheap but low-end products in China and many kinds of copy products (not really similar) everywhere in Asia.

What are the implications of "Makie" for current Japanese manufacturing? (1) Current Japanese manufacturing should not repeat the history of "Makie", which ended as an industry; (2) They should develop capabilities of manufacturing new products that match demands of an emerging lower middle income class in Asia; (3) They should also work more with the local intelligence in the emerging Asia for R&D and marketing; (4) They should maintain and enhance the competitive edge of high value-added products but maybe with new marketing and branding strategies; and (5) They should globalise their organisations, particularly their headquarters, more in line with growing Asian markets.

Business in Asia Viewed by Japan

How do Japanese people view the business in Asia? Here we address the question again in the context of the manufacturing industry. The 2009 JBIC survey for the Japanese manufacturing business shows the top 20 rankings of "promising countries".[6] Except for Brazil, Russia and the US, Asian countries dominated the top 10 with China and India as number one (74 percent[7]) and number two (58 percent).

---

[6] See p. 11 at http://www.jbic.go.jp/en/about/press/2009/1106-01/091106 eibun.pdf. The respondents were each asked to name the top 5 countries that they consider to have promising prospects for business operations over the medium term (the next three years or so).

[7] Under the 2009 JBIC Survey, China and India received 353 and 278 positive votes as promising countries out of total 480 respondent companies, representing 74 percent and 58 percent popularity respectively.

While China has maintained the top position for the last 10 years, its popularity ratio peaked at 93 percent in 2003 and declined gradually to 63 percent in 2008.[8] With the strong expectation for the continuously high rate of economic growth after GFC, the ratio bounded back to 73 percent in 2009. India, where Japanese foreign direct investment (FDI) is still limited in volume compared with ASEAN and China, has steadily increased its popularity from 10 percent in 2000 to 58 percent in 2008 and 2009. Vietnam has also steadily increased its ranking to catch up with Thailand and overtook it in 2006 to the third position at 31–32 percent level. Interestingly, Thailand, with traditionally the most attractive business climate in Asia, has attracted more actual business plans in number from Japan than Vietnam.

There is a new trend in deciding the investment destination. The future growth potential of the local market is the biggest reason for a country to be promising for overseas operations and the importance of this factor has steadily increased in magnitude while being an inexpensive source of labour has become less important.[9] This trend is clearly observed in all of the top four ranking countries, i.e., China, India, Vietnam and Thailand.

Two years after GFC in 2008, there is a clear distinction between the economic growth rates of Asian countries supported largely by exports and the others driven mainly by domestic demand. China, India and Indonesia, representing the latter part have shown stronger economic performance compared with the former. Such difference of economic growth performances between the two categories sent a distinctive picture of the future business in Asia to the Japanese business community. In fact, China made up almost US$1 trillion in total, equivalent to around 20 percent of Japanese GDP, to catch up with Japan just within 2009 and 2010. That magnitude of difference also tells us the reason why China ranked ahead of India.

How far are Japanese businesses saturated into the Asian markets? Figure 8.3 shows the size of Japanese exports to Asian

---

[8] Ibid, p. 12.
[9] Ibid, Fig. 18, p. 18.

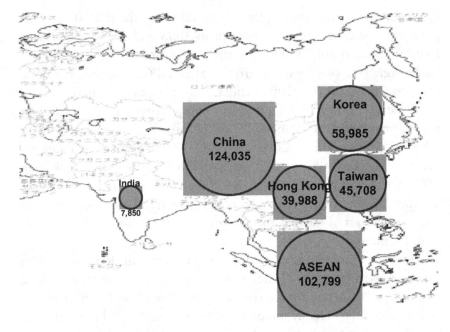

Fig. 8.3: Japanese exports to Asia (2008, US$million).

countries in 2008. Japanese exports to China already surpassed those to ASEAN 10 (121:100). Japanese exports to Korea and Taiwan are also substantial, totalling the same for ASEAN 10. However, if we look at the figures in comparison with the size of the local market we can see a different picture. Assuming that the ratio of Japanese exports to ASEAN 10 over the size of total GDPs in the region is the standard and the export penetration degree is 100 percent, the corresponding figures for China and India are 42 percent and 10 percent, respectively. On the other hand, the same percentages for Korea and Taiwan are 92 percent and 170 percent respectively. It clearly means that Japan has not exploited the markets in China and India yet to the same extent as for ASEAN 10, Korea and Taiwan. Japanese exports to India are particularly low compared with the market potential there (see Fig. 8.4).

The same exercise can be done for Japanese foreign direct investments (FDI) into Asia. Unlike Japanese exports to Asia, ASEAN 10 is

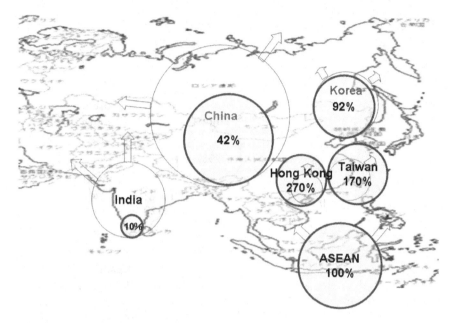

Fig. 8.4: Saturation degree of Japanese exports relative to destination market size (GDP) (as if ASEAN = 100 percent).

still the largest recipient on the outstanding amount basis of Japanese FDI, far ahead of China, although they are being steadily caught up by China. If we have another look at the same figures in relation to the size of GDP in recipient countries (assuming that Japanese FDI Outstanding/ASEAN 10 GDP ratio is 100 percent similar to the analysis on exports), China and India represent only 25 percent and 17 percent respectively (Fig. 8.5). It is also interesting to note that, unlike exports, Japanese FDI has not saturated into Korea (29 percent) or Taiwan (50 percent) as into ASEAN 10. Again it is clear that, Japanese FDI has penetrated most into ASEAN 10, but not that much in China or in particular India yet.

Another interesting feature of Japanese FDI into Asia is that the ratio of manufacturing sector over total FDI outstanding in each country is extremely high in India (91 percent) and China (75 percent), even higher than experienced in ASEAN 10 (69 percent). This could be partly attributable to investment regulations by host countries but

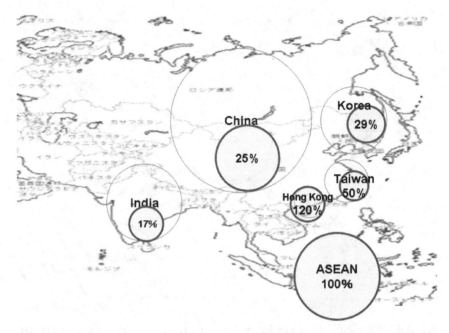

Fig. 8.5: Saturation degree of Japanese FDI relative to destination market size (ASEAN = 100 percent).

also more to the general nature of Japanese non-manufacturing sector which is internationally less competitive than the manufacturing, particularly in emerging markets.

It should also be mentioned that the fragmentation of production bases and the industrial agglomeration with vertical specialisation among firms made a very unique and highly efficient production/distribution network possible in Asia, whereby enterprises in the region can concentrate their resources on their own competitive edge (Kimura and Ando, 2005). The Japanese manufacturing sector has developed and effectively utilised this network in ASEAN 10 and Korea and Taiwan and gradually involved China in this network. The effective production/distribution network link with India has not been established yet. For example, the components trade between ASEAN 10 and India has not reached a substantial level.

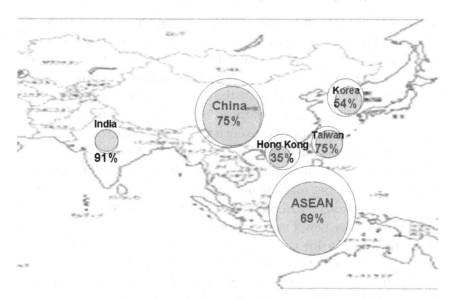

Fig. 8.6: Ratio of manufacturing in Japanese FDI in Asia (outstanding basis; end 2008; JPY billion).

In conclusion, Japanese manufacturing businesses, either through exports or FDI, have not reached deep into the local markets in China and India as they have in ASEAN 10 or NIES. They have not established the effective link with the production/distribution networks in ASEAN 10. In other words, that is why they are looking at China and India with great interest. They are also trying to utilise the existing production/distribution network in ASEAN to have synergy and efficiency in business between ASEAN on one part and China and India on the other.

How Japan Can Do Business Better in Integrating Asia?

Japan has so far invested most in Southeast Asian countries and has built, together with Japanese SMEs, local enterprises and the other Asian companies of Korea and Taiwan, Asian intra-regional frag-mented production/distribution networks, a unique characteristic of this region (Kimura and Ando, 2005). Through its great involvement in creating such networks, Japan is one of the most active users and the largest beneficiaries of the Asian Free Trade Area (AFTA). ASEAN countries are also supporting the outward-oriented economic policies to benefit from participating in the Asian production/distribution networks. In this context, Southeast Asian countries and Japan can achieve a lot together by effectively utilising and modernising existing production networks to expand business all over Asia.

The next logical question for Japan is why is it not creating similar networks in new big markets in other parts of Asia. The creation of similar production/distribution network in China and India would give tremendous new business opportunities for foreign and local enterprises and a lot of policy flexibilities for the governments. Through fragmentation and agglomeration to be expanded and linked all over Asia, enterprises can have more options for optimal location and concentrate their resources on their own competitive edge by inter-firm trade. Governments in Asia can also formulate policies without protective domestic bias and pursue much stronger economic growth. Both China and India and ASEAN and Japan benefit from this process (Kimura and Ando, 2005).

Enhanced connectivity is the key for integrating Asia. Smooth links between ASEAN and other parts of Asia are extremely important for the creation of similar networks. For this purpose, regional initiatives for creating transportation and logistic infrastructure are necessary. Not only for linking "at borders" but also improving the key domestic transportation networks "inside the borders" is necessary to reach inside big markets in China and India.

FTA among China/Korea/Japan is extremely crucial and could be a stimulus for ASEAN too. These three countries represent 80 percent of East Asian GDP. Economic synergy exists particularly between China and Japan. The countries of China, Korea and Japan decided at their summit talks on 10 October 2009 to terminate the previously-conducted private studies on the FTA to push for joint research at an administrative level. The joint preparatory meeting was held on 26 January 2010 to discuss the TOR, work plans and research fields.

FTA among ASEAN+6 is the interim goal of integrating Asia. Just linking ASEAN with India or Pacific through ASEAN+1 is not enough for Japan. To effectively organise its investments in India and Pacific, Japan needs to maintain at home their core corporate functions including basic R&D, mother factories, key corporate services and the other supporting functions at headquarters and have direct trade of goods and services. Otherwise, the country would transfer the key business functions to the most strategic point of place inside the ASEAN region and the economy would be hollowing out. To avoid such a scenario, Japanese industries need regional EPAs covering ASEAN, China, India and Pacific, i.e., ASEAN+6.

FTA among APEC is also on the agenda. FTAs including the US and Canada and Trans-Pacific countries as major trade partners are also crucial to Asia as a whole. APEC is the most dynamic economic arena, representing 56 percent of world GDP and 41 percent of world population. APEC represents more than 70 percent of Japanese trade. For this purpose, Japan should pursue the FTAAP among APEC countries, and if appropriate, Trans-Pacific Partnership (TPP) as well. As 2010 chairman, Japan should be able to conclude the review of the Bogor Goals in 2010, create new goals for the next stage and then formulate the concrete roadmap for 2020 FTAAP.

More attention shall be paid and more actions shall be exercised to trade facilitation. Various non-tariff barriers (NTBs) such as import surcharge, quantitative restrictions, import licensing restrictions and inspections at borders still exist. As shown in the analysis of Mitsuyo Ando, the impact of trade facilitation is much bigger than region-wide FTA without it.

It is also extremely important to harmonise the non-trade business issues (inside borders) all over Asia (Mahbubani, 2009). The production and distribution networks in Asia can develop further with harmonisation of non-trade business climate issues. The deregulation of investment restrictions, including sales (wholesale and retail), transports, logistics and other servicing industries, is the biggest example. More region-wide common technology standard and classification regulation is also on the agenda. Moreover, the new region-wide common standards under the concept "safety and reliability", "CO_2- reducing technology and products" and "general environmental standards", would be useful. In business-related documentation, more region-wide common business certification requirements should also be addressed. Technology transfer can also be facilitated under the region-wide common approach for protection of intellectual property rights.

Recently Announced "New Growth Strategy" of Japan

The basic outline of the "New Growth Strategy" was formatted as a cabinet decision and announced on 30 December 2009 by the newly elected Japanese government of Democratic Party (DP) with coalition parties. It is still only a basic outline and its final strategy paper with details and action plans will be formulated by June 2010.[10] It advocated departing from the former growth strategies much dependent on traditional domestic public works and market economy fundamentalism and moving toward creating new domestic demands. It tries to promote new industries in Japan. It identified four engines for growth: Environment and Energy, Medical and Family Care, growing as a part of Asia, Tourism and Regional Re-development and also set two platforms for growth, namely Science and Technology and Labour Market and Safety Net.

Growing as a part of Asia refers to (1) doubling the flow of people, goods and services, funds between Japan and the rest of Asia; and (2) doubling the income of Asia. The measures mentioned for such goals include (1) formulating the roadmap as the chairman of APEC (2010) toward FTAAP by 2020; (2) starting initiatives of standardisations to promote the concept of "safety & reliability" jointly with Asia; (3) private infrastructure business development in railways, water, and energy sectors in Asia; (4) enhancing the competitiveness of airports and ports in Japan; and (5) deregulation of the domestic rules hindering the smooth flow of people, goods & services and funds with Asia. Before further analysing the strategy itself, the details

---

[10] The New Growth Strategy was approved as a cabinet decision on 18 June 2010.

remain to be worked out on the program itself and the concrete measures to be worked out by June 2010. Upper-house election in July 2010 is also a key political momentum event for DP.

Issues for Japan

On economic integration in Asia, there are various issues Japan should address. Some of the very important issues are explained in the following paragraphs.

Some people may observe that Japan is not acting positively for concluding FTA agreement among China, Korea and itself. However, with shrinking domestic markets, the importance of external demand is being more clearly recognised by the Japanese business community. GFC and its consequences sent a strong message of the need to promote FTA in Asia for Japan. One of the business survey reported that 76 percent of business people in Japan supported FTA among the three countries. The Keidanren, the biggest business community organisation in Japan, strongly supports it. Some domestic interest groups could act negatively, but the treatment of the relevant issues for them should be manageable by politicians and administrators. Other people outside Japan may point out an international political reason which leads Japan to act negatively for FTA among the three countries but it is inevitable that Japan should be seeking economic partnership both with the US and China. For Japan, a clear commitment to pursue ASEAN+6 after finishing ASEAN+3 is necessary. In the long-run, its simultaneous commitment to pursue the APEC-wide approach is also extremely important.

What is the sequencing of economic integration in Asia? Logically natural sequencing is FTA among China, Korea and Japan, ASEAN+3, and ASEAN+6, in that order. For this purpose, China, Korea and Japan should take the lead among themselves and also for ASEAN+3. In fact, while ASEAN has been the most active promoter of economic integration in Asia, it is also clear that ASEAN has no strong incentives to advance 3 sets of ASEAN+1 into ASEAN+3. It is clearly up to China, Korea and Japan. Parallel with ASEAN+3, India, Australia and New Zealand should be included in the process.

What does FTAAP mean for Japan? Is the proposal on FTAAP realistic? Several important hurdles exist toward the formal EPA among APEC, even though the legal framework among APEC forum has not been as rigid as the other formal economic and trade agreements. For example, Japan is not yet fully ready for negotiating a FTA with the US. The political decision is not yet made mainly for the domestic industries' considerations. International political issues are also involved. The membership of Russia shall be addressed but WTO accession of Russia has not materialised yet. If APEC as a whole, pursues the more formal agreement, the membership of Taiwan needs to be addressed. More importantly, the prospect for a FTA between the US and China is still extremely small in the near future for labour and environmental issues on which US legislators have hard positions. For the time being, FTAAP is not a goal in the short-term, but one in the long-run. During such a period, some countries among APEC could start and accelerate negotiations for TPP and the other APEC member countries may follow later. In view of the importance of strategic partnership with the US, Japan should seriously consider joining the TPP process as well as the ASEAN+6.

How does Japan resolve the domestic issues, which hinder the accelerated negotiation of pending FTAs? Agriculture is one of the major issues for Japanese FTAs in the future with Australia, China and the US. The Ruling DP's newly proposed idea of "income support program for individual farmers" in Japan could be one of the key policy instruments to open the market and accelerate its FTA process. But there would be several important factors to consider before introducing it: (1) funding of the program; (2) what to do with the current rice field acreage reduction program; and (3) its consistency with WTO rule.

One major element is still lacking in the Japanese FTA negotiations. It is increasingly important for Japan to address the human resource flow with Asia. After GFC in particular, Japanese industries need more active investments and marketing in China and Asia. To promote their manufacturing business in the Asian emerging markets, major globalising Japanese companies need more of intelligent human resources from Asia, not only at investment destinations but also at corporate functions of headquarters and R&D bases in Japan. In the coming process of FTA negotiations, it is critical to address the measures to attract more Asian intelligent human resources to Japan.

Japan does still need "good deregulations", on the domestic front. While safety net and more protective regulation for consumers remain to be created on certain areas, Japan still has a lot to do in making "good" deregulations in domestic sectors in the following areas: (1) improvement of logistics and transportation at the border where the public operators are dominant and the competitiveness is critically lost against the competitors in Asia; (2) aforementioned more active use of expertise of foreign people; (3) strengthening service-oriented industries through deregulations; and (4) opening the domestic infrastructure business for private and foreign operators.

Finally, as Professor Kishore Mahbubani argued, Japan is able to and should take the leadership in Asia for creating harmonisation in Asian regional context of "inside the border" issues. Even without the formal legal agreement among countries in Asia, various business climate issues and NTB problems can be addressed and harmonised to facilitate more trade and cross-border investments. It is important to recognise that trade facilitation measures can contribute more to higher economic growth than the simple reduction of tariff at customs through a FTA.[11]

Conclusion

Pan-Asian economic integration through the linkages between South Asia and East Asia is an extremely important historic process for Japan. Japanese manufacturing firms have already established their major business presence in ASEAN countries. They contributed to the creation of Asian production/distribution network, which is an important asset both for Asia and Japan. Its presence in China and especially in India is, however, still very weak. Through the enhancement of connectivity between ASEAN and South Asia, more

---

[11] The author thanks Mitsuyo Ando (Keio University) for her briefing of CGE model analysis in Chap. 1 of the JCER Asia Study Report 2007.

Asia-wide efficient production/distribution networks should be established. Depending upon the external policies taken by the Japanese government and reactions from the private sectors, the enhancement would provide tremendous business opportunities for the manufacturing industry and higher economic growth drivers for Japan as a whole. Concurrently, Japan should also seek the APEC-wide economic integration processes including TPP in a medium-term and FTAAP in the long-run and benefit from them.

References

Kimura, F. and M. Ando (2005). Two-dimensional Fragmentation in East Asia: Conceptual Framework and Empirics and "Global Supply Chains in Machinery Trade and the Sophisticated Nature of Production/Distribution Networks in East Asia".

Mahbubani, K. (2009). "Chuoukouron", Monthly Magazine, Japan, July Issue.

Singapore's Direct Investment Links with Sri Lanka: Past Experience and Future Prospects

Tilak Abeysinghe and Ananda Jayawickrama[1]

Introduction

Overseas investment by Singapore companies received an additional boost from the country's government in the early 1990s under its regionalisation drive to create an external wing. These efforts have paid off. At the end of 2007, Singapore's direct investment (stock) abroad amounted to about S$297.6 billion, a substantial jump over the 1990 level of about S$14 billion. In 2007, about 46 percent of this investment was in Asian countries with China taking the lion's share. Most of Singapore's overseas investments have been in service industries, financial and insurance services in particular. In 2007, manufacturing

[1] Authors would like to thank Nalini Wijewardena and other officials in the Statistical Division of BOI of Sri Lanka for the assistance offered in gathering data. This research was supported by NUS-SCAPE research grant N122-000-012-001.

212 T. Abeysinghe and A. Jayawickrama

investment was only about 22 percent of the total (Department of Statistics, 2009). While these investments generate obvious benefits in the host countries, returns to Singapore have also been substantial. Net factor receipts of Singaporeans from the rest of the world have gone up from 11 percent of GDP in 1996 to 16 percent of GDP in 2005–2008.

Apart from aggregate accounting of the above type, case studies on the performance of Singapore's investment in individual countries hardly exist. The objective of this exercise is to compile a case study on Singapore's investment in Sri Lanka, especially from the host country's perspective. A study of this nature is particularly important in light of the increasing attention paid to economic integration between South Asia, East and Southeast Asia. Large firms operating in East and Southeast Asia are aiming to capitalise on business potentials offered by South Asia in terms of lower production costs and mega domestic markets.[2] Although the opening up of India in 1991 was a major catalyst for this regional integration,[3] economic links between East, Southeast Asia and Sri Lanka have been strengthening since 1977 when Sri Lanka entered a new phase of economic liberalism. Sri Lanka's trade share with the high performing economies in Southeast Asia has increased markedly over the years. In particular, Singapore has emerged as its sixth largest trading partner.

Foreign investments in Sri Lanka date back to its colonial regimes. Large plantation enterprises, insurance companies and banks were originally developed with foreign capital. With increased socialist fervor of the Sri Lankan political leadership and the nationalisation

---

[2] Besides Japan, countries like Hong Kong, Singapore, Taiwan, South Korea and Malaysia have also emerged as large Asian foreign investors. As reported in the United Nations World Investment Report 2005, in 2004, outward FDI of these countries in US dollar millions amounted to: Hong Kong $39,753, Singapore $10,667, Taiwan $7,145, South Korea $4,792 and Malaysia $2,061. Between 2000 and 2004, FDI outflows of these countries as a percent of gross fixed capital formation was 66 in Hong Kong, 33 in Singapore, 10 in Taiwan, 7 in Malaysia, and 2 in South Korea. The FDI outflow stock as a percent of GDP in 2004 was: Hong Kong 246, Singapore 95, Taiwan 30, Malaysia 12, and South Korea 6.

[3] It should be noted at the outset that Singapore's investment in South Asia is still miniscule compared to what Singapore invests in China and Southeast Asia.

drive that ensued on and off since 1959, foreign private investment inflows to Sri Lanka dried up until the onset of new economic policies in 1977.[4] Burdened by an extensive social welfare program that could not be sustained in the face of failing economic conditions, continuing budget deficits and rising foreign official debts the centre-right United National Party (UNP) that came into power in 1977 rose up to the challenge of liberalising the economy and placing the private sector again in the driver's seat. Singapore's successful take-off by about 1975 through an FDI-driven growth strategy provided the Sri Lankan Government the much needed strength to go against the dissenting views of anti-FDI lobby groups and nationalists. With extensive and continuous open market policy reforms, which led to the relaxation of restrictions on exchange rates, foreign investment, income repatriation and foreign trade, foreign private investment funds started to flow into the island since the late 1970s.[5]

The contribution of FDI industries to the country's domestic economy is expected to be large. Dayaratna Banda (2005) found a statistically significant positive relationship between the country's output growth and FDI. Other studies highlight the positive effects of FDI on employment, export promotion and technology and skill transfers (Athukorala, 1995; UNCTAD, 2004). As stated earlier, these are aggregate accounts and they do not focus on individual investors. Our exercise explores these by focusing on Singapore's investment in Sri Lanka. In the next section, we assess Sri Lanka's economic performance in a comparative setting. Then we provide a detailed account of Singapore's FDI performance in Sri Lanka. We explore the potential in the manufacturing sector for future investments. In this section, we examine the composition of manufacturing value-added, growth rates of manufacturing industries, export competitiveness in aggregate and disaggregate industries and fiscal

---

[4] See Snodgrass (1966), Athukorala and Jayasuriya (1994, 2005), Athukorala and Rajapathirana (2000), Kelegama (2004, 2006) for discussions on Sri Lanka's post-independent economic policies.

[5] See Athukorala (1995) for an overview of Sri Lanka's foreign investment climate after 1960.

incentives offered for FDI industries. The last section of the paper provides concluding remarks and policy implications.

Sri Lanka's Economic Performance in a Comparative Perspective

In this section, to provide a comparative perspective, we compare the economic performance and social development of Sri Lanka with her South Asian neighbours (Bangladesh, India and Pakistan) and the fast growing economies of East and Southeast Asia (China, Indonesia, Malaysia and Thailand) that compete for Singapore's investment commitments. We also present some data pertaining to Singapore for the benefit of the readers.

Despite the prolonged and debilitating civil war that ended in May 2009, having lasted nearly 30 years and other political disturbances, Sri Lanka's growth performance has been far from dismal (Table 9.1). Although the country lost the high growth momentum after the onset of the war in 1983, Sri Lanka has managed to record decent GDP and

Table 9.1. Growth performance.

Country	Per Capita Gross National Income (US$) 2008	PPP Per Capita Gross National Income (US$) 2008	Average Annual GDP Growth Rate 2000–2008	Average Annual Per Capita Growth Rate 2000–2008	Exports of Goods & Services (Percent of GDP 2007–2008
Sri Lanka	1780	4460	6.3	5.5	27
Bangladesh	520	1440	6.1	4.6	20
India	1070	2960	7.4	6.0	23
Pakistan	980	2700	6.0	3.7	13
China	4940	6020	10.2	9.6	39
Indonesia	2010	3830	5.8	4.5	30
Malaysia	6970	13740	6.3	4.4	110
Thailand	2840	5990	4.2	3.5	76
Singapore	34760	47940	6.6	3.2	232

Source: World Bank, Development Indicators, 2009.

export growth rates over the years.[6] In terms of per capita incomes (expressed in PPP terms) in 2008, Sri Lanka was ahead of her South Asian counterparts and Indonesia. Fast growing China surpassed Sri Lanka after the year 2000. Obviously, the country's current economic standing is not up to the point one would have expected from the initial conditions that prevailed in the 1960s (Dayaratna Banda, 2005).

As seen in Table 9.2, more than 50 percent of GDP in the South Asian region is generated from service activities whereas the industrial sector dominates China and the Southeast Asian countries examined here (excluding Singapore). This also means that South Asia's growth potential in industrial production remains largely unexplored.

Sri Lankan growth performance is largely constrained by low domestic savings and investment climate in the country (Table 9.3). As of

Table 9.2. Output structure.

Country	As a Percentage of GDP 2008			Average Growth Rate, 2000–2008		
	Agriculture	Industry	Services	Agriculture	Industry	Services
Sri Lanka	13	29	57	3.9	5.6	6.0
Bangladesh	19	29	52	3.7	7.6	6.0
India	18	29	53	2.7	7.4	8.9
Pakistan	20	27	53	3.5	6.2	5.8
China	11	49	40	4.4	11.1	10.7
Indonesia	14	48	37	3.4	4.2	6.8
Malaysia	10	48	42	3.8	4.7	6.5
Thailand	12	46	43	3.0	5.8	4.1
Singapore	0.1	28	72	0.3	8.3	7.6

Sources: World Bank, Development Indicators, 2009. Asian Development Bank, Key Indicators, 2009.

---

[6] Many have argued that Sri Lanka did not succeed in maintaining the growth momentum achieved soon after the dramatic policy shift in 1977 (Athukorala and Jayasuriya, 1994; Abeyratne and Rodrigo, 2002). In the early 1980s, the economy grew at a rapid pace of near 8 percent on average. Political instability and the lack of commitment by governing parties moved the country to a slow growth pace in the subsequent years.

Table 9.3.   Savings, investment and FDI inflow (percentage of GDP, 2007).

Country	Gross Domestic Savings	Gross National Savings	Domestic Credit to Private Sector	Gross Fixed Capital Formation	FDI US$ mn	FDI Percent of GDP
Sri Lanka	18	23	33	27	548	1.7
Bangladesh	20	29	32	25	793	1.2
India	38	41	60	39	32327	3.1
Pakistan	15	25	31	23	5026	3.7
China	50	52	111	43	83521	2.5
Indonesia	28	25	26	25	6928	1.6
Malaysia	47	37	114	22	8460	4.5
Thailand	34	32	92	27	9381	3.8
Singapore	52	44	61	21	31550	18.9

Sources: Asian Development Bank, Key Indicators, 2009.

2007, its domestic savings rate has been the second lowest among the countries listed in Table 9.3. The savings rates of China and Malaysia have been more than double of Sri Lanka. Low savings constrains domestic credit availability for investment. To make matters worse, FDI inflows to Sri Lanka have also been relatively low. Although China is a clear outlier in this respect, US$548 million of FDI that Sri Lanka received in 2007 pales in comparison to others (excluding Bangladesh) in Table 9.3. Obviously, Sri Lanka could do better in attracting more FDI.

The fallouts of prolonged war can be seen in the human development indicators. Sri Lanka was well-known for standing out as an outlier among developing countries. Instead of the usual scenario of high per capita income and high human development indicators, Sri Lanka exhibited a case of low per capita income with high human development indicators. However, the war wasted a substantial amount of the country's resources and slowed down progress in social programs. Although Sri Lanka's achievements in this front are still admirable, other Asian countries have done much better in accelerating their human development efforts (Table 9.4).

It is worth noting that although Sri Lanka is in a leading position in secondary education, it falls behind in terms of tertiary education.

Table 9.4. Human development and social indicators.

Country	Life Expectancy at Birth (years) 2007	Mortality Rate Under 5 (per 1000) 2007	Adult Literacy Rate (percent of population age 15+) 2007	Secondary Enrolment (percent of population) 2005	Tertiary Enrolment (percent of population) 2000[a]	Gini Coeff (percent)[b]
Sri Lanka	72	21	92	87	0.36	31
Bangladesh	64	61	53	44	0.68	33
India	66	72	66	54	0.94	42
Pakistan	65	90	55	29	0.18	37
China	73	22	93	76	0.95	41
Indonesia	71	31	91	62	1.42	39
Malaysia	74	11	92	69	2.47	38
Thailand	69	7	94	77	3.41	43

[a]United Nations, World Investment Report, 2004, Table A1.6.
[b]Different years between 2002 and 2005.
Sources: World Bank, Development Indicators, 2009. Asian Development Bank, Key Indicators 2009. UNESCO Global Education Digest 2008.

Because of limited places, only a very small portion of the secondary cohort qualifies for universities in Sri Lanka. In terms of income distribution, as measured by the Gini coefficient, South Asian countries appear to do better than the rest considered here. However, this hides the widespread poverty that plagues India, Bangladesh and Pakistan. Sri Lanka has done much better in lifting up its population above the absolute poverty level. Better human development in Sri Lanka was a result of an extensive government involvement in the provision of education, healthcare and other social welfare programmes. These indicators, especially of health and education, also imply the presence of a more effective labour force in Sri Lanka compared to other developing countries (UNCTAD, 2004).

As a result of progressive trade liberalisation since 1978, the trade volume of Sri Lanka increased rapidly and stood at over 70 percent of the country's GDP and fell to about 60 percent by 2007 (Table 9.5). By the trade-GDP ratio, Sri Lanka stands out as the most

Table 9.5.   Trade openness indicators.

| Country | Trade Share* 2007 | Year | Tariff Barriers (Weighted Mean Tariff Rate) Percentage | |
			All Products	Manufactured Products
Sri Lanka	0.59	1990	27.0	24.2
		2004	6.8	5.7
Bangladesh	0.45	1989	88.4	109.9
		2004	15.9	17.4
India	0.31	1990	56.1	70.8
		2004	28.0	25.3
Pakistan	0.35	1995	44.4	49.2
		2004	13.0	15.7
China	0.64	1992	32.1	35.6
		2004	6.0	6.0
Indonesia	0.49	1989	13.0	15.1
		2003	5.2	5.8
Malaysia	1.73	1988	9.7	10.8
		2003	4.2	4.6
Thailand	1.23	1989	33.0	35.0
		2003	8.3	9.3

Source: World Bank, Development Indicators, 2005, 2009.
Note: *Trade share is the sum of merchandise exports and imports over GDP.

open economy in South Asia. Even in terms of tariff barriers, it comes across as the most open economy in South Asia. Sri Lanka eliminated all export tariffs by the mid-1990s and has lowered import tariff rates significantly over the last two decades. Not only is its tariff (mean) rate the lowest among the South Asian countries but it is also quite comparable with that of China and Southeast Asian countries.

Despite all these positive indicators, the prolonged war has taken its toll on the country by making it less attractive to FDI. As indicated by pre-war measures of country risk, FDI potentials, economic freedom and ease of doing business, Sri Lanka was not in a promising state (Table 9.6). In terms of risk rating, South Asian countries and Indonesia are perceived to be riskier than China, Malaysia, and

Table 9.6. Country rankings and ratings.

Country	Country Risk (as of December 2002) Composite Risk Rating	Inward FDI Potential Ranking (2000–2002)[a]	Index of Economic Freedom Ranking (Freedom Percentage), 2007[b,*]	World Bank Rankings on the Ease of Doing Business[c]	
				2006	2007
Sri Lanka	63.3	112	84 (59.3)	89	89
Bangladesh	61.3	117	143 (47.8)	81	88
India	66.3	89	104 (55.6)	138	134
Pakistan	58.5	128	89 (58.2)	66	74
China	75.0	39	119 (54.0)	108	93
Indonesia	58.3	82	110 (47.8)	131	135
Malaysia	77.5	32	48 (65.4)	25	25
Thailand	76.3	54	50 (65.6)	19	18

Sources: United Nations, World Investment Report, 2004. World Bank, Doing Business in 2007: How to Reform, 2006, The Heritage Foundation and Dow Jones & Company, Inc. http://www.heritage.org.research/features/index/about.cfm.
Notes: Ranking covers [a]140 countries, [b]161 countries, [c]175 countries.
*Free: 80–100; mostly free: 70–79.9; moderately free: 60–69.9; mostly un-free: 50–59.9; repressed: 0–49.9.

Thailand. Pakistan and Indonesia have received similar low ratings. Sri Lanka did not do that well in terms of FDI potential ranking as well. Sri Lanka's ranking on economic freedom is very close to "moderately-free" status and is far better than other South Asian countries, China and Indonesia. Sri Lanka has been ranked ahead of fast growing China and India in terms of the ease of doing business.

All these measures taken together show that Sri Lanka offers an investment environment similar to that of the fast growing Southeast Asian economies. The country has drawn much attention for her potential as a regional trade and service centre in South Asia. Being the most liberalised economy in the region (Athukorala and Rajapathirana, 2000; Athukorala and Jayasuriya, 2005) and having a well-educated labour force (UNCTAD, 2004), Sri Lanka possesses a greater degree of comparative advantage in many service providing activities and manufacturing products. Moreover, ports in Sri Lanka have the potential to play a dominant role in the region as they lie on key shipping and oil trade routes. Sri Lanka also has the potential to develop as a small and medium scale agro-based and labour intensive industrial park (Central Bank of Sri Lanka, 2004). Further, Sri Lanka's free trade agreements (FTAs) with India and Pakistan assist Sri Lanka to emerge as a strategic place in reaching these South Asian markets (Board of Investment of Sri Lanka, 2005). Nevertheless, perceived political risk emanating from the prolonged war substantially slowed down FDI inflows. With the emergence of India as another massive FDI absorber, Sri Lanka's FDI-driven growth strategy is coming under severe stress.

Singapore's Investment in Sri Lanka: Past Experience

Singapore has been an important foreign investor in Sri Lanka since the mid-1980s. According to the Board of Investment (BOI) of Sri Lanka, Singapore has been the largest single investor in the country in terms of cumulative investment (see also UNCTAD, 2004). Singapore's major investment companies in Sri Lanka include: Lanka Bell, Lanka Cellular, Overseas Reality, Prima Ceylon, Ceylon Grain Elevators, Singapore Informatics, Intertrade Lanka Management, and Steamers Telecommunications. By 2005, 50 Singapore FDI firms were operating in Sri Lanka with a cumulative investment of Rs. 17 billion (Tables 9.7 and 9.8). Although Singapore's net FDI in Sri Lanka has fluctuated wildly from a low of Rs. 170 million in 1990 to a peak of Rs. 4,635 million in 2003, on an average Singapore injected more than 8 percent of the country's total net direct investment funds over the two decades since 1985 (Fig. 9.1). This raised Singapore's FDI stock share (as a percent of total FDI stock) in Sri Lanka from 1.6 percent in 1985 to 7 percent by 2005. Further, Singapore's FDI stock in Sri Lanka as a percent of the country's GDP increased ten folds from about 0.1 percent in 1985 to 1.3 percent by 2005. The total FDI stock as a percent of GDP was about 18 percent in 2005.

Table 9.7. Singapore's FDI in Sri Lanka, 1985–2005 (in 2000 constant prices).

	FDI Flow		FDI Stock		Percentage Shares			
Year	SIN FDI (Net) Rs. mn	Total FDI (Net) Rs. mn	SIN FDI Stock Rs. mn	Total FDI Stock Rs. mn	SIN FDI/ Total FDI	SIN FDI Stock/ Total FDI Stock	SIN FDI Stock/ GDP	Total FDI Stock/ GDP
1985	−56.0	4411.1	764.0	49431.6	−1.27	1.55	0.13	8.62
1986	31.5	3071.2	753.3	49777.1	1.03	1.51	0.13	8.32
1987	161.2	6036.9	865.7	52582.8	2.67	1.65	0.14	8.66
1988	354.7	4484.4	1131.3	51651.9	7.91	2.19	0.18	8.28
1989	52.6	2015.7	1084.6	49133.4	2.61	2.21	0.17	7.70
1990	−169.7	4012.5	734.0	44952.2	−4.23	1.63	0.11	6.64
1991	1979.0	4168.3	2640.4	44676.7	47.48	5.91	0.37	6.28
1992	2276.5	10284.4	4676.2	50887.1	22.14	9.19	0.63	6.89
1993	104.5	17518.7	4375.7	63999.0	0.60	6.84	0.55	8.11
1994	1830.1	36792.6	5833.3	95343.5	4.97	6.12	0.70	11.43
1995	1886.2	18250.0	7267.5	106204.4	10.34	6.84	0.83	12.07
1996	4341.7	25453.2	10824.6	120191.5	17.06	9.01	1.19	13.17
1997	−18.1	33045.6	9942.8	143646.8	−0.05	6.92	1.02	14.81
1998	−65.8	35860.6	9104.3	168344.5	−0.18	5.41	0.90	16.56
1999	10.7	26466.1	8722.6	187753.6	0.04	4.65	0.82	17.70
2000	1705.1	18707.0	9892.6	194726.0	9.11	5.08	0.88	17.30
2001	360.8	11888.4	9168.3	185255.5	3.03	4.95	0.83	16.71
2002	4158.8	27446.2	12623.3	198479.4	15.15	6.36	1.09	17.21
2003	4634.9	28117.8	16626.5	216665.6	16.48	7.67	1.36	17.76
2004	2072.7	29997.8	17286.6	228253.9	6.91	7.57	1.35	17.77
2005	1406.0	39434.6	17133.5	247102.7	3.57	6.93	1.26	18.15

Sources: Board of Investment, Sri Lanka, Central Bank of Sri Lanka, World Investment Report of World Bank.

The number of Singapore investment projects in Sri Lanka increased steadily from five in 1991 to 50 by 2005 (Table 9.8). Correspondingly, the direct employment in these firms also increased from 758 persons in 1985 to 5,579 persons in 2005. Undoubtedly, these investments must have created a substantial amount of indirect employment as well. Table 9.8 also shows the expansion of exports by these firms. However, it should be noted that the outsourcing

Table 9.8.   Singapore's investment projects in Sri Lanka.

Year	Number of Investment Projects (cumulative)	Employment (number of Persons cumulative)	Exports (Rs. mn in 2000 prices)	Imports (Rs. mn in 2000 prices)	Import Composition Percentage	
					Capital Goods	Raw Materials
1985	6	758	367.7	165.2	1.57	98.43
1986	7	627	263.7	222.1	25.74	74.26
1987	7	818	615.6	636.4	20.20	79.81
1988	6	1571	1487.8	1724.0	32.66	67.34
1989	6	1470	1875.2	1907.9	12.63	62.90
1990	5	1619	1683.2	1749.5	13.95	74.10
1991	5	1587	1516.4	1491.4	8.62	78.29
1992	12	1861	1670.0	1629.8	16.15	40.37
1993	12	1155	902.3	1368.5	33.45	45.59
1994	17	1295	951.5	3932.3	67.50	29.60
1995	20	1634	1258.3	3110.7	67.05	32.14
1996	23	2100	1346.4	1807.6	46.28	51.95
1997	22	2041	1013.9	1580.6	39.40	59.12
1998	21	1890	972.2	1118.8	41.13	56.88
1999	21	1877	1009.4	858.0	31.45	66.48
2000	37	2904	1048.1	906.8	32.19	65.46
2001	36	2560	1124.7	1028.7	35.38	63.49
2002	36	2607	1947.3	1253.0	35.76	61.91
2003	37	3688	2189.4	1665.3	46.75	52.02
2004	44	4238	3100.4	2500.9	38.25	58.73
2005	50	5579	6090.5	4428.5	35.73	62.62

Source: Board of Investment, Sri Lanka.

activities of these Singapore firms are also quite extensive. These companies depend heavily on imported capital goods and raw materials. Imports of these goods increased from Rs. 165 million in 1985 Rs. 4,428 million by 2005. As seen in Fig. 9.2, the trade balance of these firms turned persistently positive only after 1998. Nevertheless, these surpluses have been miniscule compared to an increasing trade deficit that Sri Lanka has been experiencing with Singapore over the last two decades.

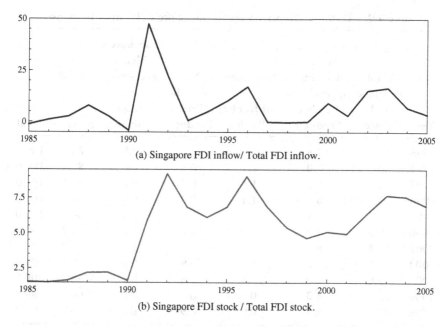

(a) Singapore FDI inflow/ Total FDI inflow.

(b) Singapore FDI stock / Total FDI stock.

Fig. 9.1: Singapore's FDI flows and stock in Sri Lanka (percentage of shares).

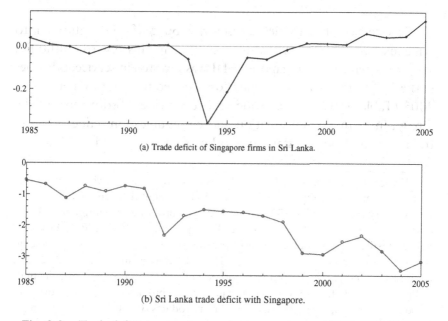

(a) Trade deficit of Singapore firms in Sri Lanka.

(b) Sri Lanka trade deficit with Singapore.

Fig. 9.2: Trade deficit (exports-imports) as a percentage of GDP, 1985–2005.

Table 9.9.   Distribution (percentage) of Singapore's FDI stock by industry.

Year	Food Beverage and Tobacco	Textile, Wearing Apparel and Leather Products	Chemical, Petroleum, Coal, and Rubber Plastics	Non Metallic Mineral Products	Fabricated Metal, Machinery and Transport Equipment	Services	Total
1995	12.3	12.3	1.8	0.4	0.0	73.1	100.0
1996	6.2	6.0	1.4	0.3	0.0	86.1	100.0
1997	6.2	6.1	1.4	0.3	0.0	86.1	100.0
1998	5.5	6.1	1.4	0.3	0.0	86.7	100.0
1999	5.5	6.1	1.4	0.3	0.0	86.7	100.0
2000	9.0	8.9	1.5	0.6	1.7	78.2	99.9
2001	14.1	8.4	0.6	0.8	1.6	74.0	99.6
2002	40.9	5.6	0.6	0.9	0.8	50.1	99.0
2003	35.0	4.0	0.5	0.5	0.6	58.8	99.3
2004	32.5	4.3	0.9	0.9	0.7	60.9	99.8
2005	28.6	8.6	0.9	0.9	0.6	60.7	99.8

Source: Board of Investment, Sri Lanka.

Service sector activities attract the bulk of FDI inflows into Sri Lanka and[7] Singapore is no exception in this regard. Although almost 90 percent of Singapore's FDI was invested in service industries in the 1990s, this heavy concentration reduced to about 60 percent by 2005 (Table 9.9). The following service activities absorb most of the foreign investments: information and communication, education and training, hotels and restaurants, other tourism related services and

---

[7] In 1995, 60 percent of total FDI stock was in service sector activities and 40 percent was in manufacturing activities. By 2005 these numbers changed only slightly with the service sector taking 57 percent and manufacturing accounting for 43 percent. The composition of manufacturing FDI (percent) in 1995 and 2005 was as follows: textile wearing apparel and leather products (17.8, 13), chemical petroleum coal rubber and plastic products (7.8, 8.1) food beverage and tobacco (2.7, 7.2), fabricated metal, machinery, and transport equipment (1.4, 4.2), non-metallic mineral products (3.2, 4.1), miscellaneous manufactured products (5.6, 3.6), wood and wood products (0.8, 2.4), and paper and paper products (0.5, 0.3). (Compiled from Annual Reports, Central Bank of Sri Lanka.)

business and trade support services. Food, beverage and tobacco products and textile, wearing apparel and leather products are the major industries that receive a large part of Singapore's manufacturing investments. In 2005, nearly 30 percent of Singapore FDI stock was in food, beverage and tobacco production and 9 percent was in textile, wearing apparel and leather production industries. Not much of Singapore's investments move into industries such as machinery and transport equipment, and chemical, petroleum and plastic products where the country has a greater degree of specialisation.[8]

Table 9.10 provides current account balance of Singapore's firms operating in Sri Lanka by main industries. After reporting deficits between 1995 and 2000, firms producing food, beverage and tobacco have run increasing trade surpluses since 2001. On an average, these firms have produced a current account surplus of Rs. 484 million during 1995–2005. Firms producing textiles, wearing apparel and leather products have also generated large current account surpluses. The average trade surplus of this industry was about Rs. 200 million between 1995 and 2005. All other manufacturing sectors also have reported current account surpluses on an average as follows: non-metallic mineral products, Rs. 25 million; machinery and transport equipment products, Rs. 25 million; and chemical, petroleum, coal, rubber and plastic products, Rs. 8 million. As opposed to these surpluses, Singapore's joint-venture service firms in Sri Lanka have run current account deficits. The average current account deficit of these service firms exceeded Rs. 450 million over the decade since 1995.

Singapore's Investment in Sri Lanka: Future Prospects

As we have seen above, the bulk of FDI inflows to Sri Lanka have moved into service industries. As of 2005, 57 percent of the FDI

---

[8] Machinery and transport equipment is the largest export industry in Singapore. It accounted for about 65 percent of Singapore's exports over the last five years. Mineral fuels and related products, chemicals and related products, and manufactured goods and other manufactured articles together account for 31 percent (9 percent, 10 percent and 12 percent respectively) of total exports of Singapore (Jayawickrama and Thangavelu, 2007).

Table 9.10.   Current account balance of Singapore's FDI industries in Sri Lanka (Rs. mn in 2000 constant prices).

Year	Food, Beverage and Tobacco Products	Textile, Wearing Apparel and Leather Products	Non Metallic Mineral Products	Chemical, Petroleum, Coal, Rubber and Plastics	Fabricated Metal, and Machinery Transport Equipment	Services
1995	−84.6	−280.1	61.1	74.7	-3.5	−1020.0
1996	−18.1	157.1	1.8	51.0	20.3	−557.8
1997	−8.2	−75.2	−0.3	36.4	18.9	−444.4
1998	−17.3	187.9	−6.8	52.4	12.7	−342.1
1999	−30.1	321.4	14.8	26.6	21.7	−212.5
2000	−36.8	354.2	9.1	14.6	24.6	−224.5
2001	44.6	251.5	34.7	−61.8	50.3	−184.2
2002	588.2	394.4	−0.4	−38.4	44.3	−72.2
2003	332.9	417.3	50.3	−52.4	72.4	−149.3
2004	1244.0	−38.4	80.8	−15.5	-3.6	−420.7
2005	3312.9	517.1	25.9	3.4	13.1	−1315.7

Source: Board of Investment, Sri Lanka.

stock was in services. On the contrary, the country's manufacturing sector still remains largely underdeveloped and needs an investment boom to lift it to account for about 30–40 percent of GDP. Not only that, the industrial sector presents large growth potentials, manufacturing growth would also enhance the service sector performance and open up further investment opportunities in the latter because of the complementary role played by it. Thus, we briefly explore business opportunities present in the manufacturing sector of Sri Lanka.

By 2005, agriculture, industry and service sectors constituted 17 percent, 27 percent and 56 percent of GDP respectively. As seen in Fig. 9.3, the output share of the agricultural sector has fallen and that of the industrial sector has remained almost the same over the last two decades. The service sector share of GDP has increased from 46 percent in 1985 to 56 percent in 2005. The increasing trend in the service share is almost equal to the reciprocal of the declining agricultural share. Output shares of manufacturing and construction sectors also remain constant at around 15 percent and 7 percent respectively. The average

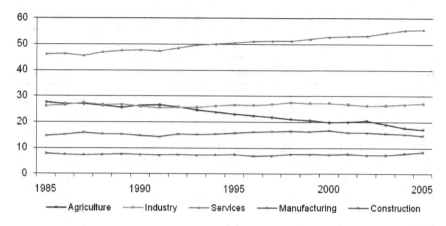

Fig. 9.3: Output composition (as a percentage of GDP) of Sri Lanka.

Note: Industry includes manufacturing, construction, mining and quarrying, and electricity and water supply. Manufacturing and construction accounted for 55 percent and 32 percent respectively of the total industrial output in 2005.

growth rates of agriculture, industry and services between 1986 and 2005 were 2.0 percent, 4.6 percent (with manufacturing 4.5 percent and construction 4.9 percent) and 5.5 percent respectively (Table 10.11). Table 9.11 also shows that unlike the services sector, growth rates of manufacturing and constructions have remained highly volatile.

As seen in Table 9.12, the composition of manufacturing has shown noteworthy changes over the last decade. The manufacturing output share of textile, wearing apparel and leather products (the country's major export product) has increased to 40 percent in 2005 from about 30 percent in 1995. The manufacturing output share of chemical, petroleum, rubber and plastic products has also increased from 8 percent in 1995 to 19 percent in 2005. The output share of other manufacturing industries except basic metal products has decreased gradually over the last decade. Food, beverage and tobacco products accounted for 35 percent of manufactured products in 1995. This figure declined sharply to 25 percent by 2005. The output share of non-metallic mineral products has fallen from 12 percent in 1995 to 7 percent in 2005. The contribution of other industries to manufacturing value-added has been very low. For example, fabricated metal and machinery and transport equipments industries

Table 9.11. Growth rate (percentage) of Sri Lanka's output by sector.

		Industry				
Year	Agriculture	Total	Manufacture	Construction	Services	GDP
1986	2.04	5.88	7.54	−0.39	4.73	4.29
1987	1.03	4.71	7.05	−0.79	−0.03	1.52
1988	0.33	−0.11	−1.39	2.95	5.83	2.72
1989	−0.50	2.55	1.84	5.81	3.64	2.26
1990	9.01	3.13	2.84	3.56	6.28	6.10
1991	6.34	2.91	1.05	1.97	4.61	5.18
1992	0.77	4.50	11.52	6.20	6.05	3.73
1993	1.91	6.80	6.02	4.58	9.70	6.94
1994	1.90	8.05	6.90	7.50	6.30	5.66
1995	2.12	6.90	7.86	7.01	6.32	5.48
1996	1.14	3.41	6.86	−3.21	5.13	3.76
1997	3.61	8.08	7.66	7.66	6.50	6.27
1998	1.09	7.26	5.61	13.26	5.00	4.75
1999	2.24	3.42	3.48	4.43	5.82	4.40
2000	2.11	6.04	8.83	2.62	7.62	6.05
2001	−0.69	−3.17	−6.55	2.35	−0.83	−1.44
2002	6.39	1.95	3.29	−2.30	4.13	3.90
2003	−1.87	6.35	4.09	6.98	8.46	5.89
2004	−1.36	6.83	3.61	15.04	7.14	5.44
2005	2.42	7.37	2.40	13.02	6.52	6.02
Average	2.00	4.64	4.52	4.91	5.45	4.45

Source: Data from the Annual Report of the Central Bank of Sri Lanka.

contribute a mere 4 percent. Further, paper and paper products, basic metal products, wood and wood products and miscellaneous manufacturing industries together add only about 4 percent to the total. The low level of manufacturing output and its composition signal the presence of a large growth potential in Sri Lanka's manufacturing sector that could cater to both domestic and international markets at highly-competitive prices.

To shed further light on the growth potential in Sri Lankan manufacturing, we examine the country's comparative standing in international trade by computing an index of revealed comparative advantage (RCA) by main sectors and by sub-categories of products.

Table 9.12.   Sri Lanka's manufacturing value added share (percentage).

Year	Food, Beverage and Tobacco Products	Textiles, Wearing Apparel and Leather Products	Wood and Wood Products	Paper and Paper Products	Chemical, Petroleum, Rubber and Plastic Products	Non-metallic Mineral	Basic Metal Products	Fabricated Metal Products, Machinery and Transport Equipment	Manufactured Products (n.e.s.)
1995	35.6	30.6	1.5	3.0	8.5	12.0	0.4	5.6	2.9
1996	34.5	32.7	1.3	2.7	9.4	11.1	0.5	5.0	2.9
1997	31.7	36.2	1.1	2.4	9.6	10.4	0.5	5.3	2.8
1998	31.2	36.7	1.0	2.0	11.0	9.6	0.6	5.2	2.7
1999	31.0	38.5	1.0	1.9	9.6	9.6	0.5	5.1	2.7
2000	29.3	41.5	0.9	1.7	10.6	8.5	0.6	4.6	2.4
2001	30.2	39.7	0.9	1.7	10.7	8.9	0.6	4.9	2.3
2002	30.9	38.7	0.9	1.6	11.4	8.7	0.7	4.9	2.4
2003	31.5	38.3	0.9	1.5	11.3	8.4	0.7	5.1	2.4
2004	31.0	39.0	0.9	1.4	11.2	8.5	0.7	5.0	2.3
2005	25.0	39.7	0.6	1.5	19.6	7.2	0.8	3.6	2.1

Source: Data from the Annual Report of the Central Bank of Sri Lanka.

According to Balassa's RCA index (Balassa, 1965), the comparative advantage of a country that exports a particular product can be measured by the export share of the product in the country over its share of world exports.[9] A country is said to specialise in exporting/producing a particular product when the RCA index of that product is above unity. The higher the value of the index above unity, the stronger is the country's specialisation.[10]

We compute Balassa's RCA index using United Nations commodity trade data for the period 2001–2005. Table 9.13 gives the computed RCA index by main sectors (SITC one-digit classification). Sri Lanka has consistently demonstrated a greater degree of comparative advantage in exporting miscellaneous manufactured articles (SITC 8) and food and live animals (SITC 0). The country has some specialisation in exporting manufactured goods classified by material (SITC 6) and beverage and tobacco products (SITC 1) too. Surprisingly, the RCA index for animal and vegetable oils fats and waxes (SITC 4) shows a substantial jump from 0.7 in 2004 to 5.7 in 2005. This was due to an export surge of these products in 2005. The RCA index of crude materials except fuels (SITC 2) has moved closer to unity over the years. The other categories do not show consistent improvement over the years.

We then computed the RCA index for 38 product categories by SITC two-digit level classification. On an average, these 38 products accounted for about 98 percent of Sri Lanka's exports during the

---

[9] If country j exports product i to other countries, the revealed comparative advantage (RCA) index of country j on product i is computed as follows:

$$RCA_{ij} = (X_{ij}/\Sigma_1 X_{ij})/(\Sigma_1 X_{ij}/\Sigma_1\Sigma_1 X_{ij}).$$

where X_{ij} are exports of sector i from country j. The numerator gives the share of country j's exports of sector i in country j's total exports. The denominator gives the share of world exports of sector i in world total exports. If the RCA index of sector i in country j equals unity, the share of sector i exports in country j's total exports is identical to the share of country j's total exports in world total exports. See Jayawickrama and Thangavelu (2007) for reference on other measures of RCA and for recent references on the use of Balassa's RCA index.

[10] In this section, we interpret high RCA values as representing competitiveness though comparative and competitive advantages do not necessarily mean the same thing.

Table 9.13. Sri Lanka's revealed comparative advantage by main sectors.

SITC One-Digit Category	2001	2002	2003	2004	2005
0 Food and live animals	3.46	3.41	3.37	3.47	3.73
1 Beverage and tobacco	0.89	0.90	1.01	1.18	1.17
2 Crude materials, inedible, except fuels	0.65	0.70	0.84	0.93	0.92
3 Mineral fuels, lubricants and related material	0.05	0.04	0.00	0.02	0.00
4 Animal and vegetable oils, fats and waxes	0.17	0.16	0.28	0.71	5.66
5 Chemicals and related products	0.07	0.07	0.08	0.10	0.12
6 Manufactured goods classified by material	0.85	1.14	1.08	1.04	1.23
7 Machinery and transport equipment	0.15	0.12	0.13	0.15	0.11
8 Miscellaneous manufactured articles	4.55	4.24	4.37	4.41	4.31
9 Commodity and transactions n. c. e. in the SITC	0.00	0.52	0.06	0.00	0.55

Source: Based on United Nations Commodity trade data base.

period 2001–2005. These results are given in Table 10.14. Apparel and clothing accessories (SITC 84) account for 50 percent of Sri Lanka's exports. Other major export industries are coffee, tea, cocoa, spices and related products (SITC 07), non-metallic mineral products (SITC 66), rubber manufactures (SITC 62) and textile, yarn, fabrics and related products (SITC 65). Miscellaneous manufactured articles (SITC 89), non-ferrous metal (SITC 68), fish and other aquatic products (SITC 03) and other transport equipment (SITC 79) accounted for about 2 percent each of total exports. The relative export importance of other product categories except vegetables and fruits (SITC 05), beverages and tobacco (SITC 11 & 12), office machines and automatic data processing machines (SITC 75) and electrical machinery, appliances and parts (SITC 77) is rather low.

Computations on RCA in Table 9.14 show that Sri Lanka is highly competitive in exporting traditional plantation products and spices (SITC 07). The average RCA index of this product category was 36

Table 9.14.   Revealed comparative advantage by SITC two-digit level industries.

SITC Classification		Export Share (percentage)	RCA Index				
No.	Product Categories	2001–2005	2001	2002	2003	2004	2005
03	Fish and other aquatic products	1.87	2.53	2.06	2.51	2.39	2.59
04	Cereals and cereal preparations	0.16	0.07	0.08	0.10	0.14	0.57
05	Vegetable and fruits	1.47	1.12	1.06	1.18	1.44	1.25
07	Coffee, tea, cocoa, spices and manufactures thereof	15.41	38.69	34.14	32.33	35.75	39.09
08	Feeding stuff for animals	0.28	0.47	0.84	0.94	0.96	0.81
09	Miscellaneous edible products and preparations	0.16	0.14	0.22	0.30	0.39	0.94
11&12	Beverage and tobacco products	0.95	0.89	0.90	1.01	1.18	1.17
22	Oil-seeds and oleaginous fruits	0.21	0.57	0.80	0.82	0.83	1.08
23	*Crude rubber*	*0.73*	*3.21*	*3.16*	*4.04*	*4.56*	*3.67*
25	Pulp and waste paper	0.14	0.27	0.32	0.51	0.63	0.66
26	*Textile fibres and their wastes*	*0.69*	*1.93*	*2.00*	*1.99*	*2.24*	*3.03*
28	Metalliferous ores and metal scrap	0.31	0.17	0.21	0.21	0.44	0.42
42	Fixed vegetable fats and oils (crude)	0.09	0.21	0.19	0.26	0.31	0.37

(*Continued*)

Table 9.14. (*Continued*)

SITC Classification		Export Share (percentage)	RCA Index				
No.	Product categories	2001–2005	2001	2002	2003	2004	2005
43	*Animal and vegetable fats, oil and waxes (processed)*	*0.53*	*0.00*	*0.00*	*0.39*	*2.98*	*36.60*
51	Organic chemicals	0.08	0.02	0.02	0.03	0.04	0.04
52	Inorganic chemicals	0.07	0.01	0.02	0.14	0.21	0.18
53	Dyeing, tanning and colouring materials	0.05	0.08	0.07	0.08	0.11	0.12
54	Medicinal and pharmaceutical products	0.17	0.01	0.01	0.01	0.08	0.15
55	Essential oils, cosmetics and related products	0.15	0.14	0.14	0.17	0.19	0.22
59	Chemical materials and products (n.e.s.)	0.36	0.32	0.34	0.30	0.29	0.32
62	*Rubber manufactures*	*3.41*	*3.23*	*3.18*	*3.95*	*4.56*	*6.53*
63	Cork and wood manufactures	0.35	0.36	0.43	0.59	0.78	0.89
65	*Textile, yarn, fabrics and related products*	*3.15*	*1.61*	*1.32*	*1.26*	*1.09*	*1.04*
66	*Non-metallic mineral products*	*5.53*	*2.13*	*3.57*	*2.59*	*2.61*	*3.09*
68	*Non-ferrous metal*	*2.02*	*0.03*	*0.94*	*1.50*	*1.27*	*1.57*
69	Manufactures of metals (n.e.s.)	0.41	0.13	0.13	0.14	0.20	0.30

(*Continued*)

Table 9.14.   (*Continued*)

SITC Classification		Export Share (percentage)	RCA Index				
No.	Product categories	2001–2005	2001	2002	2003	2004	2005
71	Power generating machine and equipment	0.13	0.19	0.02	0.01	0.01	0.02
74	General industrial machinery, parts and equipment	0.10	0.05	0.02	0.02	0.02	0.03
75	Office machines and data processing machines	1.23	0.29	0.20	0.24	0.23	0.18
77	Electrical machinery, appliances and parts	1.57	0.14	0.12	0.17	0.23	0.19
78	Road vehicles	0.29	0.02	0.01	0.02	0.03	0.06
79	Other transport equipment	1.75	0.63	0.66	0.66	0.99	0.51
82	Furniture, bedding, mattresses, and related products	0.17	0.11	0.13	0.15	0.18	0.22
83	Travel goods, handbags, and similar containers	0.89	8.33	4.40	2.15	1.51	1.32
84	Articles of apparel and clothing accessories	50.00	15.58	14.55	15.53	16.67	17.20
85	Footwear	0.38	0.86	0.51	0.56	0.35	0.34
87	Professional and scientific instruments and apparatus	0.17	0.07	0.12	0.07	0.05	0.08
89	Miscellaneous manufactured articles	2.27	0.63	0.58	0.59	0.60	0.67

Source: Export data are from United Nations Commodity Trade Data Base.

during the period 2001–2005. Apparel and clothing accessories (SITC 84) are also highly competitive as revealed by the corresponding high RCA index. The country's export competitiveness in this product category is much higher than that of China and India (Jayawickrama and Thangavelu, 2007). Based on the 2005 RCA index, we can order the other product categories in which Sri Lanka has shown to have comparative advantages: rubber manufactures (SITC 62), crude rubber (SITC 23), non-metallic mineral products (SITC 66), textile fibres and their wastes (SITC 26), fish and other aquatic products (SITC 03), non-ferrous metals (SITC 68), travel goods, handbags and similar containers (SITC 83), vegetable and fruits (SITC 05), beverages and tobacco products (SITC 11 and SITC 12) and textile, yarn, fabrics and related products (SITC 65). The RCA index of animal and vegetable oils, fats and waxes (SITC 43) improved quite rapidly during 2004 and 2005. The RCA index of oilseeds and oleaginous fruits (SITC 22) too has improved over unity in 2005. Though Sri Lanka is competitive in exporting textile, yarn, fabrics and related products (SITC 65) and travel goods, handbags and similar containers (SITC 83), the degree of export competitiveness of these products has fallen over time. Though the RCA index values of all other products are less than unity, they (except RCA of general industrial machinery (SITC 74), office and data processing machines (SITC 75) and footwear (SITC 85)) have improved over time. This means Sri Lanka is moving toward achieving export competitiveness in terms of a large class of manufactured products.

Industries with RCA values higher than unity tend to be the ones that are already competitive in the world market. These sectors are also likely to attract more investments. Industries with RCA values less than unity but improving over time are the emerging ones and show potential for further growth. Computations in Table 9.14 show that there are many industries that improved their export competitiveness during 2001–2005. Singapore does not enjoy comparative advantage in the production of food and live animals, beverages and tobacco products, crude materials, and animal and vegetable oil, fats and waxes. It is losing its competitiveness in many important industrial products such as chemicals and related products,

manufactured goods and articles and machinery and transport equipments (except electronics and parts, professional and scientific
instruments, photographic apparatus optical good and watches and
clocks and miscellaneous manufactured articles) (see Jayawickrama
and Thangavelu, 2007). Therefore, Singapore would benefit more
from re-locating such industries to Sri Lanka where their export competitiveness has been improving over the years.

It is also useful to review the fiscal incentives offered for FDI
industries in Sri Lanka. Table 9.15 highlights tax incentives, duty
and exchange control exemptions for investments under various
products and service categories. As listed in the table, there are 10
major industrial categories that qualify for government incentives.
For large-scale FDI infrastructure projects, depending on the extent
of the investment, a 6–12 year tax holiday period is offered. For FDI
industries that produce non-traditional goods for export, industrial
items for the local market, agriculture and agro-based products,
export-oriented services and small-scale infrastructure projects, the
government offers a five-year tax holiday period. Three-year tax holiday period is available for IT-related services, training centres and
regional headquarters. For most cases, only 10 percent corporate
income tax rate is applied for two years after the tax holiday period.
The long-term corporate tax rate for these FDI industries is 15 percent or 20 percent. These income tax incentives are quite attractive in
comparison to 32.5 percent (as of January 2006) tax liability of non-
FDI corporations in Sri Lanka. Further, these firms are liable for
dividend tax and non-resident dividend withholding tax waiver for
the entire tax holiday period plus an additional year (UNCTAD,
2004). In addition to income and dividend tax incentives, these FDI
firms are allowed to import capital goods and raw materials (in some
cases) without import duties. Further, exchange control exemptions
are also available for companies that produce goods for export.

At the same time, the government largely invests in the development of much-needed infrastructure facilities with the aim of taking
the economy to the next level of economic development. The
expansion of Colombo port and development of other ports, construction of a new international airport in southern Sri Lanka,

Table 9.15. Government incentives for industry-wise FDI companies under section 17 of BOI (Sri Lanka) law.

Industry Category	Requirement	Full Tax Holiday	Tax Concession	Import Duty Exempted	Exemption from Exchange Control
Manufacture of non-traditional goods for export[a]	Investment ≥ US$ 1.5 mn, and export ≥ 80 percent of output	5 years	10 percent for two years and 15 percent thereafter	Capital goods and raw materials	Yes
Manufacture of industrial tools and machinery for the local market	Investment ≥ US$ 1.5 mn	5 years	10 percent for two years and 20 percent thereafter	Capital goods-(during the establishment period)	No
Agriculture and agro-processing other than processing of black tea[b]	Investment ≥ US$ 0.01 mn	5 years	15 percent thereafter	Capital goods-(lifetime if export-oriented)	Yes, if exports >80 percent
Export-oriented services	Investment ≥ US$ 1.5 mn and export ≥ 70 percent of output	5 years	10 percent for two years and 15 percent thereafter	Capital goods and raw materials	Yes

(Continued)

Table 9.15.   (*Continued*)

Industry Category	Requirement	Full Tax Holiday	Tax Concession	Import Duty Exempted	Exemption from Exchange Control
Information technology (IT) and IT-enabled services	15 technically qualified persons for IT-enabled services	3 years	10 percent for two years and thereafter 15 percent if export oriented and 20 percent otherwise	Capital goods-(during the establishment period) if exports more than 70 percent	Yes if exports more than 70 percent
IT-related training institutes	300 per annual students in IT-related training institutes	3 years	10 percent for two years and 20 percent thereafter	Capital goods-(during the establishment period)	No
Regional operating head quarters	Turnover in convertible foreign currency > 70 percent	3 years	10 percent for two years, and 15 percent or 20 percent thereafter	Capital goods	Yes
Research and Development	Investment ≥ US$ 0.05 mn	5 years	15 percent thereafter	Capital goods	No

(*Continued*)

Table 9.15. (*Continued*)

Industry Category	Requirement	Full Tax Holiday	Tax Concession	Import Duty Exempted	Exemption from Exchange Control
Export trading house	Annual turnover: US$ 5–10 mn US$ 10–25 mn	No	10 percent for five years, and 15 percent thereafter 5 percent for five years and 15 percent thereafter	Capital goods and raw materials	Yes
Small-scale infrastructure projects	Investment ≥ US$ 0.5 mn	5 years	10 percent for two years and 20 percent thereafter	Capital goods-(during the establishment period)	Case by case
Large-scale infrastructure projects	Investment ≥ US$ 10 mn ≥ US$ 25 mn ≥ US$ 50 mn ≥ US$ 75 mn	6 years 8 years 10 years 12 years	15 percent thereafter	Capital goods-(during the establishment period)	Case by case

Source: Board of Investment, Sri Lanka.

Notes: [a]Non-traditional goods include all goods other than black tea, crepe rubber, sheet rubber, scrap rubber, coconut oil, dessicated coconut, copra, fresh coconuts, coconut fibre or such other commodity as may be determined by the BOI, Sri Lanka.

[b]Agriculture includes cultivation of plants of any description, animal husbandry and rearing and/or processing of fish.

construction of two coal power plants and many small scale hydro power projects, construction of an industrial zone in eastern Sri Lanka, irrigation development projects and construction of several highways and development of the road network are a few of such large scale infrastructure projects that are in progress. Further institutional changes are also in place to facilitate FDI inflows. Over the last decade, the governing body of foreign investment has been restructured to provide speedy services for investors. Most issues pertaining to foreign investment are handled by the BOI of Sri Lanka. The improvement of these institutional facilities is reflected in the decline of time required to start a business from 58 days in 2003 to 50 days in 2004. However, further improvements are necessary as this figure still exceeds the world average of 48 days. Moreover, as noted in the Index of Economic Freedom website, the enforcement of commercial codes in Sri Lanka is not straightforward and lacks transparency. While FDI in some areas is totally prohibited, access in many sectors, especially when the foreign equity exceeds 40 percent, is subject to conditional approval.[11] These measures stand as barriers to free mobility of FDI in the country (UNCTAD, 2004).

---

[11] FDI on money lending, pawn broking, retail trade with investment less than US$1mn, provision of personal services other than export sector and tourism, coastal fishing and education are totally prohibited.

If the foreign equity share exceeds 40 percent the approval of such FDI would be granted on a case-by-case basis by the BOI of Sri Lanka. This rule is applied for the following areas: production of goods that are subject to international quota restrictions, growing and processing of traditional agricultural products (tea, rubber, coconut, rice, sugar and spice), mining and primary processing of non-renewable resources, local timber based industries, deep sea fishing, mass communication, education, freight forwarding, travel agencies and shipping agencies.

FDI in the following areas must be approved by respective government agencies: Air transportation, coastal shipping, industries producing arms, ammunitions, explosives, military vehicles and equipments and other military hardware, industries manufacturing poisons, narcotics, alcohols, dangerous drugs and toxic and hazardous material, industries producing currency, coins and security documents, large-scale mechanised mining gems, and lotteries (see BOI website).

Conclusion and Policy Implications

This case study on Singapore's direct investment links with Sri Lanka reveals some useful observations. In terms of cumulative investment, Singapore is the single largest foreign investor in Sri Lanka. The service sector absorbs most of Singapore's FDI inflows. By the end of 2005, 50 Singapore FDI affiliates with investment of more than Rs. 17,000 million (about S$233 million) were operational in Sri Lanka. Direct employment of these firms exceeded 5500 persons in 2005. Although this is a small figure relative to the size of the country's labour force, these investments also create many indirect employment opportunities. Singapore firms have contributed to the export-led growth of the country though their current accounts have begun to turn persistently positive only since about 1999. In the absence of micro-level data, an assessment of skill and technology transfers and other spillovers was not possible. Nevertheless, the overall benefits generated by these FDIs on the country are likely to be substantial, relative to factor incomes repatriated by these firms.

Only one fifth of the country's GDP is produced by the manufacturing and construction sectors, well below the average manufacturing share of East and Southeast Asian economies and there are many unexploited investment opportunities in manufacturing and construction industries in Sri Lanka. Revealed comparative advantage measures show that Sri Lanka has been competitive in exporting agro-based products and labour intensive manufacturing products. Other manufacturing products are also gaining strength in international competitiveness over the years. Sri Lanka offers many attractive fiscal incentives for foreign investments on several vital industries and services. The government also tries to enhance FDI absorbability of the country by improving infrastructure and deregulating administrative procedures. Further, the country's free trade agreements with neighbouring large markets would offer greater market access to export-oriented firms.

Despite the very conducive FDI environment that Sri Lanka offers, the country's FDI base is too small, relative to the fast growing

East and Southeast Asian economies. Although Singapore has emerged as the largest foreign investor, what it invests in Sri Lanka is miniscule compared to its investments in China and Southeast Asian countries. For example, outside Singapore's mega investment destinations such as China, Malaysia, Indonesia, Hong Kong and Thailand, other countries like Vietnam have been attracting Singapore's investment at a much faster rate than Sri Lanka. India is picking up Singapore's investment equally fast.[12]

Obviously, the protracted war in Sri Lanka has taken a huge toll on its FDI-driven growth strategy. Although the country opened its economy in 1977, it lost the opportunity to have a head-start because of the war. Although the war is over, Sri Lanka now has to face severe competition from fast emerging economies like China, India and Vietnam in attracting FDI. In fact, China's enormous suction power of FDI is a challenge to Singapore's own FDI-driven growth strategy. Singapore's success lies in its ability to quickly branch off and capitalise on the first mover advantage (see Abeysinghe, 2008, for a detailed account of Singapore's growth strategy). Unlike large economies where firms can produce for the domestic market, Singapore's challenge is not only to attract FDI but also to secure export markets for the products. Sri Lanka's challenge is similar and there is a lot to learn from Singapore government's pro-active industrial policy.

References

Abeyratne, S. and C. Rodrigo (2002). Explaining Growth Performance in Sri Lanka: Fifty Years in Retrospect 1950–2000. New Delhi; South Asian Network of Economic Research Institutes.

---

[12] Singapore's investment (stock) in Vietnam went up from S\$0.4 bn in 1995 to S\$1.7 bn in 2005. For India these figures went up from S\$0.2 bn in 1995 to S\$1.7bn in 2005. In contrast, Sri Lanka's figures went up from S\$0.2bn in 1995 only to S\$0.3 bn in 2005. For a comparison, Singapore's investment in China went up from S\$3.7 bn in 1995 to S\$25 bn in 2005. (It should be noted that the Sri Lankan rupee depreciated from Rs. 38/S\$ in 1995 to Rs. 61/S\$ by the end of 2005.)

Abeysinghe, T. (2008). Singapore: Economy. In *The Far East and Australasia*, D. Lynn (ed.) Routledge.

Asian Development Bank (2009). Key Indicators for Asia and the Pacific. (Online publications).

Athukorala, P. (1995). Foreign Direct Investment and Manufacturing for Export in a New Exporting Country: The Case of Sri Lanka. *World Economy*, 14, pp. 543–564.

Athukorala, P. and S. Jayasuriaya, (1994). Macroeconomic Policies, Crises and Growth in Sri Lanka, 1969–90; Washington DC: World Bank.

Athukorala, P. and S. Jayasuriaya, (2005). Liberalisation and Industrial Growth: Lessons from Sri Lanka. In *Economic Growth, Economic Performance and Welfare in South Asia*, R. Jha (ed.) pp. 102–118. Hampshire and New York: Palgrave Macmillan.

Athulorala, P. and S. Rajapathirana, (2000). *Liberalisation and Industrial Transformation: Sri Lanka in International Perspective.* Oxford and Delhi: Oxford University Press.

Balassa, B. (1965). Trade Liberalization and Revealed Comparative Advantage. *The Manchester School of Economic and Social Studies*, 32, pp. 99–123.

Board of Investment Sri Lanka (2005). Make It in Sri Lanka. Colombo: Board of Investment Sri Lanka. http:www.boi.lk/boi2005/index.asp.

Central Bank of Sri Lanka, (1980–2005). Annual Reports Colombo: Central Bank of Sri Lanka.

Dayaratna Banda, O. G. (2005). Foreign Investment Inflows, Government Institutions, External Openness and Economic Growth in Developing Countries: A Theoretical and Empirical Investigation. Unpublished Ph.D. Thesis, National University of Singapore.

Department of Statistics (2009). Survey of Singapore's Investment Abroad 2007. Ministry of Trade and Industry, Government of Singapore.

Jayawickrama, A. and S. Thangavelu (2007). Dynamics of Comparative Advantage and Production Fragmentation: Singapore, China and India. Manuscript, Department of Economics, National University of Singapore.

Kelegama, S. (ed.) (2004). Economic Policy in Sri Lanka: Issues and Debates. New Delhi and London: Sage Publications.

Kelegama, S. (2006). *Development Under Stress: Sri Lankan Economy in Transition.* New Delhi and London: Sage Publications.

Snodgrass, D. (1966). Sri Lanka: An Export Economy in Transition. Homewood, Ill: Richard D. Irvin.

The Heritage Foundation and Dow Jones & Company, Inc. 2007. 2007 Index of Economic Freedom. http:www.heritage.org/research/features/index.

UNCTAD, (2004). Investment Policy Review: Sri Lanka. New York: United Nations.

UNESCO, (2009). Global Education Digest 2008. New York: United Nations (Online publications).

United Nations, (2005). World Investment Report. New York: United Nations (Online publications).

United Nations, Commodity Trade Statistics Database. Available at http://unstats.un.org/.

World Bank, (2009). World Development Indicators. New York: World Bank (Online publications).

Index